SOUTH GEORGIA
Gateway to Antarctica

LUDWIG KOHL-LARSEN

Translated by William Barr
Arctic Institute of North America,
University of Calgary

BLUNTISHAM BOOKS · THE ERSKINE PRESS
2003

SOUTH GEORGIA
Gateway to Antarctica
by
Dr Ludwig Kohl-Larsen

First published in English in 2003 by
Bluntisham Books, Oak House, East Street, Bluntisham, Huntingdon PE28 3LS
and
The Erskine Press, The Old Bakery, Banham, Norwich, Norfolk NR16 2HW

Originally published in German in 1930 as
An den Toren der Antarktis
by Verlag von Strecker und Schröder, Stuttgart

English translation: William Barr
Arctic Institute of North America,
University of Calgary

British Library Cataloguing in Publication Data
A catalogue of this book is available from the British Library

ISBN 1 85297 075 8

Cover photograph © J. P. Croxall

No part of this book may be reproduced in any form,
by printing, photocopying or by any other means
without the written consent of the publishers

Printed in England by Antony Rowe Ltd, Chippenham, Wilts

To my mother

CONTENTS

	Page
List of Figures and Maps	viii
Introduction	x
Preface	xvi
1. To the Far South	1
2. Grytviken, the Wild West in the South	7
3. Our First Camp at Coal Harbour	20
4. In the Elephant Seal Colony	43
5. The Surrounding Landscape	68
6. Photography and Technology	72
7. The First Sledge Trip	80
8. The Final Days at Coal Harbour	93
9. Storms, Glaciers and Penguins at Bay of Isles	105
10. With the King Penguins on Lucas Glacier	122
11. Further Difficulties	144
12. Waiting for a Ship	149
13. Back with the Whalers at Grytviken	156
14. Hunting the Whale	158
15. Whales and Whalers	164
16. Our Trip Inland	171
17. Fossils, Penguins and Lakes	189
18. Lonely Annenkov Island is Our Next Goal!	215
19. Camp Life on Annenkov Island	221
20. Around the Entire Island with the Sealers Again	240
21. Farewell to Glaciers and King Penguins	268
22. Fresh Blows the Wind for Home!	280
Appendix. Maps	287

LIST OF FIGURES AND MAPS

Figures   *Facing page*

1. The pasha in the elephant seal colony — iii
2. Grytviken and King Edward Cove — 16
3. On the way to Hestesletten — 16
4. Delicate mackerel clouds hung over Echo Pass to the west — 17
5. Hamberg Glacier and the Sugarloaf formed the backdrop to Hestesletten — 17
6. Access to our campsite was barred by a high snow cornice — 32
7. On the voyage to Coal Harbour icebergs drifted across our path — 33
8. Coal Harbour from a hill above the inner bay — 33
9. Beyond a hilly foreland we could see an ice-covered ridge to the north — 64
10. Paryadin Ridge terminates the west end of the island — 64
11. The landscape between Coal Harbour and Elsehul was hilly in nature — 65
12. Above Elsehul gentoo penguins had begun nest building — 65
13. A male elephant seal was the ruler of more than 50 females — 80
14. Immediately after birth the young animal finds its mother's nipple — 80
15. The blocking ridge of "Georg Schweitzer Ridge" to the east — 81
16. Only at twilight does the black storm petrel come to life — 81
17. For weeks depressing clouds hung over our camp — 112

List of Figures and Maps · ix

18. Male and female king penguins often stood side by side as if petrified — 113
19. From our tents we could see the ice cliff of the Brunnonia Glacier — 128
20. Young elephant seals in captivity — 128
21. A gentoo penguin with its chick — 129
22. Sheltered by an ice wall we felt more secure in our abode — 129
23. A school of fin whales promised a rich haul — 158
24. Fast to a whale! — 158
25. The Three Brothers closed the head of the König Glacier — 159
26. The final flurry of a blue whale — 159
27. A heavily glaciated chain west of the König Glacier — 174
28. To the east from this desolation one could see the gleam of Cumberland Bay — 174
29. Out in the Klepper boat on Cumberland Bay — 175
30. The 23 m-high ice cliff of the Nordenskjöld Glacier — 208
31. The Sugarloaf seen from Hestesletten — 209
32. Every breaker hurled dozens of penguins onto the rock slabs — 209
33. From the albatross's nest one could overlook the alpine chain of South Georgia — 224
34. A young giant petrel in down — 225
35. We encountered the odd isolated Weddell seal — 225
36. A glimpse into Possession Bay — 270
37. The sea, a glacier and the main range from St. Andrew's Bay — 270
38. King penguins on the beach at St. Andrew's Bay — 271
39. Father, mother and child (king penguins) — 271

Maps

Sketch map of the vicinity of Coal Harbour — 289
Sketch map of the vicinity of Bay of Isles — 291
Map of South Georgia — 295

INTRODUCTION

Ludwig Kohl was born on 5 April 1884 in Landau and was destined to spend much of his life away from Germany. He had very broad interests, studying medicine and natural history in Munich, Innsbruck and Freiburg before going to the Tropical Institute in Hamburg to prepare himself properly for undertaking expeditions. His first overseas venture was to Brazil as a ship's doctor, after which he returned to work at Wiesbaden as a junior doctor.

He was appointed expedition doctor in 1911 by Wilhelm Filchner, the leader of the Second German Antarctic Expedition. His initial responsibility was to work out the provisions, including testing their calorific value to ensure the sledging rations in particular would provide enough energy. Accompanying the *Deutschland* south Kohl spent much of his time working with the zoologists on the plankton and sediment samples. En route for South Georgia on 16 October 1911 Kohl suffered a severe attack of appendicitis, which got worse during the following day, necessitating an emergency operation. Bad weather ensued and it was not until 21 October that the ship eventually arrived at Grytviken with the patient in a very weak condition. He was put ashore to live with Captain C. A. Larsen and his family in the manager's house at the whaling station. Recovering somewhat he went with the ship on an exploration of the South Sandwich Islands but, with continuing bad weather, he again became very weak. By the time *Deutschland* had returned to Grytviken it was clear both to Kohl and to Filchner that he would have to leave the expedition and return to Europe. Fortunately, the expedition was able to find a replacement doctor from the whaling ship *Harpon*. However, his sojourn at Grytviken had not been in vain as he had met his future wife, the daughter of Captain Larsen who had been with Nordenskjöld in the Antarctic before establishing the whaling station at Grytviken in 1904. After his marriage to Margit he changed his name to Kohl-Larsen.

Returning home he also returned to good health and went off to holiday in Norwegian Lapland, crossing from Tromsø to Gällivare in Sweden. In 1912 he and his wife set out with Max von Oppenheim on an expedition to Central Mesopotamia (Syria/Iraq). Here he began to show the amazing talents he had for getting on with a wide variety of people. They made contact with a difficult Bedouin group, and, learning enough of the language to converse with them, became friendly. The success of this expedition was in considerable part due to the efforts of the Kohl-Larsens who had now discovered their true interest in anthropology. At the start of the First World War Kohl-Larsen was sent as a doctor to the island of Yap in the Pacific (then a German colony and now part of the Federated States of Micronesia), leaving Margit behind. In 1915 he was moved to work in Iraq and Persia (Iran), thus renewing his aquaintainship with the Arab world.

After the war he turned his attention to the Arctic and began working, over several years, with the Lapps in Finnmark, studying their cultural traditions, and recording their oral tradition of myths and sagas. This period yielded a great deal of information, which he and his wife continued to publish throughout the rest of their lives.

The call of the Polar Regions and his family link to the Larsens persuaded him to undertake a whaling voyage in 1923–4 as a doctor with the Norwegians aboard the *Sir James Clark Ross* in the Ross Sea. This was the first whaling factory ship and the voyage was both conceived and commanded by his father-in-law. He published an account of this in 1926 called *Zur grossen Eismauer des Südpols* [To the great ice barrier of the South Pole]. The following year (1925) he and his wife went back to Lapland to continue their anthropological studies of the Lapps.

Through his wife's family he had maintained good contacts with the Norwegian whaling community and it was through them that he organised his expedition to South Georgia in 1927–8, recounted in this book and a lengthy paper on the penguins and elephant seals. He wanted not only to explore new parts of the island and collect data and specimens on natural history, but also to make the first film about South Georgia. For this Albert Benitz, the third expedition member, was recruited. He produced a detailed film of the island and the work of the whalers.

Kohl-Larsen's name is commemorated in the Kohl-Larsen Plateau and he also gave names to other minor features on the south side of the island, in many cases formalising the traditional use of the whalers. After the expedition his zoological and geological specimens were sent to the Senckenberg Museum in Frankfurt.

By 1931 he was back in the Arctic, this time with the *Graf Zeppelin* expedition led by Dr Hugo Eckner, who was determined to demonstrate the feasibility of using airships in northern latitudes. The airship left Friedrichshafen on 24 July 1931 with a group of German and Russian scientists aboard (including the Russian Arctic explorer Professor R. Samoylovich) and Lincoln Ellsworth. The airship proceeded to the Barents Sea via Berlin and Leningrad, reaching Franz Josef Land at 81° N and a rendezvous with the Russian icebreaker *Malygin* to exchange mail. It them continued over Severnaya Zemlya, the Tunguska crater and Novaya Zemlya. The Arctic flight took 90 hours to cover over 5,000 miles (92,000 km) and amply demonstrated the potential for Arctic flying under the right circumstances. Not surprisingly this provided Kohl-Larsen with the material for yet another book!

Kohl-Larsen had been making an increasing reputation as an anthropologist from his work in Lapland and now turned his attention to East Africa. He first went to Tanganyika (Tanzania) in 1932 to manage a coffee plantation, leaving Margit in Germany with their son and daughter. The family finally joined him and coffee began to be replaced by anthropology. They spent 1934–6 and 1937–9 living and working in Tanganyika and their studies there provided material for several books. Their work ranged widely across ethnology, anthropology, palaeontology, geology and even climate studies. They established an excellent working arrangement with the Tindiga, a tribe of the nomadic Hadzabe, and were able to make very intensive investigations into the hunter/gatherer way of life in the Lake Eyasi basin, where the remains of the tribe survive today. They were keen fossil collectors and because of this made two major discoveries. Careful excavations in the Mumba Cave (which now lies on the present border between Tanzania and Zambia) between 1934 and 1936 led, in 1935, to the discovery of the remains of a hominoid individual of *Africanthropus*, dating from the Miocene period. This interest in early man put them in touch with the Leakey family, who were just beginning their own archaeological investigations in Kenya. Later, in 1939 they chanced upon the upper jaw and tooth of *Meganthropus africanus* (now called *Australopithicus afarensis*). Their interest in caves led them to a study of African rock paintings, the subject of yet another book. All their fossils and anthropological materials from this period were finally deposited at Tübingen University. Kohl-Larsen's papers and manuscripts are now at the Stadtarchiv Landau/Pfalz.

Returning to Germany in 1939 Ludwig was made an Honorary Professor at Freiburg University in honour of his achievements and appointed a reader in the Anthropology Institute of the University of Tübingen in 1941. From 1941 to 1944 Ludwig was required to undertake medical work but, despite the difficulties of the war Ludwig and Margit laboured on, analysing their data and writing up the material for publication, both as books and scientific papers. After the war he was classified as a 'fellow traveller' and lost his professorship in the denazification period. However, by 1949 he was back at work in Tübingen as an emeritus professor, organising their material for a display on early African history.

Ludwig Kohl-Larsen died at home in Thumen-Schlachters on 12 November 1969. He had continued to write throughout the rest of his life, producing a remarkable number of books both on the studies in Lapland and in East Africa. Even after his death more material was put into print by editors working with the archives at Tübingen. Margit Kohl-Larsen survived him by two decades and recalled her time in South Georgia until her last days. Ludwig and his wife left a major contribution to anthropology, as well as the books of their adventures in many parts of the world.

April 2002 D. W. H. WALTON

SELECT BIBLIOGRAPHY OF BOOKS BY KOHL-LARSEN

1926 Zur grossen Eismauer des Südpols. Eine Fahrt mit norwegischen Walfischfängern. (Stuttgart)
1926 Nordlicht und Mitternachtsonne. Erlebnisse und Wanderungen in Lappland. (Stuttgart)
1930 An den Toren der Antarktis. (Stuttgart)
1931 Die Arktisfahrt des Graf Zeppelin im Auftrage der Internationalen Gesellschaft zur Erforschung der Arktis mit Luftfahrzeugen (Aeroarctic). (Berlin)
1936 (with Hans Reck) Erster Überblick über die jungdiluvialen Tier-und Menschenfunde
1937 Issansu-Märchen
1938 Felsmalereien in Innerafrika (Stuttgart)
1943 Auf den Spuren des Vormenschen (Stuttgart)
1956 (with Simbo Janira) Kleiner grosser schwarzer Mann: Lebenserinnerungen eines Buschnegers. (Kassel)

1956 Das Zauberhorn. Märchen und Tiergeschichten der Tindiga. (Kassel)
1956 Das Elefantenspiel. Mythen, Sagen und Volkserzählungen der Tindiga. (Kassel)
1958 Die Bilderstrasse Ostafrikas: Felsbilderin Tanganyika. (Eisenach)
1958 Wildbeuter in Ost-Afrika: Die Tindiga, ein Jäger- und Sammlervolk. (Berlin)
1958 Der Hase mit den Schuhen. Tiergeschichten der Iraku. (Kassel)
1958 Der grosse Zug nach Mitternacht. Eine Wanderung mit den Lappen zum nordlichen Eismeer. (Kassel)
1963 Das Kürbisungeheuer und die Ama'irmi. Riesengeschichten der Iraku. (Kassel)
1964 Schwarzer Eulenspiegel. Schwänke der Iraku. (Kassel)
1966 Der Perlenbaum. Ostafrikanische Legenden, Sagen, Märchen und Diebsgeschichten (Iraku). (Kassel)
1967 Die Frau in der Kurbisflache. Ostafrikanische Märchen der Burungi. (Kassel)
1969 Fünf Mädchen auf seinem Rücken. Ostafrikanische Mythen und Märchen. (Kassel)
1971 Reiter auf dem Elch. Volkserzählungen aus Lappland. (Kassel)
1975 Die steinerne Herde. Von Trollen, Hexen und Schamanen aus Lappland. (Kassel)
1976 Der Hasenschelm. Tiermärchen und Volkserzählungen aus Ostafrika. (Kassel)
1978 Die Leute im Baum. Ostafrikanische Mythen und Ursprungssagen der Thuru. (Kassel)
1982 Das Haus der Trolle. Märchen aus Lappland (Kassel)
1991 Ludwig Kohl-Larsen – der Mann, der Lucy's Ahnen fand: Lebenserinnerungen und Materialen. (Landau/Pfalz)
1994 Das Leben des Rentierlappen Siri Matti – von ihm selbst erzähält (Frankfurt)

PREFACE

The lonely island in the southern part of the globe, on which the events of this book occurred, intruded itself into my life at quite an early point. I first visited it 19 years ago aboard the South Pole expedition ship *Deutschland* which ran into King Edward Cove on a grey, snowy day.

On that occasion I had left home with great, proud plans, but I had to abandon them all in that quiet bay. An appendix operation at sea under the most primitive conditions had sapped my strength, my resolution and my taste for the loneliness of South Polar voyages, no matter how tempting the firn and glaciers of South Georgia and the ring of pack ice around the South Sandwich Islands.

But just as a great friendship, or even love, may be kindled from the deepest pain elsewhere in life, during that period I may have gained a quiet, suppressed affection for the island of South Georgia in later life from that enforced renunciation of my plans.

Strangely enough my life up till now has often played a peculiar double game with me. Whether it is by chance or through a final unconscious decision of my own will, throughout my life the certainty has recurred that I have visited a series of lands and seas a second time, having first seen them a considerable time earlier.

Norwegian Lapland, Mesopotamia, the icy Southern Ocean are all examples of this double experience and at times, when I survey the remainder of my life, anticipating the future, I do not reject the possibility that my work and life's course may lead me back to our former colony of New Guinea from which the War once drove me from "life, love and the dreams of a South Seas island".

To break away from home is ultimately no great matter. Often all that is needed is a little jolt in order to fulfil a plan which, unspoken, has been proceeding towards maturity for years. A disappointment, a friend whom one has lost either through actual death, or who has died as far as one is concerned although he may still be alive, may provide the impetus.

Then one says to oneself: Wouldn't it be better to live away from people again in the great outdoors? Doesn't everyone experience moments when he prefers animals and solitude to people?

At other times the impetus may be even less than this. All that is needed is an alpine range lying bright and clean above a lake on a blue föhn day, or the moon gliding above a soft spring landscape. Perhaps it was no more than such a night which provoked the decision to undertake an expedition to the island of South Georgia.

The goal of our voyage was a triple one. First of all, as a geographical goal I wanted to collect data on the present-day glacier-cover of the island and if at all possible to travel around the central part of the island at the height of the southern summer, when experience indicated that the best weather should prevail. Before and after this trip I wanted to be landed on as many bays and points as possible, which had been little explored or even were totally unvisited, in order to carry out partial reconnaissance and minor sledge trips from these locations.

As a second task which could be easily combined with the first I had set myself the goal of studying South Georgia's fauna in detail, and of capturing it on film. In connection with this I wanted to investigate the island's freshwater lakes, not only in terms of establishing their positions and depths, but also in terms of studying their fauna and especially their plankton. Almost the entire extensive range of scientific material was given to the Senckenberg Museum in Frankfurt am Main; as a traveller one can experience no greater joy than that of seeing everything of scientific value being transferred to the care of individual specialists for analysis shortly after one returns home.

I wish to thank the Notgemeinschaft der Deutschen Wissenschaft [Emergency Coalition for German Science] for its contribution to my expedition; my wife, who took part in this extensive, dangerous journey; our companion Albert Benitz from Littenweiler near Freiburg who combined a marvellous gift for observation, an alert feeling for nature and a great love of animals with his duties as cameraman; the Argentinean whaling company, Pesca, of Buenos Aires, which made possible our voyage to the island; and finally all the Norwegians who lent us a hand on many occasions on the island itself.

Allensbach am Bodensee 　　　　　　　　　LUDWIG KOHL-LARSEN
September 1930

1

To the Far South

AFTER A TEN-DAY VOYAGE which started from Sandefjord in Norway, we passed Las Palmas on 27 August 1928 and by 4 September had already crossed the Line aboard the Argentinean whale-catcher transport ship *Harpon*. We northerners always look first for the Southern Cross, and the sight of the strange stars in the sky was like a prelude to a new hemisphere. The movement southwards due to the progress of our ship was made more apparent to us by the signs in the sky than by the flying fish, the sharks, the blue colour of the sea, or the temperature differences.

In this brief period the utter contrast with home was sufficient to make us perceive a transformation in ourselves which no discerning, or even mildly perceptive mind could miss. The natural delimitation of all one's values occurs more easily at sea than elsewhere. What one would have scrutinized conscientiously through a magnifying glass a few weeks earlier, whether it be people, things or objects, and would have conceived to be valuable, indispensable and necessary, now loses its importance with distance.

Thus the splinter parties and their pomposities sank noiselessly, as if they were dying, beneath the storm-lashed horizon, or were annihilated by the white crests of the waves. Value and non-value, reality and appearance were sharply contrasted as if in the clear medium of a microscope slide, unsullied by any reflections. The essential can be separated from the non-essential. A full moneybag becomes the empty skin of a balloon; for a moment at least all party programmes dissolve here into the insubstantial, and what is left of them is common to all. One can see things more clearly from this distance and after this transformation. Much that was meaningful, much that was light and friction, and vital necessity, out here are only irrelevant shadows which flit through the minds of the ambitious or the driven.

As these thoughts ran through my mind as they had so often before, the bow of our ship, aboard which 200 whalers were travelling with us to South Georgia, ploughed tirelessly through the sea. The night is blue and the sky is full of stars. The last gleams of daylight are lingering in the west and the effect along the line of the horizon with its heavy, black masses of cloud, is that of a heavy, dusky picture. The wind runs its fingers through the flanks of the waves, giving the sea something of a ruffled appearance. At times the pattern is that of a coarse-meshed sieve. I ask myself, what are the bright colours of mosaics compared to the colour gradations of a morning or evening sky in the Tropics? What is the ornamentation of an artistic carpet compared to the grandiose confusion of a cloudscape?

Thus relaxing to a more natural tempo we headed farther and farther south at 13 knots with our cargo of humanity. When, as now, the men are heading back to the whaling operation, they have no great desire to see the propeller turning particularly fast. There is no hurry. For few of them are there any surprises in store. The men know what is waiting for them: heavy, tedious work. They know and remember that only very recently they held a Nordic girlfriend or wife in their arms for the last time. Their thoughts are still full of home. They are not at all upset if our progress is delayed by a storm. There is nothing but work waiting for them. It will suddenly arrive one morning without having to be summoned: blubber, filth and unremitting toil in the snow and cold.

The youngest among them is practically still a boy; the oldest are in the final stretches of their lives. Their thoughts swing forwards and backwards as they chat in groups, but one can also see the odd man who holds himself aloof, loners perhaps, who prefer to gaze out over the sea and wander around deep in their own thoughts.

In the case of many of them their wallets are thin and empty again after the summer in Norway. There is no point in letting money rust. And what other solution is there but whaling? The circle is so clear and simple. Once again a person leaves his home, as so often before, with empty pockets, a mattress for his bunk, a seaman's bag and some memories of pleasant living, of the long magnificent summer with its light nights. If one were looking to write about adventures at sea, one would not need to look far among the men of the whalers. Almost all of them, certainly many of them, have experienced the wrath of the sea in the stormy waters of the southern seas at least once, even if one hears little about it from the men themselves. Whaler is a collective name, like the word warrior. Those who have been at the front are the most taciturn.

Nobody would guess from the appearance of the quiet man on board, the radio operator Hansen, who would play his violin in his cabin in the evenings, that the sea had played such a shattering role in his life. It was only by accident that I learned that along with mate Alun of our ship, *Harpon*, he had been shipwrecked off Kerguelen Island in the steamer *Erivan* in 1924, had spent 35 hours in a lifeboat, and only by chance had been rescued by a sealing vessel.

Johann Tömmermann makes little of the emergency bivouac he made in Johan Harbour, named after him, on the west side of South Georgia, when he was sealing. He hadn't even a match with him; no roll of tobacco; not even a quid. He had to burrow into the peat in order to survive the snowy night.

Amidst this group of men our 32-day voyage to South Georgia passed tranquilly. At 20°S we observed the last flying fish, which are larger and more numerous here than near the equator. Thereafter all life, both in the air and in the sea, seemed to be extinguished until at 27°S the first Antarctic bird, a Cape pigeon (*Daption capense*) told us how quickly the ship was now approaching her goal. Already the occasional blue whale shot its steeply inclined, bushy spout into the air; and at 30°59'S the first albatross (*Diomedea exulans*) soared in marvellous circles above our wake. A few days later, on a windless day with a smooth sea such as no Antarctic bird appreciates, all the new life seemed to vanish again, until at 38°S all the birds which were so familiar to us from previous voyages began cruising around our ship: albatrosses, both the wandering albatross and the mollemawk of the seamen, i.e. the black-browed albatross (*D. melanophris*), the sooty albatross (*D. fulig* [= *Phoebetria palpebrata*]) with its stiff-winged flight and the white half-moon around its eye; the snow petrel (*Pagodroma nivea*) with its unsteady, ghostly flight. These were almost daily visitors to both the close and wider proximity of our ship; nor must we forget the petrels and the Antarctic tern and the "shoemaker" of the crew, alias *Procellaria aequinoctialis* [= *P. cinerea*] and the black giant petrel which science has endowed with the name of *Macronectes giganteus*.

Over the course of a few days one gets to know all these strange birds like the birds of a stretch of woodland at home. And then, at times when in the seclusion of shipboard life one becomes grateful for every new phenomenon, one is really delighted when the rare Antarctic fulmar *Priocella glacialoides* [= *Fulmarus glacialoides*] or the little common diving petrel (*Pelecanoides urinatrix*) comes into view.

After some impressively beautiful phosphorence and some rare sheet lightning, at 44°S we experienced a night of heavy storm. During this assault all the birds of the high seas approached the ship more brazenly; even the shy sooty albatross became more trusting as the waves towered higher. Their joy in living seemed intensified when they were allied with the storm. Or was it simply because the turmoil in the sea and the pounding ship made the birds' food more easily visible.

Then came the most severe night of storm of the entire outward voyage; the wind tore at the masts until its monotonous song became shriller and louder. If one goes up to the bridge on such a dark night when every gleam of light is extinguished because of the iceberg hazard, one can see nothing but spume and spray, meagrely lit by the light on the mainmast. The ship's struggle becomes comparable with that of a person. One has to think in terms of struggling and losing, winning and dying. The sea, which appears to slide past us in the night, becomes the symbol of a great river which hurries past us like our own lives.

At 50°S, as a further enhancement of the southern scene, rainbows alternated with snow squalls; the latter swept over the ship, leaving a thin skin of ice on her hull.

Thereafter the weather became calmer, the sea abated and while fog rolled furtively around the ship the first remnants of ice appeared so that we continued on our way amidst some apprehension and uncertainty.

By dead-reckoning we were not more than 76 minutes from the island. Now whales blew quite often within our constricted range of vision.

Whales and icebergs, which we encountered quite often within 80 km of the coast, repeatedly lured the men on deck from the warm crew's quarters. One would often hear one new arrival asking another: "Is that a whale out there?' And the reply: "Yes, there was a little one alongside just now."

Yes, soon we will have firm ground under our feet again; we've come through the seas of the Westerlies tolerably smoothly! If only one could say the same about the jazz music which the men prefer and which has recently been blaring from the quarter-deck.

Are there as many whales again this year as last? Will Arne finally be able to build his girl that house in the woods? Will Ole be able to acquire that patch of land to which his neighbour has been clinging so firmly? Will the stoker, Johansson, a Dane, be able to fulfil his dream of driving through his village in his own Ford car?

In addition to the whalers there are three people standing on the bridge; on the afternoon of 18 September they are full of anticipation as the first Antarctic icebergs, like slender towers or wide, almost square plinths, present their sides to the seas, which break against them in roaring, hissing waves. Then, at 5.00 in the afternoon, the captain pointed to a bright gleam to the south, with a grey, undifferentiated layer of cloud lying oppressively above it. To starboard a wide, vague slot opened, probably the entrance to a fiord on the northeast coast. "Possession Bay" suggested somebody uncertainly, who had known the island since 1904.

As every revolution of the screw brought us nearer to the coast, although delayed by areas of reefs and shallows which necessitated minor changes of course, one's searching eye could discover through gaps in the clouds, rock ridges, cirques, glaciers and cliffs on the extended mass of the island.

Around 9.00 p.m. as we swung out of the wide Cumberland Bay, almost feeling our way, into narrow King Edward Cove, a sudden change of course as the ship crept slowly forward through the calved ice masses from the Nordenskjöld Glacier brought us into the inner part of King Edward Cove. The lamps and lights of the Grytviken whaling station sprang into our line of sight from a black rift in the cliffs.

Thousands of penguins and elephant seals were roused from their rest at this hour of the evening as our steamer's whistle, which had reached her distant goal after almost 32 days, resounded several times from the mountain walls around the bay!

2

Grytviken, the Wild West in the South

NEXT MORNING, as we wandered through the Argentinean whaling station, in an understandable state of excitement and curiosity, the impressive impact which the settlement had made on our receptive senses the previous night, when so much had been concealed, quickly gave way to harsh reality. We gazed at large, round tanks, which must contain whale oil. We saw a snow-covered work plan which diligent shovels were already clearing of its load of snow, and actually the first heap of elephant seal blubber which the sealing vessel *Diaz* was just landing. She had begun the hunt on 1 September. Hence the first heap of gold was lying between the chimneys which, belching smoke, indicated that work had already begun. We found ourselves in a small factory complex which even included primitive wooden houses for the workers, who this year numbered a little over 200.

Narrow railway tracks ran across the softened, oil-drenched ground, meandering between whalebones, barrels and heaps of scrap iron from shed to shed. Behind all this the unadorned building of a small church protruded as if from another world.

Whether one liked it or not there was no doubt that this sober scene was an expression of Germanic energy, which one could not but admire. Like anything built by men whose aim is to make money quickly and hurriedly, it lacked subtlety.

On the first day we experienced friendly weather, we took a walk up the nearby slopes; after a rapid ascent we found ourselves in a different, unspoiled world within barely ten minutes. In a southwesterly direction, 80 m above sea level, lay a large lake which I still remembered well from 1911 since it and the snow-covered boulder and talus slopes in the background were a frequent destination on my ski trips.

A gleaming sheet of ice still covered the lake, and one of the highest mountains in South Georgia, Sukkertoppen (Sugartop), about 2500 m high, was reflected in its clean-swept surface. Only along the shore, towards Grytviken had the ice started to break up. Southern black-backed gulls (*Larus dominicanus*) and some terns (*Sterna vittata*) sat tiredly at its edge, searching for the first little crustaceans in the clear patch of water.

But in contrast to the purity of the environment, even here technology had commandeered the narrow outlet of the northern part of the lake. An uncommonly prosaic but effective concrete dam had impounded the water, thus producing probably the most southerly dam in the world. Small cracks in the dam indicated the effects of frost and other severe climatic assaults. Two generators, each of 200 hp, and most recently another of 400 hp, provided the station with water and electricity. We happened to read the name Siemens and Schuckert on the cases which were lying around.

The stream, whose life had been drained by these human interventions, and which had delighted us in 1911 when it was still a natural lake overflow, flowing over a cheerful waterfall with rich cushions of moss and tussac grass, had had its day. It had been relegated to retirement as long as men live on the island.

We again follow the stepped stream-channel downwards via a slight detour until quite unexpectedly we find ourselves standing on a little shelf of land in front of a homely, weathered cross and are reminded by the inscription: "Slossarczyk, III Offizier der Deutschland" of the abrupt end of this young man, who found his death in the waters off South Georgia. The cross does not mark his grave; it lies somewhere out there in the restless sea. It is simply a memorial cross, erected through men's faith.

This is not the only example in South Georgia's past history of occasionally erasing its northern visitors from among the living. As we descend the slope completely to a little hut which houses the radio station linking the island with the rest of the world, some more colourless crosses project from the snow. In 1912 a typhus epidemic, the germs of which had travelled to the healthy shores of South Georgia from the slums of Buenos Aires, attacked the young men living here and resulted in this row of crosses, which a loving hand still occasionally decorates with a memento. Even if one were to renew or modify it every year, there would be little point here, since the storms gnaw incessantly at the crosses and the snow lies deep over them for the greater part of the year.

Among these crosses, amidst adventurers and seamen from all over the world, is the grave of the great British polar explorer Sir Ernest Shackleton. A stone obelisk preserves his memory. As we reflect on his many achievements, especially on his final voyage aboard *Endurance*, we read the inscription which his grateful native land has dedicated to the great explorer:

To the dear memory of
Ernest Henry Shackleton
Explorer

This cemetery, set in this mountain solitude, penetrated only by the roar of the breakers and the calls of the gulls, speaks a different language from one at home. It is the loneliest, most impressive cemetery I know, just as lonely as men must be in their last hour.

One is roused from these meditations, to which one can devote oneself more easily and more readily in this seclusion, by the factory whistle which announces that it is noon and time for the lunch break. Walking through groups of workers hurrying to their quarters, we make our way via narrow planks laid on the soft, greasy earth to the dwelling of the hospitable station manager, Captain Esbensen. There are no guest rooms in Grytviken and hence our "headquarters" are in the draughty warehouse of this handsome building where we have spread our sleeping bags on the floor in a cheerful company. The steward and the cook had a small room nearby, and these artless fellows taught us to appreciate many an hour of conversation. When we exhausted conversation and had crawled into our sleeping bags it became even more cheerful. Now the singing and dancing began, but this time executed by a very unpleasant group of animals, namely by swarms of rats. They flourish on the island in the same unmolested fashion as the colonies of penguins and elephant seals which we later encountered in the field. If we had made a point of attempting it I believe we could have got them to eat out of our hands. At any rate they shared our camp and provided the nightlife; it was not until, out of necessity, we later requisitioned two cats that they kept their activities within reasonable bounds.

During the days after our arrival we were kept fully occupied and the time passed in a peaceful, concentrated and natural fashion. Given the hospitality and interest shown in our expedition, our members worked cheerfully as they hauled individual pieces of baggage from the pier at which *Harpon* lay to a warehouse. We were certainly glad that our muscles were in good shape. For no matter how much occasional help we were offered by the muscular whalers we knew only too well from earlier encounters how these offers should be interpreted; understandably, with the start of the frenzied activity of the whaling season they become fully occupied elsewhere. Moreover our own work could only be done in short stints between pauses, so that Benitz and I soon got used to it. Despite our care many of the smaller cases of our considerable accumulation of expedition material had got lost in the capacious hold and as a result our work was held up at times. If there were no pieces standing on the deck ready for us to haul ashore we could take a rest and make short excursions into the area round Grytviken with a clear conscience.

One such excursion occurred on our first Sunday on the island, 23 September, when we took a hike to the Hestesletten, a plain in front of the Hamberg Glacier, discovered by the Swedes. The route lies along a boulder-strewn beach, first in a southerly then in a southeasterly direction. At low tide one can walk along the beach the whole way. But when the tide is rising, in places one has to hike along slopes which drop fairly steeply into the bay and which initially are interrupted by harmless little rock faces. At this season there is no vegetation to be seen. Winter still stubbornly prevails, unbroken, in the bay. The beach we walked along no longer displayed its pristine beauty. Every whaling season since 1904 had played havoc with it. The bones of whales lay piled in great heaps, while the rocky section of the beach displayed a yellowish-brown coating derived from rotting whale offal, slippery with oil and highly unaesthetic. After a few hundred metres one was delighted to leave behind these mementos of this great whale extermination. One found oneself breathing quite deeply as one reached a small stream spanned by a bridge made of two whale vertebrae sunk into the soft ground. Beyond it one was again walking on clean snow, one's eyes blinded by the sun as it sank in the harshly coloured western sky. There was no water rushing down the stream; apart from a section near its mouth it was frozen solid. The Norwegian [Argentinean] station now lies behind us, hidden by the last bend in the coast. There is no factory installation impinging on the view or on one's quiet, undisturbed contemplation of it.

We had barely been walking for half an hour, hurriedly and excitedly, when everything was new for us again, or at least was a fresh discovery: the breaking waves, the surf, mountain peaks, slopes and cliffs. Suddenly Benitz, who was taking this walk for the first time in his young life shouted in surprise, almost in a fervour: "There's one lying here!"

His entire search, his endeavours and his haste that day were bent on his first sight of an elephant seal. He sat crouched behind a rock waiting for us, so as not to disturb the animal. The kelp was playing in the water. Waves gently washed the bulk of the female seal. Lit by the sun, pieces of ice shone almost as if they were alive; when occasionally one paused to listen to the play of the waves one could hear a distinct crackling like that of a wood fire. It was either just the brash ice jostling together, or little explosions produced by the effects of the sun as the water veins in the ice which had frozen solid during the night, now widened, producing little explosions.

While the rest of the fauna, Southern black-backed gulls, Cape pigeons and also one or other species of giant petrels, as well as skuas, flew up from the rocks as we approached as if they were communally trying to warn their world against men, the only movement we could detect from the seal which Benitz had spotted was when it turned its head and gazed at us fearfully. The sun was reflecting from its black eye, so that for a moment it glowed like a large, flashing stone.

To judge by its girth this was a pregnant female, and in order not to disturb its peace we made a little detour; before we had walked more than a hundred paces we spotted a further group of seals, huddled together and lying partially on the rocky beach, partially on a snow surface which bounded this part of the shore, being separated from it by a steep drop. Almost all the animals were pregnant females; only a few of them were slim and not obviously pregnant.

But our good fortune was enhanced even more when at this spot, all concentrated in a small area we found something which we would so often admire at our various camps over the course of the expedition. Among the females we spotted two quite long masses with black pelts and with their eyes already open. When we detected a short, shrill crying tone, almost a bark, we knew that on this part of the island the first pups had already been born (it was 23 September). They were a good metre in length and one could see a cross-striping in their coats; remembering the appearance of the skulls of newborn babies I told myself that these might possibly be birthmarks. But ultimately the very simple explanation was that their pelts were lying in folds since their young, newborn bodies did not quite fill them yet.

We also saw other things at this point. Among the cluster of females, which may have numbered 20, lay a powerful male, as if embedded in their bodies. Its hooked nose doubled and tripled in size as it roared in excitement on becoming aware of us.

In the case of elephant seals, one needs only to see the nose, quite apart from any other features, in order to distinguish the sexes immediately. Individual animals, somewhat alarmed, began to change places a little; in order not to disturb them further we hurried on along the beach towards a conspicuous rock nose which projected towards the sea.

Our considerate haste was in fact unnecessary; we had gone barely a hundred metres when a group of three young lads came across the snow. They were undoubtedly young members of *Harpon*'s crew who also just wanted to see some elephant seals after their long sea voyage, and were using their free Sunday to do so. One could not object to that. But the peace around us was shattered. We and the animals were no longer alone. Still absorbed in the young life of an elephant seal or delighted at the discovery of a shag out fishing on the reefs, we had to watch as stones flew through the air. They scared up a young gull then chose as their target a giant petrel which, having eaten its fill, was almost helpless as it staggered along the beach, hampered by the weight in its stomach.

When the young men reached the elephant seals it

became abundantly clear that they viewed the environment and its life forms differently from us: more as a field of activity for their young muscles and whims, or for their courage, which they had had no particular opportunity to put to the test on the voyage out. Initially we were rather angry, but soon began to see things more calmly, thinking of our own first experiences in this strange environment. We told ourselves: one really should not take it so seriously if the lads throw stones at an elephant seal, which to them is such a hideous animal. When one is younger such aggressive behaviour is often more easily provoked by an abrupt contact with the animal world. We finally saw our way to accepting the fact that no matter the area involved, it is part of human nature to express one's self-assertion, perhaps most readily in a hard, stern environment in which a man may see himself as poor and pitiful.

After two hours, including all the pauses and delays resulting from the terrain and from watching animals, we reached a large plain, the Hestesletten. Hestesletten means Horse Plain. The area was given the name by American sealers who once left horses here. The animals could run around here freely and unfenced since the sea and the mountains provided a natural corral.

A white snow surface, almost horizontal at first sight, stretched away towards the Hamberg Glacier. From later investigations by our expedition we now know that two lakes lie at the southern edge of the plain, towards the glacier. Today, if we stand on one of the wide rock pinnacles which, like lookouts, are such a striking feature at the start of the plain, we can just detect the lakes by some slight cracking of their ice cover. Also a sinuous slightly sunken road seemed to be incised into the landscape; this could only be the course of an ice-covered stream.

In its steeply descending lower course the Hamberg Glacier is interrupted by a rock face, but below this cliff it reconstitutes itself as a new glacier which forms a proper glacier tongue. This latter is presumably fed by ice avalanches from the section of the glacier above the cliff.

The main ridge of the island was rarely visible during our entire expedition and today was no exception. Although there was an almost cloudless blue sky the ridge was embedded in clouds, clouds of snow blown from its ridges where only on very rare occasions do wind and storms abate.

For the return journey we selected a route across the eastern edge of the plain. We had to pick our way on our skis from one rounded hill to the next, scattered among which lay numerous small ice-covered pools. The origin of this landscape now became clearer. We knew that the hills we were skiing over had to be abandoned lateral moraines of the now relatively small, rudimentary Hamberg Glacier. Alerted by the first description of this area, written by Gunnar Andersson, from the dome-shaped hills we could also pick out three terraces which, seen from a distance, ran like straight lines along the rocky slopes on the eastern side of Moraine Fiord.

They undoubtedly could be interpreted as remnants of the earlier lateral moraines, deposited by the current small glacier at the head of Moraine Fiord, the "De Geer Glacier". But the "De Geer Glacier" has left more than this; the east and west sides of the little bay are linked by a row of boulders on which today only gentle waves were breaking. When we came within striking distance we could see individual boulders protruding out of the water. This bar was investigated by the Swede in 1902; he interpreted and described it as the end moraine of the previously more extensive "De Geer Glacier".

While we were thus attempting to understand the composition of this altered world, the twilight of the southern late winter descended on the plain. Above a snow-covered pass to the west, which in fact leads to Cumberland West Bay, small, delicate mackerel clouds were spread across an obscured sun. An hour later when we had long since passed the little elephant seal colony where we had watched a bull seal approaching the colony from the sea, it was a clear, starry night and pale moonlight trembled over Cumberland Bay.

    Hundreds of gulls stood almost motionless on the snow slopes, facing into a gentle west wind which slid down the slopes in gusts. It was like a peaceful massed assembly. Only a few ran into the wind, their wings spread as if to dry them. In King Edward Cove the quarrelling of the Cape pigeons was still not silenced; occasionally one would hear them fly up en masse with a great rush of wings when they were scared by the splash of a boat's oar.

    As we came around the final headland we suddenly saw the lights of the station again. Were it not for the lingering memory of the loneliness and strangeness of the day we had just spent we might have been in a remote industrial town back home.

    I must admit that it was good to lie in the soft lounge chairs at the hospitable station; there one could share the view of the whalers that one has to make life comfortable on the island. Hence we lay sheltered in a comfortable nest which friends had prepared for us.

    Movies were shown twice per week; in addition there was an extra movie showing on evenings when the whaling results and chance brought two whale catchers into harbour simultaneously. Then the men were given an evening at the movies, which was also eagerly attended by the factory workers, office workers, and also by the upper crust, the director, doctor and chemist. At least on film one could see beautiful women and one could listen to music provided by *Harpon*'s crew, and for an hour one could forget the oil and the cliffs which cut Grytviken off from the world and from every outside contact. Incidentally the movies were shown in the church which Captain C. A. Larsen originally had built because his was a pious, unspoiled faith. There was even a temporary priest here once. But as things are today, all that is no longer necessary. Church, pulpit and altar are still standing, certainly, but one only needs to cover the latter with a

2. Grytviken and King Edward Cove

3. On the way to Hestesletten

4. Delicate mackerel clouds hung over Echo Pass to the west

5. Hamberg Glacier and the Sugarloaf formed the backdrop to Hestesletten

flag and the movie theatre is ready. Isolated from things religious by this drapery, jazz music takes over where previously the priest walked to the altar.

This transformation is somewhat strange, however. I was told that people down here had neither anything to laugh about nor anything to cry about and hence had no need of a priest. Or on another occasion that the priest who lived here had thought more about his salary than his people. He introduced into his sermons the things which depressed him in his isolation, rather than what was troubling the souls of the workers.

However that may be, I cannot easily imagine the role of a priest. Moreover, as a solution it does not seem very important to me.

No, when I stand on the steep slope above Grytviken and gaze at the sea and the ice-covered pinnacles of this wild mountainscape, or when at night I listen to the rattling of a gale tugging at man's handiwork and trying to annihilate it, I can imagine that God is quite close to mankind without any church. Man can hear him breathing and see his workings in the surf. He is evident in every species of bird and animal; more recognizable in the soil than in the scheduled sermon of a priest who received the princely salary of 9000 kroner, a salary which must almost inevitably have eliminated his effectiveness if he wanted to talk of happiness and love for one's neighbour to workers and his brother men. Natural chords and their interaction may well be stronger than the human words of a priest.

In the meantime 27 September had rolled around. The days had passed quickly in unpacking and organizing our things. We left a depot at Grytviken and took with us only what we needed for our first camp, which we planned to establish at Coal Harbour at the west end of the island. Inwardly we were long since ready to make the trip but we were still short of a few things, among them the most important of all, a case containing our two primus stoves. But then on 27 September this last culprit, which had been hiding from us for so long, turned up. Now as far as we were concerned there were no further obstacles preventing us from establishing our camp in the west.

But we still had to pay three visits, dictated by form and necessity. But they were all quite simple since all three destinations lay on Sauodden or Sheep Point [King Edward Point]. This headland, from which the masts of the wireless station also towered up, derives its name from the fact that the first whalers encountered some feral sheep there; an American had released them on the island after his attempt at establishing a farm on the island had collapsed.

First we visited the representative of the British authorities, Mr. Stewart. He carried out the duties of the representative of the Falkland Islands Government on this outlying territory of South Georgia and kept an eye on men, whales and contraband. We received from him official permission, for which we had already applied from home, to collect for scientific purposes two specimens of each bird and animal species on the island. Next we visited the members of the British *Discovery* Investigations* whose leader at that time, Mr. Fraser, gave us a very friendly welcome and expressed enthusiastic interest in our work. As we sat in their tasteful lounge by an open fire and then later were conducted through the work rooms, from which on clear, sharp days the mountains around Cumberland Bay must have distracted one from one's work, for a moment one could not but think of the advantages of a rich nation. And in the warm comfort one could not but think of the two tents which would represent our accommodations and working space from now on.

Our last visit was to the meteorologist, a Norwegian, who was housed in a small, grey house, nearest to the bay. Here we compared our aneroid barometer to the station's

---

*The British *Discovery* Investigations is involved primarily with studies of whales and their biology

mercury barometer, a task which took only a short time. As an introduction the Norwegian frankly informed us that he held his position only by accident. Meteorology was quite alien to him; he was really a businessman, heart and soul, and we were made fully aware that the movements of currencies and shares were much dearer to his heart than air movements. His frankness made a very sympathetic impression on all of us, since it has become such a rare commodity on earth, like so many other abandoned ideals, and we had only sympathy as we followed his train of thought, which focussed on shares and transactions.

Even in our sheltered bay the day on which we made these obligatory visits to Sauodden was stormy and rough. Lashed by southwesterly winds the bay lay grey and cloud-covered; only a single iceberg glowed with rich blue colours. The bay was alive with flocks of birds in their thousands, especially Cape pigeons; this is always interpreted as a sign that there is rough weather prevailing out at sea.

Benitz and I had moved all our baggage aboard the whaling vessel *Tiburon* during the course of the morning, and when we returned home in the evening Captain Esbensen asked us, as the gale hurled one squall after another into King Edward Cove: "Well, you won't be wanting to go to Coal Harbour yet; you probably want to wait until it's getting closer to spring or at least until the weather is somewhat better?"

No, we would prefer to leave for our field area in the morning, assuming the weather would permit. Naturally we would leave it to him to select the day and time of our departure. On hearing this and realizing that we were serious in wanting to reach our objectives, he informed us that *Tiburon* would get us to Coal Harbour by 7.00 p.m. next day.

3

Our First Camp at Coal Harbour

L̲ET ME ANTICIPATE. Not a soul could tell me the derivation of the name of this bay. It is purely an accident that it bears the name "Coal Harbour" and I myself have nothing to contribute. It appears fairly certain that it owes its name to some insignificant incident, most probably involving one whaling vessel bunkering from another here.

The vessel *Tiburon*, a small craft capable of 12 knots, put to sea with us early on the morning of 29 September. It was a cold morning and the sun glistened on the icicles which hung from shrouds and rails. A plastic brightness lay over the world, perfectly appropriate for starting the day happily. The southwesterly wind blew quite frequently from the main range of the island. Thanks to it and to the resultant clouds and snow squalls, only the immediate surroundings of Cumberland Bay were clearly visible. We could see only the lowest parts even of the adjacent Nordenskjöld Glacier. In the morning sun its crevassed cliff, almost 2000 m wide, looked like a cemetery with numerous gravestones made of ice.

The wind had driven an abundance of bergy-bits towards the exit from the bay, but they lay quite loosely and dealt the ship only a few harmless blows. Around 8.00 o'clock as we passed the light-beacon on Larsen Point at the entrance to the bay, an addition of recent years, the coast of the island progressively disappeared and one could distinguish only vague outlines of a mountain base.

On the first leg of the voyage as far as Stromness Bay we encountered two tabular bergs. One of them, otherwise intact, had had a mosque chiselled from its side and maintained this unique formation as we steamed close past it, and thus were able to admire it from every possible side.

Around 9.00 o'clock, as we were avoiding two more icebergs which appeared ahead of our bows with uncanny suddenness, and when the grey houses of a whaling station in Stromness Bay had long since disappeared from sight, another iceberg about 25 m high drifted across our course. Hence our first excursion was blessed abundantly enough with these unpleasant hazards. One of the latter was three-pointed. Deep shadows already lay in the clefts beneath its three summits. Another still had the pristine shape of Antarctic tabular bergs; only the face turned towards the coast tapered to a point which, in profile, resembled a human face.

By around 10.00 o'clock we had completely lost sight of the coast. The captain indicated that, judging by the time, we were off the bay which is marked on the British chart as Antarctic Bay. It was now blowing very strongly in a very heavy snow squall. An old northeasterly swell was being broken up by the gusty wind which had swung round to the southwest; as a result the movements of our little vessel had become short and choppy.

Again a flat, eroded iceberg emerged from the uniform grey. A quick turn by our handy vessel resulted in a change of course which guaranteed safety. What had become of the promising morning we had experienced in Cumberland Bay? Had that location captured all the sunshine and light for the whole island?

The ship was now completely iced up; seas were constantly washing over her deck and the voyage was becoming more unpleasant by the minute. This was certainly a rough first day. How nice it would be to be lying in the lounge chairs back at Grytviken! Shortly after 11.00 o'clock I climbed up to the bridge and learned that some barely-visible snow-covered islands marked the entrance to the Bay of Isles.

Hence on this rather uncertain voyage we considered

ourselves fortunate to have sighted these white bosses which projected, hump-like from the sea and could only be the Welcome Islands. For the waters off the coast of South Georgia are foul and there are many reefs and shallows which have not yet been charted.* Since I had not seen my companions out on deck for a long time I went into the captain's cabin to look for them; the captain never left the bridge that day. I found both of them more or less in good condition but they did not appear to be very enthusiastic about this type of sea voyage.

Since the porthole was iced up and hence provided no view, after a meal of salt fish, that fine old sailing-ship fare, I went on deck again. Here I found the ship's engineer, now that the tension was increasing. We could already see a snow-covered, pointed pyramid, the summit of Bird Island, which marked the entrance to Bird Sound.

I estimated that the narrowest part of the strait was barely 400 m wide and many a whaling vessel must have thought itself in trouble here. We watched, full of admiration and hope, as the mate at the helm guided the vessel through the furious breakers, calmly and surely. The legendary Scylla and Charybdis cannot have presented more of a menace to seafarers than Bird Sound. Fortunately the narrowest section is short, so that after a few minutes one's grip on the shrouds could relax a little; we had been clutching at them with perhaps exaggerated force to prevent ourselves from being thrown overboard. Every one of our earlier experiences with dangerous seas paled by comparison with this frenzied channel.

Thank God! The wings were widening; the strait was becoming broader and we could already see the exit leading to the south side of the island where we no longer needed to contemplate and ponder over a change of course every metre, as had been necessary in the strait.

---

*It was on this stretch of coast that an uncharted reef and raging breakers finished the whaler *Sky* and drowned her crew of 13 men.

Once we had rounded Cape Paryadin the weather on the south side of the island cleared up and we could see as far as Ice Fiord, which was quite besieged by icebergs.

Then a further abrupt change of course brought us into calm, peaceful waters and we steered into Coal Harbour which from a wide mouth towards the southwest tapered into the interior. It was already 4 o'clock and since time was pressing the men of the crew immediately helped us ashore with several boat-loads of gear to a beach where a large bull elephant seal welcomed us with angry roars. But finally he disappeared from his confined resting place when he found four men in the immediate vicinity.

Our boxes now lay on a narrow strip of beach and since we were expecting high tide there was no time to lose; we had to move everything to safety. But we looked in vain in the surrounding area for any sign of spring, which individual whalers had promised us; even the sealer Johannesson expressed the view that summer began earliest in the western part of the island.

A snowdrift over 3 m high barred access to a little, short valley and delayed the selection of our campsite. We first had to cut a few steps in the snow face with a shovel in order to reach the terrace. Small ice floes lay around on the kelp, which the last storm had cast ashore. They may have been remains of icebergs or else parts of the snowdrift which had been overhanging and had broken away.

While we exerted ourselves to the maximum in order to get our boxes above the snow face, since the water level was rising visibly as the flood tide came in, despite our rush we could not resist casting a glance at this or that new and unique feature of our surroundings: at the elephant seals which swam around us in the bay, or northwards beyond the snow drift where the ice cap on a summit, rising amongst the clouds, repeatedly inspired us.

Accommodating our dinghy, a heavy craft which prior to our departure from Grytviken Johann Tömmermann had put into such a satisfactory and handy condition, caused us real problems now that we had become aware of the nature of the beach. It was too heavy to be hauled up a cobble beach or over the snowdrift by three people (two men and a woman), and we decided to anchor it using a buoy. A mooring line, running through a block, was secured to a post driven into the snowdrift. It thus allowed the boat to be hauled in case of necessity, and moved out beyond the rocky shallows when it was not being used but had to be made secure from storms.

Unfortunately our attempts at driving the post deep into the snow were foiled by a hard ice layer which lay beneath the upper snow layer, hence hereafter checking the security of our boat imposed a daily walk to the beach on us.

Once we had laboriously secured all our boxes (70 in total) from the rising tide and had moved them above the snow face, we immediately set out to find a campsite, since nightfall was not very far off. But here luck was really in our favour. In the short snow filled valley a few dark patches and a faint gurgling beneath an ice cover betrayed the underground course of a stream, faintly indicated by a channel in the snow.

The immediate landscape around us consisted of small, flat or domed hills, separated from each other by small depressions. We pitched the two tents behind one of these hills, 100 m from the landing place. We thought that this choice would give us maximum shelter against the island's prevailing winds, namely westerly and southwesterly gales. Here the storms should have spent themselves somewhat on the hills surrounding the bay, so that they ought not to be able to do any further harm to us and our belongings.

Apart from four heavy cases of bread which were sealed and watertight, we hauled all our belongings to the tents on our sledges that same evening. When it got dark two tents glowed in the white, lonely, hilly landscape. The larger of them looked like a yellow paper balloon, of the type one uses at garden fetes. That first evening we had only the absolute essentials to hand: our sleeping bags, the primus stove and some food.

The first nights under canvas in a strange, inhospitable country are a dubious pleasure, in terms of transition. One's senses are heightened and one wakens quite easily when the wind stirs, when a flight of ducks wings past the tent gabbling, or when one is assaulted by the cold towards morning.

The morning after our first night at Coal Harbour I was wakened by muffled footsteps in the snow and when I stuck my head out of the tent sleeve I saw a remarkable scene. A party from the ship's crew, eight men strong, was out and about at this early hour. A wan twilight still lay in our little valley. Their gear was strange to me and quite unique: the men were armed to the teeth. Flensing knives, ropes and ice axes formed the major part of their equipment and we concluded from this that they must be responding to some unusual hunting drive.

Then it occurred to me that earlier, when we were still back at Grytviken, I had heard that Coal Harbour was one of the whalers' favourite harbours, one which they could not praise highly enough. Not only for the shelter it gave from southwesterly gales, but also because of the numerous young albatrosses, which are still sitting on their nests in their down plumage at the end of the southern winter.

The leader of this killing party was the ship's engineer. He pursued his careful work with particular zeal and thoroughness, as was later revealed by the success of the hunt. To our regret we witnessed the entire proceedings from our tent. His Herculean physique and strength, which he certainly owed in part to his inactive life, stood out sharply against the snow; he took long, rapid strides in order to discover any sign of life and to cover the largest possible area. Each of the men who went swarming out from the starting point had been allocated his own territory.

Then we watched the swinging strokes with which the

iron hooks struck the magnificent heads of the young birds; watched the men run on to the next occupied nest; in brief within our field of vision a whole series of operations was executed to which no animal-lover could be indifferent.

Finally we even had the dubious pleasure of seeing the Sunday hunters' bag, amounting to many birds. Although they were seamen their stomachs came first, even if the delicacy consisted of these defenceless, half-fledged birds which must be something sacred, as a symbol of the sea, to anyone who has ever sailed the southern latitudes. Certainly this was not a favourable start for our bird studies, at least as far as the albatross was concerned.

Hence to a certain degree we were delighted to watch the men depart in the afternoon, even though we had no fault to find with them otherwise and were indebted to them for their ready assistance in getting ashore. But from what we had just experienced they were very disruptive intruders into the environment. How thorough the work of our visitors had been we were able to establish when a morning ski run took us over the neighbouring hills. We found innumerable nests; we could see the elegant mounds with their slight rounded depressions in every direction and all in excellent shape but there was not a single young bird left although we skied around for a full three hours on that dreary, grey morning.

Only when we found the nest of a giant petrel (*Ossifraga gigantea* [= *Macronectes giganteus*]) with a sitting bird, more by chance, among some snow free rocks, did our exhausting search start to make some sense to us again, and despite today's disturbances we began to detect the still undisturbed paradisiacal qualities in the environment of the island. But even this bird was not as undisturbed by man as one might have expected in such a remote area. As we cautiously approached to within 10 paces of its nest it flew off, smashing the newly laid egg as it took off; the egg still showed no sign of incubation.

Once the weather had become clearer in the afternoon

we headed nothwestwards towards a bay which is named Elsehul on the map. At first the route took us north from the camp up a short, steep rise, and we reached a small, almost circular, ice-covered lake which was embedded among the hills. We had barely climbed a few metres farther uphill when we saw another lake, then after some gentle ups and downs we reached a valley which ran from east to west.

If one proceeds on in a westerly direction, one reaches an almost level plain, 9 m above sea level, from where one can see two bays: Undine Harbour to the south and Elsehul to the north. To the west as one hikes along, a mountain chain provides a magnificent background; it shuts off the western tip of South Georgia in a continuous wall. For simplicity, since it runs from south to north from Cape Paryadin, we named this mountain ridge, which had no connection with the main range of the island, Paryadin Ridge. This ridge repeatedly drew our gaze; on a later occasion we were able to cross it via a pass at a height of 230 m. Still snow-covered at this time of year it seemed so massive, even although its average height was only about 300–350 m, because it rose sheer from the main part of the island, indeed almost straight out of the sea.

As we looked out from our vantage point, our view encompassing both bays (indeed on calm days one must be able to hear the surf on both coasts from here), Benitz spotted a solitary penguin who was strolling around quite alone in a hollow in the isthmus between the bays. It was a gentoo penguin (*Pygoscelis papua*) whose dark back made it stand out in its white surroundings. Like all newcomers, to whom the endless wildlife of South Georgia appears like the fulfilment of the wildest youthful dreams, Benitz wanted passionately to handle this comical little fellow, with his upright, honest gait. He could not restrain the impulse to chase after it on his skis. For both parties, the penguin and Benitz, it was an exciting chase; for us spectators at least it was quite entertaining. Once the hunter had reached his goal, i.e. the penguin, during which operation the skis were more of a hindrance than a help, we watched him stroking and calming the creature. Once he had satisfied his whim he let the bird go again, but after a few steps it stopped and stood calmly. After being handled by *Homo sapiens* it was essential that it put its plumage in order again, so as to be able to make an appearance inconspicuously in its rookery in Elsehul.

Encountering penguins, totally alone, on this isthmus ridge was not an accidental, isolated event. Later we often saw small groups of penguins land in Undine Harbour and make the trek from there to Elsehul on the other side of the isthmus, where the rookery is located. It is difficult to decide whether this was by mistake. In any case it was a long trek for a penguin through deep snow and with a southwesterly gale.

When they are travelling over level terrain penguins have an important, staid, solid gait. Taken altogether there is nothing frivolous about them and every burgher at home would feel a kinship with these creatures, if he did not feel himself so proud and exalted.

Even although it would be likely to produce quite a reaction, every spectator is inclined to transpose the souls and minds of these people, good solid citizens, into the plumage of these birds, no matter how unscientific and contradictory a procedure this might seem, in that their gait, like that of the penguins, can often be so pompous and important that one could almost believe that the weight of the entire world was resting on their shoulders and that life was really no longer tolerable.

But let us return to the Elsehul area in order to get a fuller view of the penguins. There things are really hopping: the southern spring is just about to arrive! There is still nothing very organized about the rookeries which are just at the developmental stage. Numerous penguins stand out against a snow slope as they clamber up a hillock, 80 m from the beach. Here the new penguin rookery is taking shape at varying heights from 10 to 30 m. Quickly scanning the entire scene we initially identified 60 birds, but in the course of the afternoon they increased to a good 150. Every day a new stream was arriving and in a week there would be several hundred.

If one turns one's attention away from the busy penguin rookery and focuses it on the surface of the kettle-shaped bay, which today is smooth, one can clearly identify the reinforcements making for land. Far out to sea one can see them leaping out of the water, resembling dolphins in their lively play and in their movements. If one tracks the turbulence in the water it approaches closer and closer to shore, where a bold, resolute leap right onto the beach marks the conclusion of a day, and for many of the penguins even many months, at sea.

With the exception of the king penguins, which are resident on the island throughout the year, the annual cycle of all South Georgian penguins is divided into a life at sea and a life on land. When the first autumnal storms blanket the island with snow gentoo penguins and macaroni penguins (*Cattarractes chrysocoma* [= *Eudyptes chrysolophus*]) head out to sea; they come ashore again just at the time of our visit to breed, build nests and enjoy the brief glory of summer.

If walking is too slow for them they lie flat on their bellies in the snow and propel themselves along with their stumpy wings.

Never again during the ensuing weeks did we see the birds so excited as during our first visits to Elsehul. The easygoing creatures had become quite busy, with no time to waste. None wanted to arrive late; they all needed a mate in order to make their lives happier.

Later in the day we moved from the basin-shaped bay to the rookery itself, where there were already signs of the start of reawakening life and of pairing.

Why are two penguins standing motionless over there behind the restless tufts of a tussac, as if there were nothing else in the world apart from them? Some occasional billing and some formal bows are the visible expression of a tender relationship, even if it has not yet been consummated; they are together, they have found each other safely, and they are paired for the summer!

What do these two care about the other singles who lounge around, not knowing what to do with their time, but yet rearrange a nest in leisurely fashion, almost acting as if they wanted to build in order to demonstrate their good intentions and thereby to make a female more willing.

Who can explain all the tricks of a penguin heart?

South Pole expeditions which have had to winter in the South (I am thinking primarily of the wintering of Otto Nordenskjöld's Swedish expedition and especially of the personal reports of Captain C. A. Larsen) have stated that in the case of penguins only the male builds the nest. We can accept this view only conditionally. We would prefer to say that the start of nest building is the male's obligation. But once the rough structure is completed, our frequent observations established that later it only delivers building materials. It will bring a tussac grass stem or a scrap of peat which it has stolen from a neighbouring nest, and with which the female will continue to build up their nest.

Stealing nesting material from another nest is the simplest way for a penguin to acquire such material effortlessly and indeed it is the usual way, as one can perceive from the many minor scenes of persecution which are hourly played out before the observer's eyes.

In contrast to these scenes of penguin nest-building, everything else that we recorded in our notebooks that day on the other abundant wildlife at Elsehul, sank into insignificance, whether it be a sheathbill tripping around restlessly on the rocks, leopard seals sleeping undisturbed in the bay, or female elephant seals waiting for their imminent arrivals.

Our return route to our camp on Coal Harbour was by way of Undine Harbour. By contrast with the abundant life in Elsehul no particular animal or bird life stirred on the wide beach at Undine Harbour, although only some parts of it were still covered with snow and ice. Only a few elephant seals lay widely dispersed. The grey of their hides was scarcely distinguishable from the surrounding sand and were it not that one or other of these lumps of fat occasionally fanned itself with its rear flippers, one would have passed by without paying any attention had one been standing on a rise above the bay. Indeed we would have taken back to camp an even stronger impression of a cruel, hard coast.

Around the tents the whitish grey of the landscape had become even denser. As early dusk fell, unbroken by any stars or by the moon, the first teal landed in the stream by our camp with the punctuality of a human schedule, and started playing and gabbling in the waterhole from which winter has released its grip, so that it is a joy to watch them. Like a low, timid child's whistle which is quite easy to imitate, their calls rang out in the night and we heard what we assumed was the male's answering call, a deep snarl: Ru ru ru!

They were not at all shy and they were present every evening thereafter; soon we could easily entice them to within two or three metres by imitating their calls. They would quickly change their course if one of us imitated their soft whistle. Even if we were fetching water in a bucket or if the aspirating psychrometer was emitting its whirring noise, a whistle was sufficient to set them at their ease although for the first few times they flew up at these unaccustomed noises. Long after we had crawled into our sleeping bags we could hear their undisturbed activity nearby until late into the night.

The wind tugs at the walls of the tent and it is impossible to get to sleep immediately. The noises of the night come alive, and even if they are all natural and we know that there is not another soul nearby and that nobody can reach us overland, they are alien to us and one after the other we try to identify them. They include the flight of a giant petrel which shoots straight-as-a-dye over the tent, the gurgling of an elephant seal in the bay, or just the chuckling and glugging of the stream which discharges into the surf beneath the snow, 100 m away.

On 1 October we awoke shivering and restless; it had been a long night and the cold from the snow beneath the tent had seeped into our bodies. There was a crust of ice on the water bucket; it was –2°C outside while inside the tent it was +5°C. As the flame of the primus began heating our breakfast the temperature inside soon reached 12° and 15°C, a pleasant warmth, almost like a trip to the tropics until, after a quick and direct transition through the temperate zone, one plunged outside into the sub-Antarctic climate again.

The weather was foggy and stormy with repeated snow squalls. Once we were awake the tent walls gathered the morning brightness; they glowed yellowish-white and one had the feeling that the weather outside must be beautiful. But when one eagerly and happily stuck one's head out of the tent sleeve the landscape lay, grey and indistinct, without any view of the nearby hills and certainly not of the ridge to the north. The sun has cheated us again today. The survey compass can be left in camp; the camera can stay in its case; our bodies, tired by a sleepless night, can stretch out again until finally a stored-up burst of energy drives us outside in order to fill the day with whatever work is possible.

Today we want to go fishing and to set our nets. Since the tide was at full ebb we found the boat lying on the rocks, and it took us an hour to free it from where it was wedged. As the first strokes of the oars took us through the dense kelp to the clear, open waters of the bay, we saw the head of a leopard seal (*Hydrurga leptonyx*) shoot out of the water very close to us. It was quite unafraid and approached to within 1 m of the boat, probably just curious rather than aggressive, although as newcomers we were not entirely sure of this. At any rate it was quite uninhibited in its desire to watch us, and since we had shipped the oars, although keeping them in our

6. Access to our campsite was barred by a high snow cornice

7. On the voyage to Coal Harbour icebergs drifted across our path

8. Coal Harbour from a hill above the inner bay

hands so as not to be totally defenceless, we could admire at close quarters its lithe build, its domed head which had a certain lizard-like quality, and its predator's dentition. While so doing we had time to think about all the myths and facts which we had heard repeated so often, either in terms of stories from others, or of our own experiences. Certainly the leopard seal is not harmless, even if its relationship to man has not yet been tested in a serious situation.

When I went fishing at Cumberland Bay in 1911 along with Dr. Göldel, who with courage and skill had relieved me of my appendix, then too the head of a leopard seal had surfaced quite close to the boat. It surfaced repeatedly so that at that point, when we still lacked a peaceful attitude towards the Antarctic fauna, we relieved ourselves of our fear and tension by hitting the animal a powerful blow on the head with an oar. Gunnar Andersson, Swedish explorer and a member of Otto Nordenskjöld's voyage on his South Pole trip similarly relates in his lively accounts of a minor adventure with this animal, whose existence and character were then even less well known than today. "Once during our sojourn at May Bay [Maiviken] I wanted to try my luck fishing from a canvas kayak in our little boat harbour. But I had not got many metres from shore when I heard a slight splashing behind me; when I turned I saw the hideous head of a leopard seal rearing up above the side of the kayak. A single blow from it would have capsized me, and then I would be hanging upside down in the round hole in the kayak. With a few powerful paddle strokes I shot forwards, but again the monster immediately reared up high above the after part of the kayak. Thinking of its large pointed, predator's teeth I swung the kayak towards land and paddled with all my strength at the same time shouting to Skottsberg and Andrew who were in the tent. The leopard seal was still close behind me. While Andrew scared him off by throwing stones, Skottsberg pulled the kayak ashore and quickly helped me out. As soon as Andrew stopped his fusillade of rocks the leopard seal came up onto the beach where he rolled to and fro, opened his mouth wide and made all kinds of entertaining movements. I have never been absolutely clear as to what he really intended towards me and the kayak. But after this incident I completely lost any desire to head out into the fiord in the kayak."

While Gunnar Andersson's adventure tallies with our experiences the whalers go a step farther in describing their experiences with this sub-Antarctic animal. They told us that two of their people were once fishing from a boat in Stromness Bay when they spotted the heads of two leopard seals peering over the edge of the boat. Since they were a little uncertain about handling their fishing lines they hauled them in and were about to row a little farther when one animal leaped into the boat then, after blowing briefly, slid over the other side back into the water.

Personally I have no reason to doubt this report, having had occasion to observe the graceful antics of the animals which so frequently surfaced right beside the boat when we were putting ashore, holding their upper bodies stiffly erect and in this position inspecting the boat and us occupants. The urge to play and curiosity, nothing more , are quite adequate to explain all these incidents. The fact that they do not attack man unless one particularly provokes them may be deduced from one of our experiences at Coal Harbour.

On a stormy day, as we were rowing out to the rocks at the entrance to Coal Harbour severe squalls and heavy seas forced us to go ashore in one of the little side coves so typical of the east side of Coal Harbour, since despite our most energetic rowing we could not reach our boat-place in the inner part of the bay due to violent offshore winds. As soon as we had landed we spotted a leopard seal almost 3 m long lying 3 m from the water and gazing at us inquisitively. We were completely without any weapon and had even accidentally left the boathook at home. With our flabby, tired muscles we could not haul the heavy dinghy up the steep shingle beach, but in view of the heavy weather we could not leave it to its own devices either but had to protect it from the surf so that it did not receive any damage. Nearby the sea was sweeping furiously over rounded rocks and we could do nothing more except wait, engaged in these tedious activities until the waters of the bay became calmer and we could put to sea again.

There now occurred the strange phenomenon that the leopard seal, which may have been made somewhat uncomfortable by the scent of man, began heading for the sea with snake-like movements and taking what was for it the shortest route between the boat and ourselves on one side and the obstacle of the rocks on the other. We ourselves remained absolutely calm and did not annoy the animal as, to our relief and amazement, it slipped by us through this narrow passage. Once it had reached the water the seal swam to and fro a few times, having reached safety; it would raise its narrow head inquisitively above the water as if it wanted to watch our activities a little longer.

Whalers are not particularly fond of leopard seals. Wherever its head appears it is sure to get a bullet, even if the kill cannot always be retrieved. For it is primarily a predator and in their minds its sharp fangs and its uncannily supple build, which distinguishes it from every other species of seal, can alone elicit a hunting urge. But often the object is only the animal's liver which is considered a delicacy and is so large that it can provide a good meal for the 12-man crew of a whale catcher.

Perhaps another reason for the whalers' dislike of the leopard seal is that in any bay in which it is encountered any attempt at fishing is pointless. Since it feeds almost exclusively on fish they believe that its appearance makes all the fish in the bay nervous. Our experience indeed confirmed this.

And so our fishing trip on 1 October was fruitless. No matter how often we lowered our spoon lures among the fronds of kelp, at the edge of which experience had taught us fish are most numerous, we never hauled up anything other than the lure.

Moreover, while we were fishing the sea became quite rough; although the waves were moderated by a reef at the mouth of the bay they still rolled right in to where we were anchored so that we began to drift and were carried back to our landing place almost without a single oar stroke.

Just as disappointed as we humans graceful terns (*Sterna vittata*) followed us in little groups as we drifted; they had been hoping to get some little scraps for their ever-hungry stomachs from our catch and they circled very trustingly to within 50 cm above our heads. If we had had a small net we could have caught them like butterflies as we did a few months later at King Haakon Bay in the case of the elegant little petrels.

To conclude this minor, unfortunate excursion we collected flotsam and jetsam along the beach and filled our jars with some starfish, sponges, spiders and bristle-worms in order to be able to record something positive for the day.

We were scarcely back at the tent when a violent gale with snow squalls began; the tent walls flapped furiously so that we had to go out again to check the tent pegs and fetch some supplies from the cases in lieu of the fish we had anticipated, had talked about that morning, and had been looking forward to with such certainty.

The period from 2 to 10 October was a self-contained period during which almost every day was climatically identical. Since the weather was full of the most unpredictable foul whims our existence consisted mainly of being confined to the tent, although this was interrupted by minor periods of activity and by hikes over hills and slopes which quickly became very familiar and which contributed new charms to our days.

In the early morning hours, when dawn broke without colour or light and the southwest gale carried the normally distant-sounding song of the surf to our ears, we would sit in wait in our cramped tent. We would get sore backs and would become restless until, despite the foul weather we could not bear it among the hillocks and our piles of baggage. Then we would often walk down to the boat in order to check that the moorings were a match for the storm and, if possible, we would check our fish trap which we would have to haul up from a depth of 16 m some 100 m from the beach. This minor trip would often require the entire strength of two men, since the wind gusts would hit us so strongly and persistently.

Disappointed if the fish trap came up bare and empty in our frozen fingers, despite the fact that we had baited it with a large, meat-covered bone, we would be all the more delighted if we found something alive in it: some fish or one of the chestnut-brown starfish: such items we would take home with glee and satisfaction and add to the zoological collection, the assembly of which was very dear to our hearts right from the very start.

We had just got back when further excitement arose. My wife came rushing into the tent to inform us that a leopard seal on the beach intended visiting us. I quickly stuck the triple-barrelled gun and some cartridges into Benitz's hand and watched him disappear, full of hunting zeal, towards the edge of the snowdrift, while I shouted after him; "A neck shot if possible, so that we get an intact skull."

Over the harmony of the surf, the wind and bird calls we scarcely heard the shot; we were sure of it only when Benitz called for me since he could not retrieve the animal on his own and the sea was threatening to reclaim it. This kill filled the remainder of the day. We had no room for carrying out zoological preparations and it is no trivial matter to skin a large, slippery animal in several degrees of frost in a gale and drifting snow. The only convenient aspect of the job, which institutions at home might envy, was our double water source: we had the raging surf and also to one side the cheerful little freshwater stream which flowed out of the snow bank, across the shingle beach, then plunged into the arms of its big brother.

 Until now the bay had been very quiet but once we began this job it came to life. The first to appear were the Antarctic jaegers, the skuas, who lay in wait beside us and on the snow bank, taking up their positions in anticipation. Later the giant petrels arrived and finally the southern black-backed gulls and the little terns. They all arrived despite the fact that they were all busy with nest building and mating at the time, apart from the skua, which is not in such a hurry to mate, and nests later than the others. We could hear their calls and watch the foreplay which precedes mating. When it was as easy to fill their stomachs without effort as it was today they all quickly forgot about the topic of love. From idealists they became materialists when they spotted the first accessible scraps so close to them. Nor did they worry any more about the two men at work, and they flew up in alarm only when we threw the blubber which we thought we would use for fuel on fine days over the snow bank. But then they would return to tug at the heavy, bulky slabs all the more voraciously.

 Some of them, more fearful, took off with heavy loads in their bills, but often had to drop them in the bay because, in their greed, they had exceeded their capacity. Often too we would watch a repulsive conclusion to this general gluttony: giant petrels which do not know what moderation is, and fill their stomachs to bursting, would vomit shortly before taking off, in order to be able to take off at all.

 But all the other birds in the vicinity of the bay: the sooty albatross whose call rings out like the latter part of a cockerel's call from the rocky cliffs on whose sheer faces we discovered its nest, the wandering albatross and the shags, stayed well away from this feast.

 The entire job of skinning the seal was really nauseating for us but Benitz had the advantage that as a boy he had grown up near a slaughterhouse and hence knew extremely well how to execute certain tasks. Mastering a layer of blubber is not an artistic taxidermy operation but a raw, dirty task with which one can only be reconciled when, years later, one sees the animal on show in a public museum.

When we huddle around the primus in the evening after such a bitterly cold day its roar seems to tell us something about cosiness, warmth and the delighted voices of children. And when, soon thereafter, the aroma of leopard seal liver wafts through the tent and we have made the final trip out to record the meteorological readings, we forget the entire day's labour and the icy southwest wind which rattles in vain at our secret lair.

It is a remarkable contradiction and one which I have often experienced and thought about: at times I feel more lonely in large cities and among crowds of people than here in this lonely, remote camp where, when it is quiet, I can hear the beat of my own heart. The noises of nature soon no longer disturb us. Does the noise of a giant petrel zooming by scare me as it skims over the tent like an aircraft which has switched off its engine? Shouldn't the alluring whistle of a duck or the roaring call of a bull elephant seal seeking a mate with avarice and lust, make me happy? Even the almost human call of a skua ringing over the slopes, no longer scares me since we have come to recognize it and know that the original sound has been modified by the wind and the blocking tussac slopes, so that it sounds like a shout of alarm.

I am probably a traditionalist and probably a relic. But when I watch the flickering film of life scurrying past me at the station in a large city, or when I have to move as prescribed by custom and obligation in a congested circle of people, I am almost overwhelmed by even greater loneliness and strangeness.

One can almost never be lonely in the solitude of the Antarctic where one is daily overwhelmed by an abundance of observations and new impressions. And when, despite everything, a longing for people surfaces, it is extinguished again as quickly as a faint strip of the southern lights in a gap in the clouds.

In the desolation and loneliness of the powerful surroundings one experiences more than elsewhere a God-filled yet Godless mystique but imbued with the inseparability which links us to the dust of the earth. Without any narrowly circumscribed, precisely specified idea of a God, nonetheless one is close to the Almighty without the benefit of crucifix, communion, mass, confession or mediation.

The day I have just described was one of the many which we so frequently had to endure when hills and sky merged into each other and our instruments could remain unused in their cases. Almost daily one of us would walk to the west side of Coal Harbour where we had discovered a quiet little idyll of animal life, even if one had to hang on to the tussac grass clumps so as not to be blown over in the gale. A strait running east-west has cut through the west shore of the bay which farther to seaward degenerates into rocks and reefs.

This little strait, which represents the shortest connecting route to Undine Harbour and which one can even use on boat trips, differs enormously depending on the time of day and state of the weather. The channel is rarely calm and smooth but when it is its waters glow like a green mountain stream. Currents from both ends clash in the middle where there are hidden reefs.

In the morning, if the sky is grey and one stands on the summit above this strait, it is eerily dark. Then it looks almost like a subterranean vault, covered with clouds. In the evening, in the twilight, night creeps into the clefts and gullies faster here so that the water yields the last bright glimmer to the night sooner than in the open bay.

But we love this quiet corner with all its eeriness because it has so many varied beauties and can produce an experience even on a stormy day.

Our camp is nestled between walls of snow and the snow is drifting more heavily than usual from the snow bank. The little stream is again covered with new ice so that the little ducks are anxious as to where they can demonstrate their love and trumpet the coming spring to the world. As we reach the edge of the snow bank we stoop and peer cautiously over, searching the beach for a leopard seal. If it is all clear and there is no life in the bay we work our way up over slopes mantled in deep snow where we sink to above our knees, until again we can make easy progress on rocky ridges, over moss cushions and rocks which are only glazed with a thin crust of ice.

Sauntering carelessly across the slopes to the bay one stumbles almost accidentally over a white, shapeless lump which sits on a little pedestal. It is a wandering albatross (*Diomedea exulans*), the first adult we have found in our area. Its head is stuck under its wing and the black-marked wings are barely visible since they are covered with drifted snow. It lies sleeping, facing into the gale, on an old nest to which the wind has added a border of snow. I carefully walked around this unique scene in a little detour until the restless, tightly circling flight of a sooty albatross drew my attention to a steep schist face on which I discovered the bird's nest. Tussac blades tossed restlessly around this practically inaccessible nest, which lay in a little niche. Stripes of snow ran around this nest too, and also lay on the bird's wings.

Black-backed gulls and terns, which are always the first birds to announce any danger with their excited calls, had already discovered me; this forced me to cover the few remaining steps to the cove where a new scene presented itself.

I spotted a newborn elephant seal pup completely drifted over with snow; it lay half a metre from its mother and when it changed its position slightly I spotted the stump of the umbilical cord. I deduced from this that the birth had occurred only shortly before. Its barking noises, like those of a puppy, rang out shrilly in the cold air; I watched the pup searching for its mother's nipple. As the pup began to suckle the mother lay on her side in order to make the pup's first treat as accessible as possible.

These three animal scenes which I had just enjoyed were set in a harsh, gigantic landscape. Tattered clouds lay over the summits of the Paryadin Ridge to the west and through them a brief ray of sunshine poured silver across Undine Harbour.

The sub-Antarctic landscape is filled with harshness, certainly cold, and almost tragedy; involuntarily one's thoughts leap across the stormy seas which separate it from the Antarctic, the personification of death in nature.

Pushed and buffeted by the wind I wended my way back to the tent in the twilight. A white, blowing veil again extends from the snow bank towards the bay. Beneath it I can now spot a cow elephant seal, whose body lies more than half in the water. It is probably looking for the pupping area in Undine Harbour but has taken a wrong turn. Only rarely does this sociable animal give birth alone.

These little animal episodes give the day some content, even when any more serious scientific work is impossible. We extract from the grey days not just isolated images, not just a few species of a family of birds or animals, but we receive enhanced impressions and images which set the sea and the bays, the snowy peaks and clouds in an effective framework.

4

In the Elephant Seal Colony

I SHOULD LIKE TO TALK ABOUT one of those grey days which formed the prelude to our stay on the island and about a ski trip to Undine Harbour. The skis ran well on a good surface over a firn base. We climbed the steep, little slope, heading due north to the little inland lake I mentioned earlier. After crossing a few easy terraces and troughs one came into sight of another larger, fairly long lake, farther to the west on the east side of Undine Harbour.

After 45 minutes one reaches the last summit overlooking both bays, Elsehul and Undine Harbour, and if one now heads southwest for some distance one's skis glide down into a narrow little valley which one needs only to follow in order to find a large elephant seal colony, even in the worst weather.

During our stay at Coal Harbour the elephant seal colony was our commonest destination, which we could reach no matter how heavily the snow was falling, totally eliminating any distant view. We wanted to observe the seals' complete annual cycle and every stage of development was to be filmed. Every Antarctic travel book reports on elephant seals to some extent and many strange things turn up in the stories of the whalers and sealers, but nobody has devoted months or even longer in order to capture every facet of their life and their habits. The first essential for recording the biology of the elephant seals was that one had to be prepared to occupy a tented camp on one of the stormiest coasts in the entire world for a long period, unflinchingly and cheerfully.

On the dismal day of 7 October when the clouds hung

especially low and drearily on the mountain faces we found an intensified level of activity in Undine Harbour for the first time. Dozens of females stirred from their slumbers in alarm, with a sad, fearful look (the animals' sighing reminded one of a bible reading), as three people in flapping coats walked along the top of the steep drop which the sea had formed (mainly from flotsam) 20 m from the present waterline. Immediately below this drop lay the elephant seal colony.

We soon spotted the first pup with its dark coat; the fresh umbilical cord revealed that it had only just been born. At that moment our attention was drawn to an unusually imposing animal which reared up, with a great deal of excited bellowing then, when we moved on, headed towards us.

I have to describe this animal, a bull, in more detail. Although it was never friendly to us humans, but invariably became angry and excited whenever we disturbed its magnificent idyll, nonetheless it was our friend. It was a one-sided friendship which remained unreciprocated no matter how much effort we made.

Its large, wide, nervously trembling and almost incessantly mobile nose which hung down like a trunk and to which some scars added even more prestige, told us that this was a large bull. At the time it ruled the entire colony, a harem of a good fifty cows, which clustered around him, protected and coveted by him; they had already started pupping. The animal was a little over 5 m long, an extraordinary size at a time when diligent sealers had been pursuing their trade for a long time; we found no other animals of this size anywhere else on the island.

The seal's blubber flowed down, wide and flabby, on either side so that its underside, flattened out by its lying, reached an astonishing width. One could easily lay one's arm in one of its folds. Its hide seemed to have difficulty in containing its accumulated abundance of blubber. Without reflecting over much on the topic we thought of him as an obese epicurean as seen through human eyes, naturally, and on occasion even nick-named him "the stock speculator." On another occasion we gave him a much more unequivocal name, which the reader will have to imagine for himself, since I have no desire to set myself on a hostile footing with individual human groups.

But how astonished we were when this blubbery colossus revealed an agility and speed which otherwise was totally alien to these animals in their normal ungainliness. Whether we challenged his quiet, unthreatened peace as intruders or whether the scent of man was alone sufficient to make him irritable, he charged at us. Benitz, who despite the foggy weather had begun filming enthusiastically, was so absorbed in catching the great head with its gaping jaws on film that on our first visit, when we hoped to establish a friendship with the animal, it was only at the last moment that he escaped its angry assault, which was really seriously intended.

One should not be at all surprised at this. During the breeding season all its senses are more alert and irritable, its vitality more intense, its watchfulness more acute and its suspicion stronger, as indeed is the case with humans too, although in our case only an isolated case will arouse all these emotions.

But in the case of the elephant seal he is concerned with possessing fifty cows. He is truly very strongly polygamously inclined. He wants to possess and enjoy all of them; even man is not allowed to disturb this dream of the entire year. What does he know about man, who waits only to take home his image, the impression of his magnificent, elephantine head?

The unrest in the colony that day did not die away and we soon noticed that we were at least partially responsible as we moved up and down. Hence we lay down behind a block of ice, drifted over with sand, and watched what else the day had in store for the seals. In front of us an elephant seal pup had only just been introduced to South Georgia's environment. An indescribable wailing had drawn our attention to the event, which must have occurred unbelievably quickly, since by now peace and quiet reigned there again. At the outset one of the mothers had been uttering these plaintive noises, but we had not been entirely sure that such a plaintive call preceded the birth. But all was well; the pup had arrived and we could see that it was hungry, since without further ado it sought and found its mother's teat; the latter quickly satisfied the young animal's desires.

We did not see everything which I shall now report on 7 October, but in order not to dismember my narrative too much I shall introduce a few aspects here which in fact we observed on later days and weeks.

Mother and pup are not always left alone. The pup is barely born when a bird appears, about which I shall write several times again later, namely the Antarctic jaeger or skua, which is never absent from the landscape of South Georgia on any occasion when there is something to be picked up.

What is there to be scavenged here, we thought, when the skua appeared immediately after the birth? But its hooked raptor's bill was already pecking at the placenta; then another skua arrived, and in a few moments the placenta had disappeared. The young elephant seal now had one impediment less to handle in its young life. The round, ponderous object which it had dragged with great effort through the sand, was eliminated; only the remnant of the umbilical cord which was too tough to provide any attraction for the skuas, bore witness to its brief time on earth, as it crawled away, relieved of its load.

The audacity of this predator of the South Georgia avifauna exceeds all description. It could be seen daily at Undine Harbour. If there were great activity there, i.e. numerous births, one would also see black-backed gulls, although with their brilliant, snow-white undersides, one would not have suspected them of it. But they only began their work when the skuas could not handle all the material alone.

But the skuas did not sit expectantly and modestly at the edge of the seal colony, no they sat right in the middle among the cows, which would occasionally scare them off by a threat, especially if a bird became too insolent and actually took up its position on top of a pupping cow. Hence hereafter we were kept informed of the course of events by the presence of the skuas.

It is not just the afterbirth that the predator is waiting for; occasionally it will also dive down on a stillborn pup, still lying beside its mother. We could not even observe whether the pup was truly dead.

This ghoulish meal is not exactly a pleasant sight; as a special delicacy the skua always pecks out the eyes first. From our human viewpoint this does not make the bird especially lovable.

As I have already described I saw the first elephant seal pup on our hike to the Hestesletten near Grytviken on 23 September, but one can state that the main pupping period extends from the beginning of October until the last weeks of November.

Without stressing farther here the inherited and hence established qualities of the young animals, let it be said that immediately after birth the pup searches for and immediately finds its mother's nipple, and that it can achieve coordinated movements. For example a change of position can be achieved and incontestably one may observe, in particular, scratching movements immediately after birth.

We saw the first mating, i.e. the first copulation, about three weeks after the cow had given birth. The temporally close juxtaposition of birth and mating makes the colony particularly restless and multi-facetted, so that an otherwise quiet bay echoes with the young sounds of the pups and the calls of fear of the mothers which have difficulty in eluding the often premature onset of the copulation urge of one or more males.

When I spoke earlier of the large bull, the pasha of the elephant seal colony, I also mentioned its vigilant care for its wives.

They probably all belong to him momentarily, as long as he can defend them by virtue of his strength, age and experience. But just as we humans all have sleepy moments, so too does this old fellow. He is tired from excitement, from desire and from staying on the alert, night and day.

If by chance one's gaze strays from the scenes in the colony to the surface of the bay, which today lies heavy and oily, a head occasionally surfaces. Like a dark bullet it approaches steadily closer until, by its hooked nose we can recognize a crusading bull whose goal is the colony of cows. While the old bull sleeps he approaches the edge of the herd undetected, constantly scenting the air and looking around. Without moving a muscle he had already made an approach to a cow lying near the water; indeed things had advanced so far that they were having fun in the water together. Playfulness and passion were aroused. Full of lust the young bull drives his fangs powerfully into her neck and extends a flipper across her back as if to embrace her.

But then the old bull wakes from his slumbers, smells a rat and hurriedly charges over cows and newly-born pups towards the challenger. His excited breath jets whitely into the cold morning air. His angry roaring echoes eerily from the cliffs around the bay. We tensely watch his progress, hoping that a battle will develop. But his challenger, who is of much lower rank, hastily retreats. Soon his head is just a small, dark point out in the waters of the bay, heading out to sea. Almost contemptuously the gurgling of the lord of the colony rings out one last time as he reclines amongst his cows once again.

Apart from the main colony where we observed all the events just described, there were also some smaller groups of elephant seals around Undine Harbour; here too a bull was the supreme monarch in every case. By the middle of October the entire population numbered 100 animals, 88 of which were cows and 12 bulls.

It was interesting to note that outside this colony, about

150 m away, a concentration of mostly younger bulls appeared. They lay there, closely packed, and took advantage of any opportunity to steal a cow. We called this site the "knights' hall" because they were all young heroes, three to five years old, lying in wait here. Even here every new arrival was seen as an intruder; all day long, until late into the night, little battles were played out here, although in this case there was no actual possession involved but at best a very dubious chance of access, since none of these "knights" had free access to a cow but first had to fight for or steal one.

On every day that we visited the elephant seal colony there was something new to see, even if the overall picture remained the same. But the numbers and the ratios of the sexes revealed constant changes; there were always rearrangements of groupings occurring. Only one aspect maintained a steady course although day-by-day it displayed an intensification: birth and mating. As a rule we would spend the entire day in the colony if the weather did not permit any other activity. We would sit freezing on a tussac hummock and would hastily consume the snack we had brought with us. Often we did not even get peace and quiet for that and would wait until we returned to camp to eat, since everything was much more comfortable there.

The thread of our stories and observations at night in the tent, would not be exhausted until late at night. Each of us had something to say. Often each of us had seen or interpreted something differently, so that once we had exchanged thoughts and impressions we were very grateful that fate had brought us to this untouched animal paradise.

Finally on 10 October an improvement in the weather arrived. When I awoke at 7 o'clock the tent roof seemed to be brighter than usual. No wind stirred. Anxiously I opened the sleeve entrance and looked out at a blue, cloudless morning. We crawled out of our sleeping bags faster than usual. The first day with bright sunshine since we had arrived in Coal Harbour. As we gazed at the brilliance of our surroundings and at the chain of the Paryadin Ridge it was as if we had awakened from a dreary life in a cellar and were seeing the world around us for the first time. While my wife and Benitz set off eastwards on skis to film the newly discovered young wandering albatrosses and the giant petrels, I set off on foot with tripod and theodolite in order to take full advantage of the unexpectedly good lighting.

I selected a hill which was 40 m high and possessed a moss-grown boulder on its ridge. The hill lay northwest of our camp and could be reached in 10 minutes; from here I managed to take bearings on some of the peaks visible at this hour. Thank God it was calm, since this was indispensably necessary for accurate work with the tripod. When I had finished the job and the mountains to the north, west and east were still towering sharply into a matt blue sky, I walked to another hill of the same height as, and to the north of the first one.

My work here also completed I walked back to the tents. Since I did not find my companions there I wandered across a steep, westerly slope, marked by a conspicuous terrace, to a dome-shaped rise covered only with sparse tussac grass, and continued taking bearings, especially since further peaks were emerging from the clouds. From there I soon saw that a bank of fog to the south was expanding. A tabular iceberg which was still visible, shrank to a little silver object. One could barely make out three icebergs which were drifting past outside Cape Paryadin; and then the dense fog rolled over Coal Harbour with uncanny speed. Warmth and sunshine were over for today; freezing miserably and with numb fingers I walked back down the steep, hard snow slope to camp. Similarly fleeing the fog my two companions had returned from their filming trip. They talked excitedly about the magnificent landscape background to their albatross pictures.

Later that same day my wife and I walked to a giant petrel colony while Benitz tackled a number of technical problems pertaining to housekeeping. Since our primus was occasionally being temperamental he constructed a blubber stove and he wanted to convert a small barrel he had found on the beach into a wash bucket. Yes, Benitz was never at a loss when it came to discovering new possibilities and modifications for our Robinson [Crusoe] life.

The giant petrel colony, which on the day we visited it numbered a good 40–50 birds, lay east-northeast of our camp and we could reach it in 20 minutes. In order to be sure to reach it one needed only to watch the loose powder snow in which our ski tracks increased in number with every trip.

The giant petrel is a wary bird, not so much due to its original nature, but because it has come to know men only too well. They appreciate or like the bird's eggs rather than the bird itself, and many giant petrel colonies receive visits from the whalers every year, especially if they are easily accessible.

One evening Benitz came into the tent filled with delight and spread 12 large eggs on the groundsheet; he proposed to make pancakes.

We had discovered the first egg on the day we arrived in Coal Harbour; now there were many birds sitting on their nests, which lay 30–100 m apart. They are not built as carefully or as artistically as those of the albatross; they are about 15 cm high, little more than a small depression in the peat, in which a few grass blades or pieces of moss have been laid.

We were soon distracted from these peaceful nesting scenes which indicated that mating had already occurred, to a few turbulent locations in the slightly undulating terrain from which a peculiar noise repeatedly emanated. It could best be compared to the miaowing of a cat when engaged in a lovers' quarrel with her mate. If one hears this noise: "Rrrrrrrrrrr-iiiiiiiiii-au" when the bird is in flight, it often sounds like the neighing of a horse.

Using the telescope one could spot three small gathering sites where 4–8 birds were uttering this noise particularly loudly. These were the sites where the females were being wooed.

While the female herself was the picture of tranquillity, only occasionally spreading her wings in order to show herself to advantage, the males were behaving quite crazily: they would bow in three directions then ponderously, with an excited, sideways, jerky step, would try to gain the prize for their strenuous dance.

One could fill pages if one wanted to describe the varying plumages of the giant petrel. No other bird on the island displays such a variation in plumage coloration. We encountered individuals from white to dark, almost black and of every intermediate shade. The German South Georgia Expedition of 1882–83, or rather its doctor and zoologist, Dr Karl von den Steinen, has reported in detail on the coloration of its plumage in his report on the avifauna of South Georgia (Die internationale Polarforschung 1882/83, die deutschen Expeditionen und ihre Ergebnisse).

We never found more than one egg in each nest; the eggs were from 9.75 to 10 cm in length and by our measurements their circumference varied between 18.25, 20 and 30 cm. They are whitish in colour and are of economic benefit, especially since the yolk appears an appetizing yellow.

We found a well-developed brood patch on the male birds we killed. Hence both males and females share the chore of incubation, an activity which we observed frequently later at the Bay of Isles.

No matter how much we admired the bird as it cruised over rough seas out in the open ocean, we could not get close to it because of its foul qualities. In animals, even more than in people, one should just ignore external features, but this is not always so easy. The reception which the bird gave us when we approached its nest, was alone enough. With repulsive retching it would often vomit an oily, foul-smelling liquid at us, and since it had an excellent aim the observer would be enriched by a long-clinging souvenir. It is also said that it vomits over its eggs to make them less appetizing, although we did not observe this ourselves. These foul qualities have given it the name "stinker" among the whalers and sealers, a name which is both popular and appropriate. After the skuas it was always the first to appear when man's bloodlust or a natural death in the animal world provided an effortless meal, and hence carrion and giant petrels soon became inseparable concepts.

In order to provide new attractions for the zoos of Europe thus far nobody has been successful in transporting the stinker across the equator. All attempts have failed. One bird after another has died even before the critical tropical zones were reached. The giant petrel, which soars around ships in southern seas on its widespread wings, almost like some primeval bird, would reject meat or any other food which was forced on it. But when one of its fellows, accompanying it on the voyage north, died, the surviving birds (or so it is said) would throw themselves greedily upon the individual which had taken leave of the unnatural surroundings which had been forced upon it.

Once our rich, well-filled days were over we would begin our lonely camp evenings, squatting around the little milk case which we used as a table, and on which our camp lamp, a hurricane lantern, cast its miserable light. When, with this mystical illumination, our hungry gazes fell on the large, bright-yellow yolks of the storm petrel eggs one had to be able to disassociate the eggs as a *res ipsa*, i.e. as a thing in itself, from the idea of the grey-speckled bird and its evil qualities and habits. Benitz and I had the good fortune to be able to achieve this separation completely, but my wife found greater obstacles in tackling the dish. Three stinker eggs make an abundant dinner! When Benitz received his ration on his aluminium plate it could not contain the entire meal so that he had to use his knee in order to hold this overflowing delicacy in check.

One day (my diary entries place it on 10 October) the

bird sounds of the area were enriched by a new one which we had not heard before. Since we knew that a little pipit (*Anthus antarcticus*) was resident on South Georgia we initially attributed the new, strange melody to this sparrow-sized bird, which on first acquaintance sounds like a joyful trilling. But with every passing day the call became more ardent and lustful until, one dusky evening, we observed the dark shape of a bird which stood out sharply against a snow slope. When we walked closer to this silhouette we recognized it as the whalers' "shoemaker", the white-chinned petrel, known to science as *Procellaria aequinoctialis* [= *Procellaria cinerea*]), whose filing and whetting at the entrance to its dark burrow rang out all night long.

The night belongs to this bird. Only as twilight is falling does it dare to emerge from its almost metre-long tunnel, since the skua is its enemy, just as it is of the dove prion (*Pachyptila desolata*). At the end of the tunnel, often around a final bend, it lays a white egg the size of a good hen's egg, without first collecting any special nesting material.

There is not a single bird on South Georgia that one associates so much with the nocturnal noises right up until the first grey of morning as the shoemaker. Nor is there any other which becomes so ardent and passionate in its wooing or which in its amorous moments "wears its heart on its tongue" to the same degree.

It was a bird which one had to like right from the start, even if its brownish plumage was as unassuming and sober as an everyday outfit, and if its twittering was a complete discord and conjured up comparisons with a file. Just as a file may occasionally slip out of one's hand or may move irregularly at the end of a job when one's hand is tired, the end of its song might often become a discord, a shrill whistle, coming unexpectedly and disturbingly.

When it fell quiet around our camp in the evening and we had crawled into our bags for some much-needed sleep, we would soon hear a noise which got on our nerves more than any other; it turned out to be due to something gnawing mischievously at the tent canvas.

None other than the researcher Gunnar Andersson has broached the question of whether some unknown mammal was to be found on the island, since he too had discovered the tracks of one in the snow.

"Meantime," wrote Gunnar Andersson, "as a tip to future researchers I shall impart a report compiled by the expedition's zoologist, K. A. Andersson on the tracks observed at Bay of Isles: 'On 8 May I observed the tracks of a land mammal on the beach at Bay of Isles. They were partly snow-covered so that in general one could not see their complete sequence. But in the individual tracks I could distinguish larger tracks of four toes quite clearly and the smaller mark of a fifth. Where the tracks lay at a normal distance apart the measurement between two successive front paw tracks was 28 cm.'"

We ourselves had often seen the tracks at Coal Harbour and had even seen the outline of the animal itself on one of the first days of October on an overcast evening when despite the total overcast light was being radiated quite brightly from the snow. Perhaps magnified by the marginal light the animal ran hopping across the snow, heavily and not at all afraid, almost like a small hare.

Finally the time was to arrive when we had the luck to establish the particular details of this South Georgian rodent. One evening when I would have greatly preferred sleeping to a hunt for the nocturnal animal which had been occupying us on the previous few days I heard Benitz cursing in the adjacent tent as he crawled back into his clothes and went off to lie in wait. He armed himself with a long bamboo pole which we had obtained in order to mark the route to Undine Harbour or other destinations in foggy weather. A good ten minutes must have passed when we heard an angry blow among the boxes followed immediately by the shout: "I have one!" Then for better or for worse I too had to crawl out of my nest (my wife showed little interest in the event) and after some searching we found a dead animal among the provisions boxes: it was a rat. So now the question was solved. In a few minutes it was preserved in alcohol and we could leave it to the researchers at home to determine whether the long sojourn on the island had produced any changes in this obviously immigrant animal.

Over the following days the island revealed its worst side and even though we loved this life and were not suffering either from want or home sickness, almost throughout the entire period of the expedition we had to suffer a major hardship, namely that of foul weather. For us it was only a minor consolation that at the end of our stay the whalers said that the summer we had just experienced had been the worst summer in 16 years on the island.

I shall select the month of October quite arbitrarily: only once did we have a cloudless day; on 22 days it was completely overcast, while on the remaining eight days we had a cloud cover of between four and eight tenths. This partial cloud cover would break for a few hours to reveal the sky and a few stars.

It was just as bad with regard to wind conditions. The prevailing gales were from west and southwest, more rarely from the northeast. The highest pressure reading for October was recorded on the 10th, a magnificent day of blue skies; it was 769.50 with a temperature of $-2.0°$. The lowest, 725.00, at a temperature of $0.0°$, occurred on 25 October.

We were often all agreed that the worst aspect of expedition life on South Georgia was not the loneliness, or hauling heavy sledges, but the climatic obstacles: the merciless weather in a grey, colourless desolation, and the associated and inevitable waiting in cramped tents which could last for hours, days or even weeks.

For major projects the October–November period was extremely unfavourable. We were never able to wrest more than a few hours for our work from the weather.

From this comfortless, grey, stormy period which often reduced us to despair I shall cite here some of the diary entries which I confided to my little book every evening so that they would not escape my memory and which I have not altered since returning.

11 October. A severe stormy night, so that we have frequently been starting up and involuntarily grabbing for the tent walls and the tent pole. Since some tent pegs had pulled out we had to overhaul the tents around midnight. We had to brace the tent pole since it is bent into an arc by sudden wind gusts. Rarely have we heard the roar of the sea as loudly as last night. Totally superfluously yet another unpleasant object disturbed my slumbers: this morning I found in my sleeping bag a rusty pair of scissors which the seamstress had forgotten, and which thus had come south with me.

This morning it is melting, with a temperature of 2.75°C and heavy rain. Yet the tussac clumps are still frozen hard and as one strides across them they feel like rocks under one's feet. Due to the melting of the snow cover the little stream has widened to 4 m; the water temperature is 2°C. Its average depth is 50 cm; there are many boulders with generally sharp edges lying in its bed.

Today there was a small bull elephant seal lying right beside our campsite. It was very irritable and a bleeding wound ran across its nose.

At noon we walked to the beach in a fine drizzle, planning to reach Undine Harbour by the sea. In the meantime the southwest wind had raised a heavy surf in the bay. Off the inlet we spotted the lithe body of a seal among the welter of rocks; initially we mistook it for a leopard seal but the pointed head and pointed snout were striking. In addition its bristles were unusually heavy. When we also spotted very small ears we knew that it was a rare fur seal (*Arctocephalus forsteri* [=*Arctocephalus tropicalis gazella*]) which had not been identified by any previous expedition to the island. It had a remarkable number of fresh, bleeding wounds on its body.

Could it be that this seal too was indulging in battles in some quiet, unknown bay? Had it been torn on the rocks during the storm or had it been attacked by that enemy of all seals, the killer whale (*Orcinus orca*)?

Today the little strait was full of turmoil. One was inevitably reminded of Stephenson's descriptions in the story "The mad man," or else one experienced again in brief the memory of our trip through Bird Sound 13 days before.

The turmoil of the sea made our planned trip all the way to Undine Harbour impossible and hence we headed for a small bay on the east side of Coal Harbour, carried along by the waves. Here Benitz wanted to take a photo of the surf in its heavy, dark mood, which is in fact the characteristic mood of the island. While in terms of photography light and strong shadows are the most welcome in order to achieve beautiful effects, sunny shots give almost a false impression of the island.

While the landing was not an easy one because of the rough sea it was even more difficult to protect the boat from the violent assault of the waves. While Benitz clambered out onto the rocks we others had to look after the boat; we were soon soaked to above the knees since our soft rubber boots with their wide tops were excellent for scooping up the water. Then quite unexpectedly one snow squall after another came driving in; it became greyer by the minute until Benitz returned after 45 minutes.

In quick succession four to six breakers would come rolling in, turning the little bay into a seething cauldron, but then there was always a slight quiet spell. During one such pause we hurriedly stowed the camera aboard and grabbed the oars as a raging sea came racing in over the rocks barely a few metres from the sucking beach.

Safely home again we busied ourselves with this and that. We went to see the shoemakers and vainly searched the shale for fossils, while Benitz continued with his stove experiments; the latter now reached fruition and his stove was tested for the first time.

Since it was a somewhat milder day it was only nightfall which drove us into the tent, and as we sat around the primus and chatted about the world back home, which seemed to have escaped our thoughts for a long time, a high flame suddenly flared up outside. Rome was in flames! The entire cooking stove was enveloped in bright flames. It was a rare sight for us and we all laughed heartily over the premature end of Benitz's device, of which he had promised so much for the future. In particular he had often spoken of the many buckets of hot water which would be available for us on washday.

15 October. Bound for Undine Harbour with sledges on which we have stowed our cameras and tripods in order to sound the waters and if possible to film an elephant seal fight. But bad weather curtailed all our expectations and plans. The outlines of the bay were barely visible. At times the wind blew out of the north, at times out of the south.

One repeatedly finds new features and peculiarities in the elephant seals, new sounds which one would like to be able to place and interpret.

As one overlooked the colony today one could divide the scene into three sections spread across the beach, 430 m in length and running east-west. To the east lay the "knights' hall" as we designated it earlier, today occupied by five bulls. Then came the middle group with 60 cows, the pasha and around him a further three bulls. To the west, separated from this group, lay a second group of 31 cows with nine bulls; one of the latter lay in the middle and ruled this group for the moment. Pups were continually being born and again we observed the skuas at their usual urgent business. Again we watched the behaviour of the elephant seal pups in their first hour of life on earth.

They are just elephant seals, of course. But we inevitably think of young human babies, even if not in a very scientific fashion, when a two-day-old pup, lying comfortably on its back yawns and fumbles around in its mouth with its flipper which at this first stage of life reminds one uncannily of a hand. It even leaves it in its mouth for a while just as an infant sucks its thumb.

And again we have to make comparisons with people whenever we look closely at the old epicure with his constantly changing feats of mimicry.

Today he is the picture of happiness: half asleep, half awake, he is enjoying life. Tired, he lies in his blanket of blubber, probably contemplating what a beautiful beach Undine Harbour is.

Several times today we saw him accosting the cows lying around him. They had only recently given birth but this great mass of blubber was still trying to mount them; during the mating season he charges impetuously and without consideration over the wailing pups and we were always afraid that they would be crushed by his enormous weight. Remarkably, they always emerged alive from beneath his resilient body.

The cows tried to flee from him in fear; we saw a few rushing away and hiding from their impetuous master among the other cows. Many were still awaiting the arrival of their pups. In his annoyance his roaring now rang out like a reprimand. We watched the old boss hurl his head or even his entire upper body on top of a cow, hold her firmly with his weight and embrace her with his flippers.

If a cow continually rejects the approaches of the bull, as often occurs, he is not at all upset but simply tries his luck with another one. His choice is indescribably wide since the entire beach is now covered with cows.

At another hour of the day the pasha had serious problems. Nobody should think that all his days are peaceful. One needs only to look once around the circumference of the colony to understand his worries and his constant restlessness; these fears would sometimes overcome him just as people suddenly take fright at the thought of the loss of their possessions.

Out in the bay, rippled by a gentle wind, we see a seal's head, drifting in like a buoy. The head and neck extend high out of the water as the seal stretches and scents the air. The image disappears, then, while we are still watching the restless eddies which it left behind, it reappears closer to the beach. A loud roaring, often like the most perfect belch, resounds in the noonday air. Gazing over the colony, swaying on its rear flippers, it reveals its size and strength.

Now the old bull really has to be on his guard!

The boss of the colony lumbers as quickly as possible to the beach, in spurts broken by pauses, and quickly rears up like a vertical column with angry, blood-shot eyes, near its opponent. The next movements are cautious; there is something cunning and sly about them, until the two animals are lying only a metre apart. In their excitement their breath is expelled in brief white clouds.

Then they rear up quite slowly, stand still for a moment with heads inclined to one side, until the first lunge with the fangs interrupts the stillness. Without a pause, blow upon blow, a continual series of severe thrusts is delivered. These are intense moments; each knows the prize and neither wants to yield. Each wants to be the victor and ruler; one wants to protect his possessions, the other wants to acquire a welcome inheritance. After ten minutes we see a stream of blood running down a brown body and collecting red and dark in the black sand. On the underdog we spot a long, bleeding furrow which runs the length of its proud nose. It is the intruder who is forced to withdraw. He heads back to where he came from, into the sea; billows of blood in his wake betray his course. Not until he is a long way out do we see his dark head again, perhaps bound for Coal Harbour. It is quiet and peaceful there.

A tranquil peace descends over the colony again. The bodies lie sluggishly in the noon silence, broken only by the "kva kva kva" of the black pups. Fog rolls towards the bay from the south; clouds race over the spine of Paryadin Ridge which still wears its white winter mantle.

Once we had completed our observations at Undine Harbour we rarely missed an opportunity to visit Elsehul, which consists of a double bay. Separated from the cauldron-shaped main bay by a narrow tussac-covered rock ridge a smaller bay lies to the west. In both bays there were colonies of elephant seals, in which life and battles, birth and mating are proceeding at a fairly modest level.

Organized conditions now prevailed in the penguin rookery. Most of the birds had formed pair bonds; the nests were further advanced; building material was still being stolen enthusiastically from neighbours; and the first eggs had already been laid.

I feel that I must present an ever-recurring picture of the gentoo penguins which may be taken as typical. It is a brief scene but it reflects all the intimacy and cohesion of a pair of these birds. If both are in the rookery and at the nest the female lies flat on her belly on the eggs, like a tortoise. This is the incubation position. The male stands nearby like a guard, proud and responsible, if we may use these adjectives, borrowed from the language and the qualities of an upright citizen. From time to time one sees it leave its post and wander over to a neighbouring nest. But this is a duty-associated trip since the bird brings back a grass blade or a little piece of peat and lays it on the edge of the nest with a series of bows. It accompanies this with repeated spitting which, however, is much more subdued than in the case of geese, with which it can most easily be compared.

In connection with these proceedings I have been speaking simply of male and female and in many cases, especially with regard to nesting scenes, one can do so with a certain justification. But if one is judging totally without bias, one occasionally has to admit some doubts as to which bird is the male and which the female, since externally it is impossible to distinguish them. No matter how much one compares the speckled white flecks on the back of the head or the sheen and the tones of the back plumage, the colour of the bill or the legs, in terms of external sexual differences any system of standardization breaks down.

The objection is often raised that one interprets certain scenes through human eyes to an excessive degree. In the case of the gentoo penguin with its upright gait and its communal life one simply cannot avoid it. No animal lover, no normal person can do so, unless he simply wants to describe animals systematically. In this area of zoology one simply has to set aside for a moment the crown which creation has assigned us. In the case of penguins comparisons with the upright citizens of a town constantly intrude, with regard to their peculiarities and habits. If one looks out across this large rookery of birds one can easily determine that individual groups of penguins stand out. Even if they all belonged to the same species there were individual associations here. At one moment I thought: could it be that here, where the hubbub and noise rose so continuously, a party system or clan system could have caught hold? As I was tending towards such ideas, so unscientific that any ornithologist would reject them out of hand, a vast number of penguins was walking across the slanting snow slope as if in a procession, one behind the other, towards another group, and the word "demonstration" sprang to mind, a word which always involves the bread basket and much less often any conviction.

Although as a final touch I also saw a penguin which stood with its plumage ruffled and puffed up, like a public speaker on an elevated podium, on a tussac-grass hummock, I forcefully broke this train of thought; perhaps I had allowed it to evolve to this length because that morning I had happened across a scrap of newspaper and by chance I had read about the target practice at Eigelfingen, where people had got so excited about increased beer prices in particular and about things in general.

The gentoo penguin (*Pygoscelis papua*) usually lays two eggs, more rarely three; the yolks are bright red, the colour of ripe tomatoes. The whitish shell is quite unusually strong, in contrast to the egg of the giant petrel.

The German South Georgia Expedition of 1882–83 calculated the incubation time to be 33 days; we were able to confirm this from our own observations at Bay of Isles and from whalers' reports.

We were often able to watch the exchange of incubation duties; it proceeds very slowly and is accompanied by much bowing and caressing.

This peaceful avian citizen has one particular enemy, the leopard seal, which occasionally deals it a vicious blow; I can never forget the cruel scene which we watched one afternoon in Elsehul. As usual during the early afternoon hours groups of penguins were returning to the rookery and we were admiring their landings which are a real credit to the birds. Often, delighted to have firm ground under its feet again the penguin will shoot rapidly and elastically out of the water; on other occasions the poor creature slides out on to the ice, rowing with its flippers a few times before throwing itself into an upright position with a jerk.

On this day the usual flow of landings was interrupted and we saw that small groups of penguins were being pursued by a leopard seal out in the bay. It soon seized a penguin, threw it into the air several times like a cat with a mouse, until after a few minutes only the feathers were drifting on the water, the carcass having disappeared.

Just as with humans there are outsiders who prefer not to swim with the current and do not like associations and societies and hence tend to be called asocial elements, so one encounters recluses among the penguins who hold themselves aloof from the rookeries and try to live entirely on their own for the period of the mating season. Thus we spotted a pair sitting 200 m from the rookery on a slab of rock; here, in desperation, they had quickly and not very carefully

9. Beyond a hilly foreland we could see an ice-covered ridge to the north

10. Paryadin Ridge terminates the west end of the island

11. The landscape between Coal Harbour and Elsehul was hilly in nature

12. Above Elsehul gentoo penguins had begun nest building

built their nest. At first we mistook the pair of birds for a little rock formation; the male and female sat pressed together so closely and intimately, almost cemented together. In order not to disturb their quiet happiness we stayed off to one side and watched a second pair not far from the first, which was also thinking of settling in. But then the little clump of penguins came to life; they did not want any spectators or any plans for new nest construction so close. We watched them defend themselves and repeatedly the interlopers were driven off. We humans took the side of the outsiders and with them were quite upset that they were not left in peace when there were so many unoccupied slopes in the neighbourhood.

As we were hauling the sledges through the sticky snow after this idyll, through a snowstorm which almost obliterated the nearby swellings of the hills, a peculiar surprise lay in store for us just before we reached Coal Harbour. Several times previously I had noticed an almost circular hole in the otherwise unbroken snow cover but fatigue or simply the vast abundance of the day's impressions had always forced me to continue past the spot.

But this time, with a certain positive defiance which cannot be satisfied with any negligence, I threw the hauling line from my shoulder and walked the few steps up the slope. As I widened the edges of the opening a little with my ski pole I involuntarily started back: I saw a dirty, yellow, snapping bill and soon also the downy head of a young wandering albatross. The entire bird was enclosed in a prison which was cold, dark and barely more than 1.5 m in diameter. Only the bottom of the pit was free of snow and revealed peaty earth without any nesting materials.

How did the young bird get into this hole? Was this its original quarters or simply enforced quarters? Had a vicious southwest wind blown the young bird off its original nest hurling it helplessly into the snow, and had its own body heat then made its downy body gradually sink into the snow?

Over the next few days our route took us past the pit several times. We never saw signs of any albatrosses in the vicinity and the mother must have severed all ties with the young bird. At its age, which was comparable to other unconstrained albatrosses, it ought still to have been fed by its mother. Even we could not prevent its fate. On the fourth day we found the starved, emaciated bird dead; when the sun had melted the snow the skuas would discover it and would excitedly utter their wheezing noises as they fought over the rare morsel.

Spring is stealing over the heavy hills and – strange that one should remember it occasionally despite everything that is happening – in our distant home the leaves have turned yellow and brown and the autumn sun is gilding them. Soon the trees will be relieved of their weight of fruit and the wine will be fermenting in the cellars.

In every direction the external appearance of the landscape is now changing: moss cushions stand out more clearly and freshly in their green coloration and tussac clumps are growing out of the snow. In troughs and down slopes water is gurgling valleywards beneath the snow cover. The course of the stream glistens blackly in the snow, while on the snow surface we find large numbers of small, brown or rather yellowish beetles and coal-black spiders which the storms have blown out of the grass clumps onto the snow. On the hills around the bay black-backed gulls are billing and mating; along the courses of the streams terns pursue little worms in the moss while masses of skuas rest, bathe and sun themselves along the sinuous stream.

On days when the snow collapsed soft and friable beneath one's feet and white clouds piled up around the Paryadin Ridge, even we began to believe in spring on South Georgia.

But this dream of a better time, which can so quickly inspire and enrich us humans no matter where on the planet we spend our days, is dreamed for only a short time on this island. The very next few hours or days may eliminate any belief in spring.

On this island of storms spring seemed to be extremely reluctant to arrive; even by mid-November no unequivocal change for the better in the weather had made its appearance. Only the birds and animals were urgently and single-mindedly pursuing their activities, unrestrained by all the turmoil in the sky and at sea.

5

The Surrounding Landscape

APART FROM ONE CONGENIAL DAY which revealed the picture of the landscape around us, the view towards every direction of the compass was never completely clear when one stood on a hill. Hence we pieced the landscape together from the largest possible number of individual observations and views, with the help of hikes and trips of every possible duration both on land and by boat and also with the help of many height determinations. By the end of our stay we felt that we had acquired a composite picture of the western end of the island from all these individual parts.

The southern boundary of our camp was Coal Harbour, which runs from northeast to southwest. The entrance to the bay is obstructed by a reef although water depths of 10 m on either side allowed the whaling vessels unrestricted access. Our soundings of the bay, heavily encumbered with kelp (*Macrocystis*), were carried out from our clumsy little dinghy and with a hand lead; they revealed a depth of 10–18 m in the middle part of the bay while beyond the reef the bottom dropped away sharply to a depth of 49 m. In total we carried out 65 soundings; the task took several days since it was repeatedly interrupted by offshore winds.

If one stood on the 22 m high hill at the head of the bay and looked out across it, both sides revealed numerous small bays and coves, which were particularly striking on its east side. The sides directly facing the bay, rising from 20 to 54 m as one moved from the outer part of the bay towards its head, projected into the sea in places in steep-sided stacks.

The interior between Coal Harbour, Undine Harbour and Elsehul had a hilly, often hummocky character; the highest elevation rising from it was a hill with a flat, moss-covered ridge, 66 m high, which at one unvegetated location displayed a whaleback formation.

At other locations too, the identification of whalebacks, the finding of striated rocks, the abundance of small inland lakes and water bodies, indicated to us that the western end of the island, now completely ice-free, had once been covered by ice. The suspicion that we might perhaps find some of the remnants of the former glacier cover in the form of a small glacier, led us to make a reconnaissance sortie on 21 October. In order to complete the picture of the landscape to the north and west I shall quote from my diary entries from this trip:

Not until 2.00 p.m. on 21 October was the visibility good enough that we could decide to set out on our reconnaissance trip, travelling on skis and without sledges or sleeping bags. We struck northwards from camp, over a short, steep slope and past three lakes; after descending a few metres we emerged into a wide valley running from west to east.

To the north the valley was bounded by an ice-covered ridge about 850 m high, running from west to east. After crossing a stream on a snow bridge we set an easterly course, passing on our left a wide cirque the upper parts of whose walls were mantled in an almost total ice cover. After we had skied for an hour the valley narrowed; we had named it the "Valley of High Hopes." Its steep northern flank supported hanging glaciers which flowed down as if in cascades. An isolated rock pillar, 5 m in height and visible as a landmark for a great distance, projected from the snow like a beacon just before the valley narrowed.

We had reached a height of only 87 m as we skied on eastward into the almost level, U-shaped valley; after another half hour of exhilarating skiing we reached the glacier forming its head. It ended a little above the floor of the valley and had left a few slight moraine ridges below it. Two diagonal crevasses ran across its snout while the whole of the rest of the glacier revealed no crevassing at all.

Since the weather had become uncertain we travelled at a good speed up the glacier, which had an average gradient of 15–20°. It led up to a transverse ridge which rose in front of us; we had often admired it for its sharp ice ridge and peak; when seen at close range it turned out to be completely covered with ice.

No crevasses interrupted our rapid progress, which reminded us of a race since we were so keen to see how things looked on the other side and whether we could continue, especially since a black wall of cloud was again lying over Elsehul. But no matter how threatening the weather nothing could have restrained us, despite the late hour, from taking a look eastwards into the vague, unknown area between Coal Harbour and the Bay of Isles. A southwest wind blew at our backs, helping us along as we covered the final section of the glacier, which was almost level.

Then suddenly we were faced with a powerful panorama: the notch we had reached (at a height of about 400 m) turned out to be a sharp divide. A small ice summit to the south of it overhung on the east in a deep snow cornice. We walked forward a few paces, much too carelessly as it only dawned on us later in retrospect, and found a steep, almost vertical drop beneath us. No technical aids, no ropes, no intensive experience at any mountain school would have been capable of overcoming this obstacle which would have lain in the path of any sledge expedition. Benitz remarked that it was the most majestic, most thrilling view he had ever seen in any landscape. Beneath us to the north we could see Right Whale Bay; to the south the waters of Ice Fiord. Seen from this bird's eye perspective both had shrunk to a very narrow width.

Looking to the east in an excited atmosphere, through the clouds and veils of drifting snow we could see innumerable summits which seemed to grow out of a void in which death lurked, banishing all life. Further ridges blocked the way; it was a chaos of nature and structure, glaciers and clouds.

We got back to the tents in darkness to find that the southwest wind had flattened them. We fished our tarpaulins out of the water; the cases had been tossed around; and the sea was roaring like a single, massive waterfall. It was some consolation that it was a southwesterly gale. If everything went flying we would at least land in the little stream-course rather than in the bay, or would be left clinging to the nearby tussac hills.

That evening in the tent we christened the glacier the "Benitz Glacier" after our cameraman; and to the blocking transverse ridge running north–south we gave the name "Georg Schweitzer Ridge", in grateful memory of Major Georg Schweitzer, who had contributed so much to the realization of the South Pole Expedition at home.

It became a stormy night which none of our friends would have envied and which none of those who made envious remarks about experiencing a new journey, would have expressed any desire to share with us.

Nobody would have envied us that evening as we shovelled out of our tent, the snow which one gust after another had drifted over our sleeping bags. Anybody would have preferred more comfortable accommodations than ours during that long night, during which the gale lifted the entire groundsheet, including us, off the ground.

The term "Robinson life" sounds romantic. In reality on South Georgia it implies a tough, isolated existence. It may be different on a South Seas island where a warm, blue sea reflects one's tent and where palms and bananas make the daily scene a constantly cheerful one.

6

Photography and Technology

IF ONE WANTS TO SEE SOUTH GEORGIA as it is for the bulk of the year one has to mentally eliminate sun and sunshine from practically every scene. Then one has the grey, everyday picture of the island, and not the festive sunshine which nature so rarely provides here in the south, at the gates of the Antarctic.

I shall relate something of the difficulties which a large number of the pictures had to undergo before they found their way to the printing establishment. Benitz always had to develop test-samples of his movie film, especially during the early stages. In addition I placed great emphasis on having my still photos developed immediately as plates since the double trip through the tropics and the uncertainty as to the length of the expedition could easily have damaged the exposed film. Once Benitz had developed the plates or the movie film in his tent, he generally passed them over to me for further treatment, although we did not suspect that this was the more delicate part.

Water was the least of our worries in this connection. We could easily procure snow water and the water from the stream was as pure as the best tap water. The difficulties began with drying the negatives. We could not tackle it in the tent where hair from our sleeping bags was constantly eddying in the air and where the cramped conditions and lack of cleanliness were further obstacles. Hence during one calm period we stretched the roll film between two skis; while we were congratulating ourselves on this simple solution an unannounced gust of wind came along and snatched away our priceless pictures.

Once the wind had thus demolished our experiment of drying film between skis, and even under the most favourable conditions had swept the film across the ground, in desperation we simply put it back in the water bucket and waited for better weather. Once it finally arrived we stretched it out, safe from the wind, in our zinc-covered boxes. We had scarcely finished this task and had set up the first drying apparatus to our satisfaction when a fine snow began sifting in through the overlapping lid and rendered any further efforts fruitless.

Once the film had been deposited back in the water again, during one of the subsequent nights the water turned to ice so that the film lay enclosed like an anatomical preparation encased in celluloid or paraffin wax. Once the ice melted again when the temperature rose we were back where we had been three weeks before. All this and much more complicated our photography.

Perhaps after all this trouble some critic back home will still say that the author's photographic material leaves something to be desired.

The month closed with some terrible days. Thus on 22 October I entered in my little book: "An overwhelming gale out of the SW with a temperature of −3.5°. Condemned to life in the tent we can only do what the moment demands: bracing the tent pole again; fetching water; warding off the cold with another item of clothing; and waiting."

Our backs bent, we occasionally straighten ourselves up somewhat or attempt to do so, and one of us expresses the hope that as a result of this eternal crawling and hunching we will not be irreparably deformed for life, with associated loss of character.

Then once again we enjoy a period of technological achievement, rendered necessary by the primus. This temperamental thing is stinking up the tent and is invariably near to exploding. Benitz brings out his instrument case and screws and files away like the white-chinned petrel up on the slopes. The vaporiser is clogged. We suspect the fuel which we acquired in Grytviken is of the worst possible kind. We have used up or broken all our prickers and have had to use medical syringes. We have even come to the last of these. But it did the trick. The primus can breathe again and is warming the tent without any temperamental tricks.

Midwinter scenes. Today for the first time we reached for our home library; out of respect for the fine literature it is stowed in an old chest for protection against the damp. While a few large, scientific works are leaning against the tent wall, the tea chest contains more condensed works: a few volumes of Balzac, Epiktet's manual of morality which I stuck into Benitz's hand, and especially that little gem of Eduard Smiles' "The character" which has become our family bible. There is a little verse on p. 3 which often became our morale-booster in that first grey, cold morning hour; "What a poor being the man is, who cannot raise himself." Even if this verse were more intended for other lifestyles, it exerted a favourable influence in foul weather. Under the influence of the little book's title, one needed only to repeat it like an Islamic prayer verse in order to be able to crawl more easily from the soft, warm confines of one's reindeer-skin sleeping bag and to undertake one's first sortie into that wretched landscape.

28 October. Another trip to Undine Harbour and Elsehuls in uncertain, overcast weather. On a rock about 1 m high on the east side of Undine Harbour we found the first egg in a black-backed gull's nest; the nest was a shallow depression in the ground carelessly lined with blades of tussac grass. It contained two eggs. They were among the first which we were able to add to our birds' egg collection. We later acquired a whole range of eggs of this species and observed wide variations in their coloration. While in one case they were greenish or grey-brown with dark, almost black

splotches, in another case we found them to be more olive-coloured with irregular brown or more often smoke-grey splotches. Only their size was constant; lengths varied between 7 and 8 cm and widths between 4.75 and 5 cm.

Near the black-backed gull's nest we also observed the first mating activity of a pair of shags, which are not very common on the western part of the island. In one bird, which allowed us to approach to within a few metres, we noticed a blue eye ring. This colouration appears to be a temporary feature of the breeding season since in later months we searched in vain for this striking coloured ring.

In the evening we organized the day's zoological "bag". This is quite a torture in a cramped tent. One squats like a Turk in one's sleeping bag; the formalin fumes irritate one's eyes and are not even neutralized by good English tobacco.

The great joy and satisfaction in compiling a zoological collection derives from something more than sightings and recordings, which are comparable to compiling a filing system, except that the air outside is certainly superior to that in an office and that one's working day is not regimented by lunch times or by the clamour of a bell. The joy lies in the awareness that through the collection material which one brings back one gives many people who stay at home an idea of the fauna of remote areas.

The joy lies in searching and finding under difficult conditions. But the greatest joy is the actual act of finding and the possibility of observing lifestyles and their connection with the environment. To rake up an opalescent worm in its tube-case, which, to counter its hostile environment has made itself unrecognizable by means of a fine coating of very small stones and shell fragments; to observe the little vortex which the tentacles of an anemone produce; or to turn over a slab of slate and to gaze at one marvel after another on the moist, slimy, surface beneath.

Out on the beach everything near us had retreated into their little burrows at our approach and we were digging for some of the alarmed creatures when in front of us, almost in rhythm with the breakers, the head of an elephant semi surfaced; it roared at a slender female whose head projected from behind the corner of a rock like a rotund boulder.

It is the larger framework around the minor tasks of zoological collecting which makes it, as a necessary part of research, not only valuable but also congenial for a non-expert, even if it often consists of mechanical, individual movements which are not very refreshing. Perhaps those who analyse the final collection in their well-heated laboratories will occasionally remember this analysis of collecting activities as experienced, felt and described by me here, even although I personally have had nothing but good experiences with my scientific partners.

In the evening of this day of work at home it fell calm; along with the increasing brightness in the evening we enjoyed the calm as the finest gift which the southern latitudes could bring us.

31 October. There are nights when one sleeps fitfully, when past images obstinately pre-empt sleep, even if one's body is tired. They appear unbidden, like lightning, in a long endless string, and no amount of will power can shut them off. They run through one's consciousness in brightly coloured series. They may fade, then return again between waking and sleeping: images one thought were long-dead, adventures from other latitudes and warmer days. Even the confusion of voices outside in the southern night is not capable of banishing them. It may be midnight but one's senses are still awake.

But a restless night may also be the precursor of an event which one is not expecting. And indeed this was the case today. It was 5.30 a.m. when my wife woke me and said there must be a boat nearby since she had heard the rattle of anchor chains and other accompanying noises. At that moment the steam whistle of a whaling vessel sounded.

One can readily believe that we were soon on our feet;

we pulled on our clothes any old how, in great haste. We could already hear voices and especially one that was familiar, that of Captain Abrahamsen, captain of *Harpon* which had brought us to the island and since then had been waiting at Grytviken for a cargo of oil. We greeted each other warmly and we noticed that he had mail for us. It was a beautiful, calm morning and soon we were sitting around our milk case in the tent; questions and answers came rattling out in quick succession. After the torrent of questions had subsided a little, we asked how things were with the whaling.

He said it was moderately good but that the weather was wretchedly bad, and that one could not expect a great haul in October in any case. The weather was exceptionally foul this year and it was especially because of this that he had come to see us at the request of Captain Esbensen, who was worried about us. Thus far five whaling vessels had been damaged by storms and ice, one of them seriously; it had been in a severe collision with ice to the south. At present nothing further was known of the fate of the vessel, which was bound for South Georgia from the South Shetlands for repairs. In addition a large factory ship which was bound for the South Orkneys had been damaged by ice, but once its leaks were stopped it had been able to continue its voyage. And how were things with us?

Excellent, couldn't he see that for himself and wasn't he convinced of it by our accommodations?

Yes, we certainly looked fine and healthy thus far.

But we noticed that Captain Abrahamsen who couldn't manage to tuck away his legs properly, seemed to find our home somewhat cramped and too primitive.

He had arrived on a very unfavourable day after a lot of rain. Our tent, which for the moment was standing on an ice pedestal, with little melt streams isolating it from the surrounding area, was all damp. Certainly he did not get the best possible impression of our residence. But he must have seen how much we enjoyed his visit, and not just because of the fresh beef and pork and the loaf of fresh bread which he had brought for us as a change but because on the voyage to South Georgia he had promised (almost jokingly, as we thought at the time) that he would visit us in camp one day. Promises are quite commonplace in the world but their implementation is somewhat rarer and hence we appreciated his visit and also his participation in our work.

The weather lay leaden in the bay; one really could not tell what the grey calm would lead to and hence we felt it quite natural not to prolong the visit any further since a quiet passage through La Roche Strait was certainly preferable to fog and a turmoil of waves.

Once the two men had left things fell quiet again in camp, and soon the event had receded as if it happened days before.

Just as before we would gaze out across the slopes on which the white specks of albatrosses were now visible, resting on old nests. Soon they would increase in number and in mid-November would begin their displays.

Once again in the twilight period we could pick out against the snow the white-chinned petrels who have the most to say about love and passion.

Later, in the tent, we all gave a start when an ice avalanche rolled down in "Hope Valley" to round off our day.

During the next few days, on which we had rain and later snow, our first laundry session fell due. Everyone undertook his own share while Benitz continually supplied hot water from his restored blubber stove which had been remodelled more safely since the fire. When everything lay spotless and immaculately clean in a tub the laundry looked so appealing to him, he always preferred just to gaze at it in admiration, rather than wear it.

While we worked away quietly at a wide range of tasks, 4 November finally arrived. I had set it aside as a rest day in camp because on the 5th we planned to undertake our first sledge trip in a westerly (sic) direction in order to find out whether it was possible to cross the blocking "George Schweitzer Ridge" in the west (sic). We told ourselves that there were never any spells of good weather on the island, and hence we had to use the time no matter how good or bad it might be. Our enforced rest of the past few days had had the effect that we set off on our trip hopeful and cheerful.

7

The First Sledge Trip (5–9 November)

Before we set off on the trip we had placed all our things in order on 4 November, just as one overhauls one's house and gets one's papers in order before starting a fairly lengthy trip. We buried the leg of beef which Captain Abrahamsen had brought in a deep hole in the snow in order to protect it against rats and skuas. Then we dug another hole for the two cans containing our little stock of cognac for medicinal purposes and the 96% alcohol, in order to make these treasures invisible too. We told ourselves that bad weather might drive some whalers into the bay. Much as we valued the honesty and the sterling character of the whalers, we knew that in their secluded, lonely life they possess a sixth sense for anything containing alcohol; the latter is treasured on the island as a rare delicacy so that even the highest virtues and good intentions may waver.

It was almost 10 o'clock when we set off, the hauling belts of a heavily laden sledge across our shoulders, heading due north over well-known terrain which we had covered frequently before; we moved deliberately to economize our strength. The weather permitted us a good view; a föhn-like atmosphere lay over the landscape. Everything seemed closer, clearer, more tangible; this time we thought we were really to be favoured by the weather. Benitz interrupted our contemplation of this idea with the remark that it was about time. Shortly after 10 o'clock we reached "Good Hope Valley" and, climbing steadily, headed for a large boulder which is the best landmark from which to get one's bearings.

Here our route parted from that of 21 October, when we

13. A male elephant seal was the ruler of more than 50 females

14. Immediately after birth the young animal finds its mother's nipple

15. The blocking ridge of "Georg Schweitzer Ridge" to the east

16. Only at twilight does the black storm petrel come to life

had followed the valley to its end and had established the presence of a small glacier tongue at its upper end.

To the southeast we discovered a large trough, which one might also describe as a cirque. In great expectation of finding new things we hiked towards it, without our skis, in order to get better traction. Snow conditions were miserable. At 11.30 we reached a conspicuous transverse step, the edge of which was snow free, enabling us to identify the rounded rocks of an old moraine. After barely half an hour sleet filled the air; as a result the last lap of our trip, in decreasing visibility, was even more difficult than the heavy sledge and the sticky snow had made it previously.

With the last steep climb we had reached a height of 258 m. It was exactly 12 noon when one strong gust of wind after another struck us from the east, so that we sat down on the sledges for a moment in amazement. Before one could really grasp the change, wet snow was falling heavily and we could no longer see the outlines of the trough . All we could see was three sledges and three disappointed people, all cursing with greater or less vehemence that we had been forced to wind up the day so quickly. For there was no sense in taking even a single step forwards, since our trip was pointless unless the landscape was visible.

Clouds and snow merged and within a few seconds we were in the midst of a thick blizzard. Within a few minutes we had pitched the tent on the snow and we were hoping that the storm would subside just as quickly as it had arisen. Hence we hesitated to make ourselves too comfortable in the tent and achieved only a preliminary, primitive level of comfort; but one gust of wind after another hit the tent, without a pause, so viciously that we thought some invisible enemy was slapping us repeatedly in the face. While we were cursing the damned country the next punishment struck; the sturdy tent pole snapped like a matchstick. If my wife had been sitting a few centimetres closer to it the stiletto-like broken end would have made it an even more serious accident.

After lashing the broken ends together we braced the tent pole but from that moment on we no longer felt secure. It was to be an enjoyable night! We had come to know many things thus far, such as the voices of the birds and the sounds of the night, but we had not been exposed to the whims of the storm and could never have anticipated its effects.

We crawled into our bags early, removing only our boots, so as to be prepared if the necessity arose. Then we smoked and chatted until one after another we fell quiet and the snow squalls sang us to sleep.

Next morning, 6 November, we found that the barometer had dropped from 730.00 to 719.00 during the night and that the wind, which had swung from NE to WSW, was now quite light. Grey clouds and fog blanketed our campsite so that we could not see the route ahead. Only a few nearby rocks appeared clearly for the odd moment within our range of vision.

At 10.30, since it was becoming steadily brighter over the slopes, we set off, heading first eastwards then later more towards the southeast, hauling our laden sledges which greatly slowed our progress on the steep gradient. We were forced to adopt a time-consuming zigzag course to get up sections with gradients of up to 40° and hence it took us two hours to reach a pass at 283 m which led over a side ridge of the "Georg Schweitzer Ridge".

From here our route led due south over a crevasse-free, moderately inclined glacier to a saddle which we reached in 45 minutes. Its continuation was bounded on the south by a bold rock pyramid. The view to the southeast was unique: beneath us lay a lake whose ice was swept free of snow by the storms and whose sides were almost equal in length, at about 150–180 m. It was bounded on the north and northeast by ice slopes and rock faces. It was natural that we should head down to it since any continuation of our route eastwards, especially with sledges, was blocked by the "Georg Schweitzer Ridge". Off to the south we could see rounded, snow-free coastal hills, over which we could at least continue our route farther east. Working our way down a steep snow slope, then down a stepped stream channel, we reached the edge of the lake, along whose shores the water was already emerging from under the ice, as if trying to get free.

If one were to eliminate mentally the icy surroundings of the shores of this lake and to imagine a few pines and stunted firs on the visible rock faces, the lake itself ice-free and inhabited by trout, it could be compared without much difficulty with the Feldsee in the Schwarzwald in terms of its shape and the imagined landscape.

We found the outlet of the lake to be a swollen, fast-flowing stream which in finding its way in its full springtime force over a rockstep a good 40 m in height, had sawed its way between two rock-faces which were only a stone's throw apart.

To the south, where the stream hurried towards a level valley bottom, its course initially was not visible. It was covered by a snow bridge; farther down in a little valley one could trace its glistening, sinuous course and its presumed outflow into the sea. As we worked our way towards a slope which dropped at a 30° angle to the roaring stream a few snow petrels (*Pagodroma nivea*) flew around us; they were not at all shy and flew within a few metres of us. These charming birds had their nests in the rock faces on either side of the stream, secluded from all other animal life.

The steep slope, which provided the only opportunity for continuing our progress forced us to kick steps for footholds. I took the hauling belt off my shoulders, carefully kicked some steps and let the sledge slide down the slope below me. I shouted to the other two who were following me, that they should do the same for reasons of safety. Involuntarily one is more cautious when a slip will land one in a roaring stream which disappears beneath an ice cover as if disappearing into the underworld.

My wife was following in the middle when suddenly I

heard a shrill cry and realized that Benitz was sliding at breakneck speed down the slope, still hanging on to his sledge. He was heading for the open stream with the turmoil of whirling water.

"Let go the sledge!" was my immediate shout; Benitz responded as soon as the shout of alarm was out of my mouth. Through skill and agility Benitz managed to come to a halt 1 m before the stream where, fortunately, the slope became a little gentler, while the sledge collided with a boulder in the stream and was badly damaged. But what was worse was that two bags from the sledge load, with their valuable contents, had broken loose from the tarpaulin and had been swept downstream into the invisible, inaccessible depths.

It is futile to discuss how the whole thing happened or even to reproach Benitz for it. Captured by the beauty of the distant view, most probably he had been gazing south in a moment of forgetfulness, to where we had spotted the silhouettes of penguins against the slope.

What was more certain was that almost our entire supply of provisions for this trip, the major part of our eating and cooking utensils, our primus and my wife's spare clothes had disappeared into the whirlpool. Benitz was able triumphantly to recover one pan, the sole survivor of our cookware. Our attempts at finding anything more in the open stream course in the valley bottom or to drill through the tough ice cover in various places, were fruitless. Dejected, we pushed on across braided stream channels which the almost mild weather had filled, now heading due south towards a small bay, where the penguins appeared almost like paradisiacal creatures in this wilderness.

Perhaps it would have been better to return immediately to our camp at Coal Harbour. But we pitched our Klepper tent behind a rock ridge which sheltered us from the southwest wind. Familiar bird species were common on the ridge.

There was also an elephant seal colony here among the tussac grass; in this idyllic bay, which was never visited by sealers, the animals took no notice of us although when walking through the colony we were practically stepping on their rear flippers.

That same day we hiked eastward up the snow free coastal slopes which form a southern outlier of the "Georg Schweitzer Ridge", characterized at its end by a rock summit, with the sea beneath us. Our purpose was simply to get a view towards Ice Fjord, rather than to reconnoitre the possibility of pushing onwards with the sledge. The loss of our provisions in itself made this impossible.

The smoothly polished rock slopes and individual boulders which we found displayed clear striations; in places whaleback formations were particularly well developed. They were also strikingly evident in the reefs which lay off this peaceful bay.

Hence it was scarcely a rash conclusion to assume that even this part of the island which is now almost ice free, had once been glaciated and that the ice had flowed beyond the present coast and across the reefs. Steep snow gullies which ended at the bottom in vertical rock faces descended right to the sea. Hence we could also see that even if one stayed close to the sea the route along the coast was impassable in terms of travelling with sledges and essentials such as the tent and sleeping bags without which travel on South Georgia is impossible . One could probably overcome some stretches using purely rock-climbing techniques but one could never hike across the island in one trip with full equipment without the support of one's own ship. Hence one could never do it without major expense. Minor snow squalls barely allowed us even a glimpse towards the east. But we could make out Cape Demidov and the Wilson Glacier and also had a vague view of Ice Fjord in which some icebergs were embedded in the grey air like independent ice islands.

As we were heading down the slopes again it seemed as

if the bay, which we had named Penguin Bay, was a landlocked lake; the circle of reefs off the bay seemed to extend in such a continuous line. Perhaps it had indeed once been a landlocked lake, after the ice had begun to recede; the sea then broke through those parts of the reefs which offered it least resistance.

What we had to do that evening was pure Swiss Family Robinson, the sort of thing we had admired as first-formers. In those days it was something we yearned for, away off in the distance; now we had to experience it in the flesh as adults. We had to collect driftwood, since we no longer had a primus, and we had to collect penguin eggs and dry tussac grass in order to kindle the fire and keep it going.

There were about a thousand penguins spread over three rookeries but they gave us one disappointment after another. Almost all the eggs revealed the fine, red veins which indicate the initiation of embryo formation; indeed some already contained well-developed embryos, but hunger forced us to keep on looking until we found some late-laid eggs which met our requirements to a fair degree.

God knows, it was a primitive evening. Instead of coffee we drank ice water out of a tin can; a spoon which had survived made the rounds. Finally the two men used their fingers, leaving the spoon to my wife.

Then night fell; fortunately it was calm and once again snowflakes, whispering softly, fell on South Georgia's spring earth. But what delighted us most in that camp was that Benitz was still lying with us in the tent, whole and in good spirits.

7 November. There are mosses in bloom; the stream is roaring; in sheltered spots the tussac stalks have sprouted flower heads, yet there are still large flakes of snow falling heavily and the temperature is $-2°$. Today, to the west of our campsite we spotted the rudiments of a hanging glacier in a little cirque, beneath which lay a small lake. Otherwise a low overcast blocked all distant views of both land and sea.

While we pondered on the ill luck which had landed us

in such an abhorrent situation, we again had meltwater and penguin eggs for breakfast, along with a little piece of salvaged hardtack.

After this meal we slipped our hauling lines over our shoulders around noon; the sledges had been lightened somewhat but only by a small amount, since we had added a little box of rock samples from the bay and the surrounding area and also two king penguins which we were hauling back *in corpore* for our collection. The latter had been standing around among the gentoo penguins like emissaries from some foreign bird nation.

This time we tackled the slope which had done so much damage yesterday with more care and respect. The crust was even harder now and hence we had to kick steps with our heavy boots and carry up each item of baggage separately. Once this steep slope was behind us we again reached the level stretch by the lake, where we could catch our breath, then the gully and the steep snow slope; although the latter was short it was deep in drifted snow and our last ounce of strength was needed to overcome it.

We could already see the pass above us. Despite the delaying effect of the snow we still hoped to reach the camp at Coal Harbour that afternoon, when the most violent snowstorm again arose and forced us to pitch camp immediately. The foul weather was again vicious and every feature of our surroundings was swallowed up as if by a demon. Once again all we could see was ourselves and what we were hauling with us, and soon, too, the newly pitched tent with the snowflakes sweeping past it.

Then came a long, grey late afternoon and an even longer night. Abandoned, without any covering, the ferocious song of the gale is still singing in our ears; with every passing hour we watched the tent grow smaller as the weight of the snow pressed down upon it. But it still stood strong and firm; despite the ceaseless wind there is no snow coming in today, and we are quite happy.

8 November. We are listening the fluctuating blasts of the storm as one listens fearfully and tensely to a man's breathing, which sometimes becomes calmer, sometimes more erratic, but still gives no indication of the end of the crisis.

It is 11.00 a.m. and we are still lying here, battling the southwest gale which is battering our tent more violently than ever. We had breakfast around 9.00 o'clock; with some stearine candles we produced some melted snow-water with little lumps of ice in it. As an addition there was the taste of the last meal of eggs, since we had to use the frying pan since it is our only utensil. Then we had some horribly dry oat flakes which stuck in one's throat, along with some chocolate, and each of us got two pieces of hardtack. Hurray! We're really à la mode; we're into raw foods!

But we are certainly not enamoured of this type of diet which has been forced upon us; we would have preferred a leopard seal's liver. But we had to indulge in even more raw foods; we next chewed our raw Maggi soup cubes which on normal trips, properly cooked, play a pleasant and highly valued role. Although we are in rather a sad situation, despite all the privations all we are really missing is a primus stove.

All morning we lay in our sleeping bags; our conversation was as simple as our menu. When one's stomach is empty one has little inclination to tell stories and crack jokes. Rarely does a melody or a pleasant memory flash to the surface. Somebody muses: "How strong and stable this Klepper tent is. How superbly it lets the light through although it is dark-green in colour. And see how close the weave is!"

This is said simply for something to say, just to break the silence in the tent. But it is true. Although it has been snowing, with the most violent wind gusts since 4.00 p.m. yesterday, and we are lying unprotected, the floor of the tent is completely dry. But we had to adjust the tent poles to the sub-Antarctic gale, reinforcing them with hazel sticks.

Somebody else suggests: "I think the weather is getting better; the tent walls are not flapping so much." This too was uttered just for something to say. The fact that the walls are no longer flapping so much is due to the load of snow on the tent and to the towering walls of snow, not to any relaxation in the storm.

Then the third person feels he must say something: "My body heat has melted a depression in the snow and now if I move a little it is as if I am lying in a mould." In the meantime, in order to fill some time, each of us receives two little crusts of hardtack, very carefully rationed.

Our "still-life" here in the hiking tent is quite different from that in the base-camp tent in Coal Harbour. One can encompass it more completely since there are few individual details to confuse the issue. It actually consists only of three sleeping bags and three disappointed people who are starting to get hungry, and four snowbound tent walls. It is the simplest milieu that one could conceive.

Like the snails with the colourful shells which we found on the beach at Coal Harbour, our sleeping bags are now our dearest possessions in the whole world. Then one's pipe. But we smoked our last pipes today. Last time Benitz was able to roll a cigarette from my saved-up leftovers. Thereafter he could only take one pull on my pipe, but since he could not stand this, what little tobacco remains is all mine. It is already heavily mixed with reindeer hairs which have found their way into it, and my last pipe is going to be a really dubious pleasure.

At 8.00 p.m. the storm was still raging. Still lying in our bags we told ourselves that we really ought to be contented. Summing up the events of the last few days it seemed to us that ultimately we really had nothing to complain about. What point was there in complaining because the rough melody of the storm is so persistent and that it shows no sign of abating.

No. When we left home we were expecting this defiant, unweakened refrain; we were looking for loneliness and an untouched environment away from all ingrained habits, lies, characterless features and ill manners.

But it is an honourable battle without any stabbings in the back. We love the storm and our battle against it. It fights fairly. We will bypass the obstacles and attack the island from another direction, until we have conquered one piece after another.

9 November. During the night the gusts of wind became less violent and at 6 o'clock we got up and stepped outside the tent which was almost invisible under the snowdrifts. There were no longer any sledges or skis visible; everything was enveloped in this new winter snowfall. There was a wan light all around us and the weather certainly did not promise any security but because of hunger we had to start the trek back to camp, over the pass which subsequently in our accounts we called "Hunger Pass."

Once we had dug all our sledges out from under the heaps of snow and finally had found the axe and our ski poles and even the two king penguins and the box of rocks, shortly after 8 o'clock we were ready to go. We crawled with effort up the glacier whose slopes we had recently descended so effortlessly and hopefully.

Today due to the storm of the past few nights the bare ice was visible in places, and since we had no crampons we slipped more easily as a result of the occasional jerk from our sledges. It was a tedious operation to cover this ludicrously short stretch. On reaching the pass, as we looked back and again took quick bearings on all the visible peaks and made our sketches, to the west we spotted with great satisfaction and joy the black basin of Elsehul. The future became easier again when we realized that we should soon be back among our animal friends, the penguins and elephant seals again.

But our eventful first sledge trip had prepared a surprise for us even for the last day. The slope beyond the little cirque revealed a totally new side today. Instead of the passable, soft firn-snow of 6 November, today between snowdrifts it revealed a brittle, bare ice layer. As the sledges tried to increase their speed by the minute even our nailed boots could not assure us of a safe grip.

It was obvious that we could reach the valley only with empty sledges. Hence we let everything which would not readily be damaged, such as skis, the axe, the penguins, sleeping bags and tent, slide down the slope. Meanwhile we did not entrust the rucksack full of instruments, the compass, the chronometer and the rock samples to this mode of travel, but carried them down on our backs.

We watched the liberated items disappear around a rock nose at a ferocious speed and then began tackling the slope ourselves. To our Alp-accustomed eyes it did not look very dangerous, especially since it ran out in a trough, as we knew from the outward journey. But events proved very different.

We had not counted on the sledge; even unladen it was an unpredictable, disruptive item of baggage which with its wide runners and difficulty of control, obeyed different laws of motion from those of bodies and muscles. Perhaps our tired brains and empty stomachs may have been dwelling for a second on material things such as the first full swallow of water or the first cup of hot coffee back at camp, or perhaps some imponderable jerk from the sledge may have initiated the entire proceedings. At any rate next moment I was sliding and began heading down slope, still hanging on to the sledge. My progress became more and more terrifying and it took all my remaining strength as well as every friction surface I possessed to prevent it from becoming even more dangerous than it already was. First braking with a ski pole, then sliding down headfirst, then in a normal position, I worked at trying to avoid a rock which projected about the middle of the trough. I succeeded in this due to little accidents such as minor shifts of weight, and with black spots before my eyes I became the last bundle to pile up in the heap of all the loose items which had preceded me.

Once I had established that I was still in one piece, apart from severe skin abrasions, some damage to my clothes and a few bruises, I went back up the slope to caution my companions to be careful since I was worried about them. Then I spotted my wife shooting down the slope at top speed, arms and head first. A sudden inspiration, perhaps not very wise, put me in her line of travel and by throwing myself against her I managed to arrest her dangerously fast progress somewhat. In so doing I myself again began sliding down slope, but tangled together we shot down the last 100 m at a slower pace.

Her injuries, too, were only surficial, thank God; her only complaint was of severe back pains. Once we had sorted ourselves out we gazed at the new still-life around us in subdued resignation: two sledges, skis, frying pan, axe, king penguins and the rolled-up sleeping bags. All this lay scattered around two people who owed their salvation to a snowdrift and a relaxation of the slope angle. When Benitz saw us disappear from view he had the bright idea of tackling the problem with great caution and at slow speed. After unloading his sledge he tied the hauling line and some other cord around the runners; then braking with all his strength using his ski poles he managed to achieve the safest descent.

There is nothing special to relate about the rest of our tedious trip. We reached camp late in the afternoon, exhausted, since in the heavy snow every step was a strain after what we had been through. On the final lap we were quite indifferent to the beauty of the mountains; the demands of our stomachs were too loud and persistent.

This was our first sledge trip on South Georgia; it might have killed any enthusiasm for any later enterprises. We had had to endure so many blows! And the weather had given us such a rough time.

It was small consolation when we learned later that during one of our worst nights of storm in Prince Olav Harbour all the anchor chains and cables of the freighter *Southern Isles*, a ship in excess of 10,000 tonnes, had parted. She had to be scuttled in the fairly shallow bay to prevent her being driven onto the beach and wrecked.

8

The Final Days at Coal Harbour

THE FIRST THING we did back at camp after this trip, which we named the Starvation Trip, was to get the blubber stove in operation. Without saying a word Benitz, whose special project it was, diligently tackled the task. After a few seconds we could see an impressive, sooty flame. It was almost calm and the flame and column of smoke rose straight towards the sky. While he set an iron pot on the stove, after a brief rest I walked over to the tent to check whether the rats had done any damage during our absence.

I had just opened the tent sleeve which we had carefully closed before we left, when I spotted an unfamiliar box. I concluded from this that we had had visitors during our sledge trip. I discovered a letter on the box, from which I learned that the Compañia Argentina de Pesca's ship *Diaz* had called at Coal Harbour in order to transport us to another location on the island if we wished. While I quickly read the note I experienced another miracle. Behind the box stood two brand-new stoves, which we had asked to be procured for us the day we left Grytviken. They were antedeluvianly large but given our situation they were gifts of immense value. The time and exasperation they would save us, given the uncertain weather! And in the evenings they brought friendliness and warmth back into our tent!

The tall flame outside was extinguished as fast as it had been kindled, and during our coffee break three elated people dug out all the goodies they could find from the provisions boxes. "We must be in luck!" How often we uttered this platitude during this period of surprises.

10 November. Today is a rest day. We can designate the day thus since we are back safe and relaxed in our familiar surroundings and are tackling only essential communal tasks. We are repairing torn clothes and washing laundry. It is blowing out of the southwest again but none of us has any complaints, not even at the bruises we received on the ice slope yesterday, since now we are back at our base-camp.

12 November. Rain almost all night with a temperature of 3.5°C in the morning. The stream can barely cope with all the water and we can hear a little waterfall which tumbles over a rock ledge. Individual wind gusts of perhaps a more local character, which have now expanded since the major storm centres to southwest and northeast are at rest, just like the young bull elephant seals who only come into the colony when the old bull is asleep. We cannot hear any surf. There is a magnificent silence all around us. The sky is its usual uniform grey and there is not a single mountain ridge in sight.

Once we had completed the final soundings in the bay in order to obtain a more detailed picture of its bathymetry, we went fishing. As always my wife had the best luck; she pulled out six fish one after the other and all were added to our collection. No, we simply cannot match her skill. She, for her part, gives us a hard time, accusing us of devoting more care to our pipes than to fishing. Almost all the fish had parasites of a brilliant yellow-red species which clung firmly to the scales with their suction cups. For the first time in my life I was struck by the shimmering, golden gleam of a fish's eye. Do all fish possess this uniquely shimmering golden ring which represents the iris, or is it only at the moment of death? It looks as if the eye is set in a circle of fine gold dust.

13 November. Our campsite now looks abhorrent. Boggy spots are appearing; old toilet sites are emitting a hellish stink and we welcome the rain which is washing away all

the filth into the environment. Only our tents continue to stand on isolated pedestals of ice.

15 November. We have made our decision. If a whaling vessel arrives we will have it transport us to the Bay of Isles. We want to continue our work there and especially to explore the area between the north and south coasts. The short remaining period will be used to maximum advantage; in particular we will make height determinations of the immediate area and collect the last rock samples.

Today we found the first egg of a sooty albatross. Over the sea to the south there is a brightness like an iceblink.

On the grey day of 16 November, which occasionally produced that blink of sun so important to filming, there occurred a bird incident which I simply cannot pass by, because of its peculiar nature and because it contributed to the expedition's major animal film "Roah-roah" in every detail.

I was on the way to the beach to check the fish trap when Benitz came to the tent, quite excited, to get a bamboo pole.

"Do you plan to fish from the shore," I asked.

No. Those damned brutes (he meant the skuas) were giving him no peace. As he was walking over the hill they had skimmed past his head like arrows.

I abandoned the fish trap for the moment and followed him over the hill at the head of the bay; shortly after we began walking together the skuas launched their first attack at my head despite my swinging an ice axe which I was waving in every direction as a precaution.

We were already familiar with the insolence and boldness of the skuas but today they were intensified; they became more understandable when we spotted a nest on a hillock with the female sitting. We still did not have a skua's egg for the collection or on film. I removed the egg without any scruples since we had so often seen this very bird robbing penguin and gull nests.

Despite near misses with my ice axe the male dived uncannily at my head while Benitz stood on the camera box and went into ecstasies over his pictures. The female had left the nest and stood ten paces away uttering complaining and even pitiful noises, so that I was almost tempted to return the egg out of pity. At that moment the male struck me with its wing during one of its violent attacks. I hit its widespread, fan-shaped tail and some feathers fell out but despite this it returned after only a few seconds to fly around me in excited circles with me as both its target and its centre-point.

It appeared to have commandeered an abandoned albatross nest for its single egg; the latter was 8 cm long, 5 cm wide, with a pointed narrow end; it displayed a bright yellow-brown background colour with dark-brown, often even grey splotches. Presumably the robber had even extorted the nest from its original owner! But one has to ascribe one good feature to this bird: the male protects its nest and its mate admirably.

As I passed this spot later the same day on a trip to the west to photograph whalebacks, I was assaulted by attacks which were just as violent, even before I was near the nest. Benitz had to return to the same area towards evening to recover something he had forgotten in the excitement this morning and told us how he was again attacked viciously.

With fresh memories of the morning's experiences he had armed himself with a particularly long, springy bamboo pole. Although he is a great animal lover, to him, as to so many, or indeed all whalers, the skua is the quintessence of everything horrible, and he managed to hit the bird with a well-aimed blow; it dropped on the remains of a nearby snow patch. It was only stunned and, regaining its feet, it raced to the overhanging snow cornice near our camp.

But the amazing thing was that dozens of black-backed gulls attacked the wounded or stunned bird, although on other occasions, when an elephant seal has given birth, they share the pickings with the skuas. This mass assault provoked the skua into a last desperate effort and we watched as it disappeared across the bay towards the little strait to the west.

When we blew the skua's egg for our collection that evening we found that the yolk was yellow and the white clear and fluid like a hen's egg. Despite this we had no desire to eat it. But we cracked open some gulls' eggs at the same time and in contrast to them the skua egg looked quite appealing and appetizing. Hence after some hesitation we decided to add it to the mixture. In order to dilute our reluctance even farther we took some penguins' eggs from our little provisions barrel in order to make the mixture even less objectionable.

None of us could have eaten that skua's egg, the egg of a murderer, alone. While the pan was steaming a rather coarse comparison occurred to me, namely that we often find a person unbearable on his own but in company, i.e. in a mixture of people, not only bearable but even pleasant and likeable.

17 November. Each of us filled the day according to his own inclinations. I myself wanted to visit Paryadin Ridge; my wife wanted to visit the penguins; while Benitz wanted to hike to Undine Harbour with his camera.

From a pass in the Paryadin Ridge I climbed via a short firn ridge to a summit which I named Hessegipfel [Hesse Peak]. Although it was only 252 m high, seen from the sea it appeared like the upper section of a 3000 m peak. Generally on the island it is not advisable to indulge in approximate height estimation but to use an altimeter, since otherwise one usually estimates too high. The summits, snow-covered until late in the summer and with no foreland worthy of mention, appear much higher to a visitor than they are in reality.

While Paryadin Ridge drops steep and sheer towards Bird Sound, the descent on the east side displays a stepped foreland, in which several small lakes are located.

I also found by accident the nest of a tern (*Sterna vittata*) at a height of 73 m. It is almost impossible to spot its small grey-green egg, speckled with black and 5 cm in length; not only does its colour match that of the lichen-covered rocks surrounding it but there is a total absence of any nesting material. The egg lay in a little crack between some stones, practically without even a depression; only the calls of the parents which utter a call of "ga ge ga ge" as they dive, betray the position of the endangered nest.

On her solitary walk my wife observed for the first time the little pipit, *Anthus antarcticus*, whose cheerful trilling reminds one of a lark. She then sat among the penguins at Elsehul [Else Hill], busily sketching for a few hours. Then, to combat the cold, she walked to Undine Harbour, and reported that on the narrow neck she found three planks set in the ground. There was a nail visible in the exposed end and the heaped-up earth indicated that this was a grave. It is probable that an American sealer may have found his last resting place here on the narrow isthmus, with the eternal southwesterly gales roaring over him, long before the whalers reached South Georgia.

After the two of us had been sitting in the tent for quite a long time the third solitary walker came down the slope, hauling his camera on a sledge across grass and moss. He told us the same story about the changed scene at the elephant seal colony at Undine Harbour as had struck us on the basis of a brief examination today. Although we still encountered bleeding bulls we did not detect the same excited mood among them and none of the irritability of the start of the mating season when a pasha would have had to defend 50 wives.

No, everything had now become more tranquil, as is the case in human life too. There were probably still occasional fights and pups were still being born. These aspects remained the same and even the skuas were still there, even if they had nests and eggs now. Only the lord of the colony was different; he had become more peaceful and more indifferent.

His harem had shrunk. There were only 20 cows left and all had pups beside them. His blubber had melted away significantly and when one saw him lying there so reduced and almost unresponsive one almost had an attack of pity. At least one found oneself reflecting on strength and vigour, thrust and parry.

One could see 30 pups lying in the stream channel at Undine Harbour, in grey coats and about 1.5 m long; they were now into their fourth week and had left the colony. From here on they would live their own lives, which consisted exclusively of sleeping and lazing in the nearby tussac grass.

The "knights' hall" was occupied by twenty bulls and had moved its position more towards the remains of the pasha's harem. It needs to be stressed again: the old bull looked distressed and deflated! He had become careless and could no longer prevent the "young lions" from moving closer and closer to his harem. He has had his good days, even if now he has to watch one wife after another being abducted by the young cavaliers with their haughtily hooked noses.

A truce has been declared in the "knights' hall". One no longer sees any battles such as one saw a few weeks ago at the height of the rut; perhaps communal interest has now made them less urgent. One can see bulls lying side-by-side, asleep, without any conflict or stress. One had even laid his head across a neighbour's neck. Everything eventually comes to an end!

In the evening it was calm and almost cloudless. The beat of the waves against our snow bank had died away. The evening sky glowed pale blue; a pale sickle moon lay in the southwest above the dark hills. Stars which we had not seen for weeks were shining through the light clouds: the Southern Cross above the tent, Orion in the northeast. Only the entrance to the bay was closed off by an inky black cloud. When we stepped outside the tent on an evening like this and listened to the roaring of the stream and the chaos of bird voices it seemed as if the island were filled with many miracles.

During a terrible snowstorm next day (19 November) a welcome sun's ray penetrated the gloom, not from the massed clouds in the sky but from the grey of the bay well offshore: a steam whistle in this hellish weather!

Was it a vessel searching for the harbour in this storm? No, in that case it would not have needed to announce its presence so openly. Soon we could recognize the colours of the Argentine flag as the vessel headed past the reef on a gentle curve towards the inner part of the bay.

We now remembered that it was Sunday and that before we left Captain Esbensen had scheduled his visit for a Sunday, the only day when he would be free. Whaling had to be in full swing and time was valuable.

"Yes, we thought you would be coming, but we never thought it would happen today, in this foul weather." An indeed it had been miserable weather outside; they had had difficulty finding their way through the strait, and off the northeast coast there was a storm raging with heavy snow. But as old sealers and whalers, working against time they had stolen from bay to bay and finally had reached Coal Harbour.

Without further delay they took us aboard and there we were again introduced to a completely different side of life. We found ourselves at a table with cakes, coffee, cups and forks, surrounded by an even warmth. There was little reference to the world at home in the conversation; it concentrated on relevant things: on what was happening in the world of South Georgia.

We discussed storms, our life and that of the whalers, which resembled ours to the extent that both had to cope with foul weather and uncertainties. There is always a link, even between otherwise dissimilar people activated by differing goals, as a result of a commonly shared tough environment.

Esbensen went on to ask what we wanted to do now, after seven weeks. Had we had enough of our strenuous life? No, certainly not; on the contrary we wanted to start studying everything again in new, different surroundings on another part of the island since we had now finished our work here as well as we were able. Would it be possible for his ship to take us on board and drop us off at the Bay of Isles?

Yes, he would do that gladly; not today, since it was impossible, but first thing in the morning.

On board we also met an Englishman, Mr. Salvesen of Edinburgh, son of the well-known whaler Salvesen, who had started whaling from South Georgia soon after C. A. Larsen, since he had foreseen that he would be successful. He spoke fluent Norwegian and we spent several delightful hours chatting with him. A few days previously he had returned from a reconnaissance trip to the South Orkneys. Later we heard from others that he had played a prominent role in the rescue of a whaling vessel which had lost her propeller and was drifting helplessly in these inhospitable waters.

Shortly after a magnificent dinner which consisted mainly of whale meat with brown gravy, the weather unexpectedly brightened and calmed down, and a little excursion to Cape Paryadin was proposed. The macaroni penguin (*Eudyptes chrysolophus*) rookery there, undisturbed since 1913, gave promise of providing a rich haul of eggs for the crew.

Today this section of coast was ideal for a landing, since with a northeast wind blowing it was in the lee. Barely 12–15 m out from shore we saw thousands of penguins above some steep coastal rocks.

The boats were quickly lowered and borne by a gentle swell we steered towards a little cove in which the sea gently rose and fell. Two leopard seals inquisitively accompanied our boats and came to within a metre of us. We felt as if we were making a landing on a totally alien coast; there was a sense of adventure and vitality in us.

After clambering over smooth, wave-washed rocks, then over a soft strip of snow, we found ourselves standing right in the midst of a deafening noise which exceeded anything we had experienced at other penguin rookeries. Having been brought to a peak of excitement thousands of birds in this dense community were looking for the cause of the disturbance among their neighbours, and hence were continually fighting among themselves with their sharp bills. The men ran through the rookery with large buckets, and despite numerous pecks persisted in collecting the eggs which the birds were reluctant to part with. There was only one egg in each nest, if indeed there were any. A test sample had revealed that they were all recently laid.

The buckets were filled and carried back to the dinghy. Six hundred eggs were gathered in a very short time. The work was done; it was productive and useful. In a few moments the coast was free of men once again; our blades pulled at the water; leopard seals played around the boat again; and the long swell carried us safely along. Everything proceeded without incident, very quietly and naturally and when the sea grew rougher again when we were well off shore on the homeward trip, it was as if nature had allowed us a two-hour breathing spell in order to permit us this rare landing. As dusk was beginning to fall we went ashore and began our preparations for the departure next morning.

It is our last night at Coal Harbour. Ducks are playing on the stream again; strips of moonlight gleam on the water. The soft whistles ring out once again, and the white-chinned petrel proclaims his passion. It was long after midnight when we nailed up the last box.

How many times have we had to pack in our lives? Tying up bundle after bundle; setting off on journey after journey! The whole of life is a journey, through which runs the refrain of the wandering Jew. It will only be completed when the call comes for the great journey for which one needs no luggage.

On 20 November we made the trip by sea to the Bay of Isles. We got up at 4.00 a.m. and hauled the final loads to the snowdrift by the shore; at 6 o'clock, the start of the working day aboard ships, the first seamen and whoever else was available arrived. Everyone turned to: stokers, seamen and the captain.

The sea was calm and the sky grey and overcast; not a hill or a summit showed through the grey veil as we headed out of the bay at 8 o'clock bound for a new destination.

As we were negotiating a narrow passage between two reefs before reaching Bird Sound itself the sky became blacker, and at the exit from the strait we were met by a powerfully violent sea and a heavy snow squall. Visibility decreased suddenly and we could see neither bays nor mountain peaks on the island. There was only a low, bright strip above the water, like the reflection from snow slopes.

We again hugged the coast in order to identify some headland or conspicuous point such as the entrance to Right Whale Bay or "Welcome Bay". Icebergs loomed out of the grey nothingness; it was eerie. One change of course after another. More icebergs drifting across our path.

Then the Welcome Islands were reported from the bridge, and later Cape Buller. Soon we were swinging into Bay of Isles; only a vast brightness streamed towards us out of the bay; no details could be distinguished.

I asked Esbensen whether there were any prospects of landing today. "Better than usual since a northeast wind produces the most favourable conditions. The islands and reefs moderate and block the worst of the seas, whereas with a westerly or southwesterly wind, blowing down from the big glaciers, a landing is usually impossible. Bay of Isles is a real cursed hole; you'll have lots of fun there. Back in 1907, when I was still sealing, I lay trapped in the bay for a whole week with two Swedish scientists; one of them was Skottsberg, I think. The weather was so stormy that we could neither get out nor properly right inshore."

Around 3 o'clock, as we lay in a small bay marked on the British chart as the landing place, to the south through lightly falling snow we could see the gently domed slopes of a glacier, which had to be Grace Glacier. At 4 o'clock we said goodbye to the men, thanking them for their hospitality and for the help they had given us.

"In case I forget," Esbensen shouted to us, "even if it is blowing out of the northeast today you have to protect yourselves primarily from the southwest wind, which can be vicious here. I hope you manage to find a site for your tents."

With this advice in our ears we started our search, and as we watched the boat disappear in the direction of Cape Wilson, we thought we had found the best site within the radius which we had examined; it lay below a hill to the south from which a snowdrift extended towards the northeast, and 4 minutes from the landing site.

Although we could see nothing of our surroundings we noticed that everything here was different from where we had just come from; the landscape seemed freer and the fauna less wary. Gentoo penguins were constantly coming to the beach and running around our legs and our baggage. As soon as we began hauling the most essential items up to the campsite we had to avoid large numbers of elephant seals.

The scene was confusing; everything vague and gloomy, mysterious and exciting, like a great, new adventure.

9

Storms, Glaciers and Penguins at Bay of Isles

THE FIRST NIGHT was quite different from what we had envisaged. The snow around us was the same; the tent was the same; and our hopes juggled with all the future possibilities just as they had seven weeks before when we had landed at Coal Harbour.

Nor was there anything special in the fact that around midnight the storm swung around into the southwest; but it was the animals close by all around us – we heard them more than saw them – which from here on put a totally different stamp on our life and which made that night one of the most restless for us.

More than once we started from our sleep, firstly when an elephant seal blundered over the tent guys and unburdened its presumably only newly learned and unarticulated noises on the night. God knows, such a young elephant seal would not have paid the slightest attention to the three sad figures who walked up the beach yesterday to invade its young life.

Shortly after midnight I fell asleep for a second time. Then I felt a weight against the tent wall – no, it was not a nightmare –, which collapsed onto my tired body and threatened to crush me. I started up in alarm and rolled away from me the mass of a young elephant seal, which must still have weighed 2 centners [*c.* 100 kg]. Then I tried to scare the animal away completely by banging on the canvas.

But the seal pups still continued to turn night into day. In addition a strong southwest wind carried the din of a small rookery of gentoo penguins. Hence, immersed in the adjacent fauna, we survived a terrible night full of minor alarms during which, to add to our vexation, rain squalls and wet snow transformed our familiar world by adding to the range of noises.

On 21 November it was raining and mild (2.5°C at noon) but our surroundings were still invisible. We could still hear more than we could see. The noise of distant iceberg calving, borne on the west wind, must have originated from the Brunnonia Glacier. Through a crack in the tent we could see the white crests on the heavy seas which were rolling in. The intruders of last night lay in heaps around the tent.

While we were no longer subjected to the nocturnal noises of the shoemakers or to the wing beats of the giant petrel, nonetheless we now had a greatly enhanced substitute. When we left Coal Harbour the slopes had already been showing every sign of spring; around us here there was a complete, solid snow cover, a cover of winter snow not just a late spring snowfall which a temperamental storm had dumped on the coast.

When we stepped out of the tent into the fogbound landscape towards evening, first a powerful bull elephant, then not far away an ancient female began rumbling towards our tent; despite our love of animals we had no choice but to drive them off with snowballs. They retreated before us but only slowly, the bull being the first to yield; its initially menacing courage soon ebbed away and, making a quick turn, it fled towards the beach. The female was more persistent and stubborn; even though we fired plenty of fair-sized snowballs at its torso and tried to encourage it to flee by shouting, it began moving off only slowly. It retreated in the same direction as the bull although in the twilight and in our zeal we did not realize this immediately. Without intending to we drove the bull, which was attentively following the female's line of retreat, towards its presumed prize; we later watched as the female was embraced by the bull's flippers.

Little as we begrudged the animal its hard-won prize, the high-ranking beach master elephant seal had different ideas. He was presumably an old harem-master with many females; leaving them in the lurch he made a beeline for this rival which due to excitement and uncertainty had trespassed into its territory. The female, which presumably had escaped from the powerful old bull, was driven back into the harem while the bull which we had bombarded with snowballs, now fled, abandoning its briefly enjoyed prize. Although it was again heading for our camp in rapid lurches we were now less concerned and did not drive it away again, especially since night had fallen in the meantime.

The level foreland between Grace Glacier and Lucas Glacier, lying farther west [sic], is broken by three conspicuous hills. Next day, a cold, wet morning, we quickly familiarized ourselves with them. All three hills were less peaceful than one suspected from the first distant impressions, and were teeming with life.

We reached the first hill above our tent in just a few minutes. Dropping steeply to the bay on the west, it rose to a height of 32 m. It consisted of shale and on its east side we found and handled many striated rocks which the retreating Grace Glacier had left there in the drift. It was quite sparsely covered with tussac grass and its gently sloping ridge housed a small gentoo penguin rookery which carried on its life on this conspicuous lookout point. Apart from a few widely scattered gulls' nests the hill appeared to accommodate no other bird life and hence we named it Penguin Hill.

If one walked northwards, one next encountered a long ridge, 49 m high, with a heavy growth of tussac grass which was predominantly occupied by giant petrels and white-chinned petrels. Since the white-chinned petrel, or shoemaker, as the whalers call it, was in the majority, there was nothing simpler than to call this hill Shoemaker Hill.

From its ridge one could look eastwards to a third small hill, which we also climbed. Since dozens of black-backed gulls flew up from the rocks around it, where they were nesting, we henceforth called it Gull Hill. It was 38 m high.

Around 2.00 in the afternoon it cleared up and although we felt a great lassitude, not to say laziness, in our bones, we pulled on our boots. It turned into a wonderful day, although the sky was not a solid blue; instead the whole sky was covered with clouds with which a glinting sun struggled for supremacy. Racing shadows flew restlessly across the sea and the snowfields, while the surf had lost none of its force.

By arrangement each of the three of us went his own way, following his own inclination; brief separations are always good on an expedition. My wife climbed the moraine hill between Grace and Lucas glaciers and in the evening brought back gulls' eggs; some were fresh and some less palatable. The latter went into our collection. Benitz wanted to film the gentoo penguins against a magnificent background. I headed in the opposite direction from that taken by the other two; I walked up the Grace Glacier which ended to the south at a saddle-shaped pass. Today I found the latter more appealing than all the wonders of the animal and bird life. I skied far enough up the level, crevasse-free glacier to give me an overview of its head and returned home convinced that one could travel its entire length without difficulty.

On my way back I walked towards our cameraman in order to help him carry his film equipment. He told me that he had been very fortunate and that in particular he had managed to fill a gap in his footage by taking many superb shots of the surf. We then walked together over the three hills again, and in the last evening glow rested on Shoemaker Hill, whose summit displayed the most abundant life today.

All the petrels had flown from their burrows. The black birds were bathing in the snow and the gleaming firn fields. In the last dull rays of the sun their dark brown plumage acquired a warm, almost metallic glow. The chirping of the males was so loud that one felt their throats would burst;

their utterances became even more penetrating when new competitors landed on the firn, crouched as if for a leap.

In the case of the shoemakers, as with all petrels, no difference was discernible between the two sexes in terms of plumage. If one wants to tackle the matter of sexual selection, it would seem that the selection of the female must be determined entirely by the endless persistence of their modest little musical utterances.

In the evening the fat little elephant seal was again lying in front of the tent door. It became even more trusting when we imitated some of its noises. At night, just when we wanted to go to sleep, it wanted to give us some further instruction.

Next day the weather was terrifying. It was so wild that we could not even skin the penguins which we had buried in the snow to protect them from the skuas. It was a Friday, a holiday, spoiled only by our cramped quarters and our lack of activity.

When the gale slackened somewhat in the evening the view from the tent provided us with two brief cameos. We could see the penguin spouses, which had almost all returned home from their fishing trips, faithfully and motionlessly standing guard at their nests. When a late arrival entered the rookery the calls of "roah-roah-i roh", repeated from many of the nests, sounded almost like a greeting.

Out on the wide, almost level foreland, too, one could see small, moving figures and a greenhorn would not have known what to make of them. They were in fact penguins waddling homewards; tired and floundering in the deep snow, they would stumble along like little Christmas gnomes, who wanted to reach their destinations before nightfall obscured their route completely. We could see this much but no more in the grey environment in which our tents were embedded like alien bodies.

Is it the cessation of the crash of the surf which makes us so carefree and happy today? The fact that the greyness and the desolation are only accidental natural features which are no longer so oppressive to us, and from which a strange fauna still keeps emerging? Perhaps we were momentarily entertaining the thought that the great glaciers surrounding us had once coalesced and as a continuous entity had advanced across the wide bay and out to sea? That the scale of time and events here is so vast and confusing that we lay down to sleep, poor and small, yet delighted that we can see and imagine all these phenomena? Or that the schists which form the mountains and hills around us were covered by an inundation millions of years ago, before this obstinate chunk of an island arose from the sea?

The wind gusts which now hit us so suddenly were quite detestable: squalls which could tear a tent from its pegs! But there was no time to collect such thoughts; one pushed them away as one's hand grabbed convulsively for the tent pole as if one were trying to protect it. If one pulls together every aspect which daily affects us: glaciers, storms, and surf and considers them on a time scale of thousands or millions of years, it is almost immaterial whether one lives in a tent, a hut or a palace; whether one is rich or in rags; or whether, returning to the present, the tent pole crushes one's skull; whether one is left lying buried somewhere in the ice, at the bottom of the sea; under the soil of a village graveyard, or under red hibiscus blossoms in the tropics.

On 24 November, a day which began with a bright morning, I headed for Penguin Hill with my theodolite and tripod; from there I could look out over the greater part of the surrounding landscape for the first time. By the time the first clouds rolled in, after noon, I had absorbed an impression of the landscape and had committed it to paper. I will present it here, at this point, even although some final touches were added during later observations on other days.

"The hill on which I am standing is a commanding one; one could not find a single more powerful segment of natural landscape. The most immediate feature of my surroundings, right at my feet, relates to the fauna rather than to the terrain. It is a female penguin, sitting on her nest, barely 50 cm away from the leg of the tripod and my foot; she has just expressed her view of the latter with a vigorous peck.

To the south-southwest I can see the front of the Grace Glacier, which sits on land, a fact revealed by a narrow, visible strip of beach. At low tide one can even walk along the beach past the glacier snout without any particular danger if one chooses an early hour, since there are some parts of the ice cliff which, although only 6–7 m high, overhang in a threatening fashion, ready to break away.

Grace Glacier is an "inactive' glacier; during our prolonged stay we never observed a major calving from its snout; at most a few pieces of the front would collapse and block the beach with large chunks of ice. Above the glacier snout lay some dark specks which at first I mistook for rocks until I examined them through the binoculars; they were in fact young elephant seals which, in their inexperience must have strayed there in response to a youthful urge to wander.

The glacier is a good 800 m wide at its snout. From my hill I also had an unusually clear view of the Brunnonia Glacier to the west, closing off the head of Sunset Fiord. Above a vertical terminal ice cliff which is severely crevassed especially in its central part, its surface is typically very level, totally lacking any lateral or surface moraines. It rises slowly to a plateau about 300 m high whose uppermost limit one can perhaps assume to be an elongated saddle which no doubt provides a short connection to Ice Fiord.

With the good light prevailing I was able to make out the general outline of the landscape, but during our entire sojourn by the bay the mountains between the ice pass at the head of Brunnonia Glacier and the west wall of the Grace Glacier were never sufficiently free of cloud to be visible. On one occasion, still partially obscured by clouds and fog, it appeared to us as if an almost totally ice-covered ridge projected between the Brunnonia Glacier and the west wall of the Grace Glacier; on another occasion we saw three magnificent ice peaks, the centre one of which bore a severely crevassed glacier with numerous step-like breaks, on its steep eastern face.

Our view of the northwestern part of the main bay was clearer and more distinct; from it two side bays penetrated into the interior, a southern one and a northern one, namely Rosita Harbour which the whaling vessels use as a refuge in rough weather.

As the backdrop to Rosita Harbour we could see a long ridge, while the section of coast as far as Cape Buller is distinguished by two rock ridges separated by a valley; the more northerly one swings up into a bold rock peak just at the cape itself. The steep slopes descending from this ridge to the bay give this section of coast a hard, repellent appearance, although if one were to guess its height at about 400 m, this would probably be an overestimate.

If one's gaze wanders farther north one gets a view of the whole of the Bay of Isles. From my vantage point, not including the long extent of Albatross Island, I counted seven little islands, all covered in tussac grass and with a fairly rounded shape. Despite the sea cliff on the horizon they made an almost delightful picture when the sun shone on the bay.

The weather remained fair and hence I could take a bearing on Cape Wilson, due east of me. Beyond a little foreland it surges up steeply into a rock chain about 600 m high.

Closer to my position a parallel ridge separates two fiords, Beckmann Fiord and Sea Leopard Fiord. Of the closer features I could make out only the snout of Lucas Glacier, 4 km away. Later examination revealed that its front is somewhat higher than that of Grace Glacier; it too lies on terra firma. The sea could be seen breaking just in front of it, indicating shallow water.

25 November. We have just survived one of our most terrifying nights of storm. We had to stay awake all night. We were very concerned about our large, double-walled polar

17. For weeks depressing clouds hung over our camp

18. Male and female king penguins often stood side by side as if petrified

tent. On three occasions the tent pole was bent into a bow-shape, a truly alarming sight. Even now, but especially last night, the storm was raging so wildly that the wind pressure lifted the groundsheet and our sleeping bags off the ground. If the gale tears the tent away completely it is a good thing that there is a wide foreland between us and the sea, since in the worst scenario it will give us time to extricate ourselves from the enveloping balloon of the tent. On this hideous morning we had to go out and bury the petrol cans which the storm had wrenched out of the snow. We also buried the sledges, secured the tent, and took some food inside with us, to save ourselves a second, later foray.

The elephant seal pups are engaged in lively activity around our snow fortress. The animals know that we will not do them any harm, and they live with us, as if among their own kind. Today we discovered a seal lying asleep on a sledge. The sledge box lay nearby in the snow; either the gale or the seal must have pushed it aside. When the elephant seal woke up and saw us, it yawned several times but otherwise paid no attention to us. But in the interest of our sledge box we finally had to pull it off the sledge. In view of its unwieldy, slippery bulk we grabbed it by the rear flippers, at which it looked at us uncomprehendingly.

At noon we leaped up again when the excited call of a black-backed gull made us aware that something was amiss at its nearby nest. And indeed, the first time it was an elephant seal which was rumbling close past the nest. Barely had this excitement subsided when the birds began uttering their alarm calls again, this time even more piercingly. This time it was a dignified gentoo penguin which had paused for a short rest on its travels, and was reclining on its full stomach near the gull's nest in this foul weather. While the female gull remained sitting calmly on its nest the male circled continually around the solitary wanderer, diving at it until finally it moved off a few metres towards the rookery to continue its rest.

At camp in the evening I was reading Morgan's "Instinct and custom" in which much of what we are seeing here daily is presented in clear, relevant sentences. It is a magnificent book. But since we are not living among chickens and ducks, but in a wild, forbidding landscape, we cannot classify everything exactly but can only record what chance permits us to see. South Georgia is not an island in which one can encompass partial problems in learned sentences.

Right now some macaroni penguin eggs from Paryadin Ridge are swimming in Danish butter in the frying pan, looking like apricots in jelly. Now I have to admit finally that my wife has taken over the work which is unsatisfying to, and inappropriate for a man, and indeed which she is not very excited about tackling either. We appreciate all the more the fact that she has assumed these duties so punctually and, to our great delight, throughout the entire day.

Naturally we men also give a hand with the preparations and hence everything runs like clockwork. One of us fetches water from a lake which is still ice-covered, and brings the provisions in from the boxes outside; and we fill the primus and the lamp. In short we handle the rough work.

By the day after tomorrow we will have been lying here for a week and have enjoyed a total of seven hours of sunshine.

But right now I do not want to talk any more about the gales and foul weather which continued almost without a break until 30 November, bringing snow, rain and fog. Nor about our concern about the big polar tent or about the fact that we all agreed how magnificently the much cheaper Klepper tent performed by comparison; it withstood the wind gusts much more confidently.

I prefer to talk about our friends, the mammals and birds, amongst whom life has set us down. They provided consolation during lonely periods; even on the foulest days one could find a hill which gave some shelter so that one could lie watching the seals and birds.

These incidents and accounts are not of world importance and many people would certainly prefer to hear whether there were exploitable minerals on the island. But we have to do many things which are of importance and interest only to us or to other individuals.

To whom is it relevant that during the gale we trudged out into the evening in order to take meteorological observations as regularly as mortgage payments? Then came back into the tent, coated with ice? To whom is it of interest that at 9.00 p.m. on 28 November 1929 at Bay of Isles, South Georgia, the thermometer recorded a temperature of $-1.5°$ or $-10.0°$?

On a very stormy day we climbed Penguin Hill, whose rounded lines make it appear probable that the ice of Grace Glacier, which is now retreating, once overwhelmed it. There is scarcely any shelter for us here. It is a chaos of nature, and before we reach the summit we have to squat down on the ground in order to breathe and so that the gale does not tumble us back down the slope. Beneath us the sea is sweeping waves and meadows of kelp in a seething cauldron onto the rocks.

But what are the gentoo penguins doing on such a storm-lashed afternoon on the exposed summit of the hill? Quite a variety of things, as we can see. The females are lying flat on their nests facing into today's southwesterly wind. If one did not have a compass one could deduce the wind direction from their position. The egg is best protected in this fashion, and if it is raining the water can flow off the wide, flattened back.

But what has become of the faithful husbands which, as we have mentioned so often, usually flank the nest so patiently? Has the storm delayed their return? Certainly there are a few standing in their upright guard position by the nests, defying the storm. But today they are the exception, the pick of the bunch. The majority – I counted 40 in the little area we could see – have retreated from their posts and have moved to a less exposed spot where they stand around, bored, preening their feathers and hunting for parasites in the most comical postures and, like us, waiting for better weather.

Since, as mentioned previously, there is no external difference between males and females we can only provisionally claim the right to describe these outsiders as husbands. But if they are, as we suspect, one can cite this as a fine illustration of the egotism of the male.

Finally I told myself that it was purely a formality as to whether the father were standing beside the nest, since the egg would not hatch any sooner as a result.

In other aspects, too, the female sitting unprotected on the nest has a less than rosy time. Among the penguins there are many which have not found wives. I do not know whether in the case of penguins, as is the case elsewhere in nature, there is a surplus of males and whether as a result the search for a mate is often unsuccessful. But down on the beach, or even all around the rookery one can see many penguins standing around, killing time. They do not know what do to with their time and, as tends to happen, they get up to mischief. In an otherwise peaceful scene one may often see two birds fighting and at first one thinks that the love and fidelity of this monogamous bird have collapsed. Then, in an all-too-human fashion, the suspicion grows that perhaps the strange bird at the nest, which the female penguin is still defending with her bill, may be one of these strange birds, in need of support. This is confirmed, and the whole situation becomes clear when the real husband comes waddling up and repels this intruder into its family life, punishing him excitedly. The latter bird, in the case of the encounter which I watched, left a few back feathers behind, pulled out of its hide by the harried husband. In this case we sympathize with the husband, even if he were a Philistine, and take sides against the outsider who tried to have a little affair.

The punishment was even more severe in another similar case, because unfavourable nesting conditions made the adventure, which did not succeed, a very rash and dangerous one. In this case the defeated penguin, improbable as it may sound, fell off a stepped pedestal. Pursued by the pecks of its normally good-natured opponent, he even tumbled down a little rock face and we watched as he disappeared at top speed towards the sea in a truly pitiful condition.

If this stepped landscape presented unpleasant problems for the little marriage-wrecker, it also had some negative aspects for me on one November day when it was blowing violently. I was again lying watching, trying to grasp the finer points of penguin married life, and again a gale was battering both humans and birds. I was absorbedly following the lively progress of a penguin's day when the wind dumped a penguin faeces from the storey above over my blue ski pants. For weeks I carried around a chalky patch which, like oil paint, defied every attempt to remove it.

More than once, subsequently, we had occasion to see a penguin from the first floor excrete its faeces on a brooding female on the ground floor; but this scarcely disturbed the birds at all. They feel no immediate need to cleanse themselves but instead carry the evidence around for a long time in the form of a white sprinkling. As newcomers, we initially identified such birds as a new subspecies, until on their wanderings the sea washed the guano off.

After relating these little jokes which the penguins play upon each other and to which even the elephant seals are occasionally exposed, I should like now to discuss nest building among gentoo penguins. Abilities in the area of nest building vary greatly between different birds. At Elsehul we saw nests which consisted simply of a depression in the earth, while close by we also found perfect, carefully built nests. The situation was the same at Bay of Isles too. Here it was interesting to see how the penguins had adjusted to the soil and material conditions. At Bay of Isles there are almost no areas with a markedly peaty character; even the tussac hummocks are quite meagre. Hence here the majority of the gentoo penguins had used little pebbles as nesting material, in such a way that the bottom of the nest was lined with them.

Apart from humans who steal its eggs and, when they are in need, readily consume its breast-meat and liver, the gentoo penguin has only one enemy, apart from the leopard seal, and that is the skua. It is not the penguin itself which is at risk since it can defend itself with its powerful bill and its strong, stumpy wings, but its eggs during the incubation period.

No egg is safe from the skua, whether it be that of the black-backed gull, the giant petrel, the king penguin, or any other bird. The theft of an egg from the nest of a gentoo penguin is carried out at lightning speed. With its restless, watchful eyes the skua cruises in ever narrowing circles above the unprotected prize. These spirals bring it right above the egg. For a moment it hovers, apparently motionless, a few metres above the nest, then it dives and one sees it carrying the penguin egg off in its bill to a hill where its greedy bill crushes the shell.

It would be pointless for a skua to try to fly with a giant petrel's egg in its bill, since it is 10 cm in length. The skua cannot even get its bill around it and hence it consumes it right on the spot. If it were disturbed by us during its hurried meal, we could be sure that a moment later the bird's wings would be whistling past our ears. In this aroused mood the skua is aggressive even to its own kind. Its screaming call, which has led the whalers to christen it "the raven" can be heard even before the first competitor appears. Then the greedy bill interrupts its activities; with tails fanned and wings half-open the rivals hurl themselves at each other; then follows a scene of aggression and voracity which are reminiscent of young cockerels fighting. Anywhere one goes on earth there is nothing but battle and strife! There are always frictions in nature; always life and death. The latter gives rise to the former; never does nature come to a standstill.

While this case of egg-theft was the result of an unprotected nest, left unattended because of either animals or humans, penguin eggs also fall prey to skuas without such intermediaries. It was on one of the stormy days. The female penguins, drifted up with snow, were sitting on their nests; white rings of drifted snow surrounded them. It was only noon and there were few males standing near the nests.

We saw a whole circle of skuas distributed around individual penguin nests in this unsettled weather. A sort of community of interest seemed to have reconciled the group for a while, although normally they grudged each other the smallest morsel.

First one, then another, would swoop low over the head of a sitting penguin, which would lunge at the skuas. Soon they were circling a neighbouring nest; one would harass it from behind, the others from the side or from the front. One could constantly hear the penguins' drawn-out alarm call of ro ro ro, or even more ru ru ru, which we had frequently heard at night previously. The communal, almost organized assault described here, more than once had the desired result. A somewhat timid, distraught penguin would expose its egg and with uncanny speed one of the skuas would fly off with it in its bill.

On South Georgia I was unable to spot the numerous variations in plumage coloration in the skua which I had recorded on my earlier trips to Macquarie Island. The predator's outfit was very uniform here. Even the single young quickly attains the coloration of the parents; the initial more grey-brown juvenile plumage later gives way to a dark tone.

One can instantly forget every one of the skua's misdeeds and cunning tricks as soon as one hears the alarm calls of the parents when the young bird is threatened by our appearance. After only a few days it will be strolling actively around the nest on its black, webbed feet and can take cover very skilfully. As we approach a touching call utters from the depths of this rapacious bird and one is even tempted to talk in terms of these birds possessing a soul.

At home a bounty would certainly be offered for birds like skuas. Agricultural unions would pass petitions alleging that it was pointless to run a poultry farm. Societies for the protection of animals would raise their voices in opposition and the life of this predator would be regulated by the authorities and would constantly be endangered.

But this does not apply to this bird on South Georgia. Down here in the wilderness it is free; nobody threatens its existence and nobody puts a spoke in its wheel. No sailor would expend powder and shot on a skua whereas shags, ducks, sheathbills (the sailors' snow bird) are popular targets.

Once various events had faded and we had forgotten the skuas' attacks on animals, humans and carrion, we too were able to contemplate it more calmly. We then admired the qualities which enabled the bird to achieve its feats. And even more than this. Its activities seemed natural to us when we compared what happened to human behaviour. The theft of eggs was open and harmless. Even in civilization there are usurers and extortionists around, who use need, love and happiness in order to achieve totally different types of theft.

There were two almost grotesque incidents which I must relate about the bird here; quite apart from its nature they were inflicted upon it by us humans, yet still reveal features of its character.

On the first occasion we were sitting in the tent when shrieking calls and rapid wing beats dragged us away from a game of cards, which we rarely played and was called "spritze" by the Norwegians, who taught it to us. Moreover it is a harmless game at which one wins cards which one can sell; it certainly does no damage to one's soul.

The noises were being uttered by skuas which seemed to be very pugnacious; when the quarrel became too violent we went outside and spotted a bird which apparently was fighting against itself, dancing up and down in agile leaps with half-opened wings. Curious, we walked closer; it did not fly up until, to our great amazement we could see that it was dragging a line behind it in the snow, tethering it to the tent. It was our fishing line, attached to the hook of which we had left a piece of meat when we had left Coal Harbour. The hook, with line attached, was now lodged in the skua's throat.

We killed the bird with a blow from an ice axe and since we already possessed a good skin for the collection we left it lying in the snow a little distance away. Soon we noticed a few of its kinsmen approaching the dead bird. But none of them went beyond examining it. They stood, undecided, for a while, then flew off again.

This continued for three days. On the evening of the third day we decided to resolve the matter and skinned the skua, leaving the carcass lying enticingly in the snow. Immediately the battle began over the best morsels. Hence a bird's plumage, the uniform, worn by a dead colleague, can keep even a skua in a state of terror for days, holding it spellbound.

10

With the King Penguins on Lucas Glacier

SHORTLY AFTER NOON on 30 November there was an improvement in the weather and we set off across the foreland towards Lucas Glacier in mild weather, with a temperature of 4°C.

After an hour's level walking, during which we crossed five streams on snow bridges, we reached the edge of the Lucas Glacier, which rises towards its ridge at an angle of 15°. At the edge of the glacier we discovered a king penguin rookery and the next few hours passed in a flash as we observed the birds.

One's first impression of the general scene was of great activity; young birds in down, looking like teddy bears – little well-fed philistines – trundled around among the adults, whose plumage seen against the surrounding snow and ice had the impact of a magnificent colour display.

A deafening noise, like that of a country fair, rose from this lively company, especially from the young birds. They contributed the major part of the noise in the form of a continuous whistling and of a second noise which might best have been produced by a chanter.

One could stand for hours in an unreal dream, absorbing this scene, without becoming tired of it: this quiet corner, the snout of the glacier, the waters of the bay and the steep ridges leading out to Cape Wilson. But then one had to tear oneself forcibly away from it to examine detailed scenes which were even more delightful.

In all this confusion we focussed our attention on one

little brown fellow, standing in front of an adult king penguin, its head slightly bowed like an obedient child. The mother would take a few paces up the snow slope and the young bird would run after her as if a thousand cares were weighing on its shoulders. It looked as if the serious matter of existence was weighing on the young bird, but not on the mother, which marched along, as proud and stiff as a ruler.

But the young bird really did have worries: worries about food. Its bill waved constantly around the mother's head and neck in order to show her where the trouble lay. Then the young bird would wait again in its respectful, submissive posture. Since the mother refused to produce any food, its head would sink a further two centimetres down into its shoulders. Another pause would follow. Some more whistling from the young bird while it billed its mother again until the latter decided to feed it. It engulfed the young bird's bill in its own and in the normal manner of penguins regurgitated the food down its offspring's throat. The actual feeding act is quite a complicated procedure. Prior to the actual feeding one can identify the mother's preparations in that she makes peculiar movements with her neck. Once the young bird has been fed, as a concluding sequence there follow rhythmic, pulsating contortions, probably designed to clear the food pipe again.

No young bird is satisfied with a single feeding and the procedure is repeated many times at short intervals. But at one point the mother absolutely refuses to produce any more food and runs off; now we can observe one of the most splendid scenes. The mother's stiff gait, not knowing where to go simply out of pride, while behind her the heavy, little king penguin chick, submissive to his fate, comes hobbling along.

But what is going on elsewhere, while these genuine family needs are being taken care of? The first manoeuvres of love-play have already brought two penguins together. After some preliminary billing they stand, as stiff as candles, at the top of the slope. The life and activity around them is no longer of any significance. A third bird which approaches, waving its wings, is driven off with blows of their wings. The wings vibrate excitedly in the air, then the two birds again stand, rigid and motionless.

Having absorbed these cameos we are able to identify a good 30 birds for which love-play and fighting are long past. A bulge in their lower abdomen betrays the fact that they are already carrying an egg and have begun incubating. King penguins do not make a nest but they carry the egg in a longitudinal fold of skin. The feathered skin hangs down like a skirt over the egg which in addition is provided with excellent support by the feet which are pressed closely together. If one approaches too closely and forces the bird to move slightly or change its position, it takes short, jerky steps, so as not to lose the egg. Once it resumes an immobile position one notices that the dorsal sides of the feet are turned up, forming a little shell-like cradle in front of the lower part of the abdomen.

And now the male returns. Without hesitation it locates the mother, lays its head on her neck and expresses its joy with outstretched neck by a loud 'eh e e e e eh', then head and neck drop like a baton. The bird remains standing in this position for two seconds, then switches to a less constrained position.

In our conversation we found that we could not suppress analogies with distant scenes from everyday life. They all came to the fore: the schoolmaster strolling around loftily in front of the pupils' desks, and the judge walking to his office building. We saw penguin analogy for all those people who do not know what to do with their bodies but vainly stretch their heads up. We were haunted by grotesque, lifeless poses like those of gargoyles, rigidly maintaining the position they have been given.

In the evening when the multi-voiced "roah-roah" resounded over the hills as one of those calls which at that time are uttered a thousand-fold with a similar meaning by every living creature on earth, the man/bird analogy was continued even farther. At a stroke all the people who were now moving through streets and villages wherever they lived in the world, came to mind. As I saw them moving about so rapidly penguins and men became almost interchangeable.

What advantages do I, Ludwig Kohl, really possess over a penguin, even a gentoo penguin? Like myself it is a part of the whole, and as a spouse it possesses many good qualities which I envy. Can one forget its patient loyalty at the nest or its care for its young which we later discovered?

It possesses abilities which we do not have, so much so that only a fool would draw the boundary between man and bird so sharply and loftily. Even though we have invented the compass and are aware of the forces which lie behind its operation, on lakes, steppes and the sea we are dependent on it. We surely have to admire the penguin who, gifted with a magnetic sense, daily can find one bay in the expanses of the sea, or its own nest among thousands, in storm or in fog. But when the first stormy night again arrives, with Benitz knocking against the tent pole, I will even envy the penguin, so defiantly turning his back and his tail to the southwest gale in his dense feather jacket in order to protect his egg, while we lie shivering in the tent and curse the weather.

1 December. Due east of here, barely 100 m from our camp, there is a little pool, from which the ice is reluctant to melt. In places the water is breaking through and in a few places there are little water holes. These are our new water source from which we haul water every day in a cask. We no longer need to break a hole in the ice. Now it is a quick, simple process. Earlier we hauled it from a little stream near the Grace Glacier, but it was a much longer trip.

But when, as today, there are so many young seals lying on the ice and splashing in the water, we will soon have to start hauling our water from the stream on the Grace Glacier again.

The young elephant seals no longer have any contact

with their mothers. After mating the latter go their own way. One can see a few of them lying in the tussac grass or out on the rocks, moulting; there are also many of them out in the waters of the bay looking for food. They lose contact with the herd earlier than the bulls.

We are no longer observing any mating or any births. The few exceptions do not alter this statement. Thus today we again saw a bull in quest of romance. He was pursuing a female which would have nothing to do with him. Then this late-performer abandoned his efforts too and hauled off towards a group of bulls. But on the way there a yearling crossed his path; he attacked it but was again rejected. He was received in hostile fashion by the group of bulls, since he clumsily lay down on the tail of a sleeping animal. But finally he wriggled a resting place for himself in the dense tangle of bodies.

But the fact that every serious aspect of the great epic of the rut and mating has faded away is best proved by a couple of females which were lying peacefully among the group of bulls.

It is the young seals which now set the tone in the Bay of Isles; they are active night and day, enjoying their young lives. When we see a ponderous, old seal lying on the beach we can scarcely believe that during the first months of its life it too was once as full of silliness and joie-de-vivre as the calves around us.

In stormy weather and when the frost again cements the dwindling ice cover together, they come closer to our tent and lie around us like a battlement. By preference they lie in the groove between it and the snow wall which we have piled up. It never occurs to any of them to flee. We have become friends. Still half asleep, they enjoy being scratched. If they wake up during this we can see their contented, black eyes in an almost spherical head, domed like a sphere, onto which a less-than-beautiful nose, whiskers and a wide mouth have been sketched. If a few of them tend to reject our intimacies, they must be those which have had occasion to observe reactions of rejection towards men among the adults, and have adopted these among their store of experience.

Their young bodies expand daily, so that one can literally see them grow; the blubber hangs in folds around their necks. What nutritional reserves the mother's milk must contain in order to ensure the calves' growth for weeks on end without any supplementary food!

The calves are now largely velvet-grey in colour, often velvet brown on the sides while the belly is lighter coloured. Very few still possess the black youthful pelt, in which their corpulent bodies scarcely appear to have enough room any more.

Living in close proximity as we did we could not avoid making the language of the elephant seals our own, namely the babbling and utterance of their first sounds, whether they denoted joy pain, vitality or surprise. Their sounds are inexhaustible, although admittedly they are often just new inventions of the moment, just as babies distort and run together their first stammering words.

It is easier to comprehend the words of a South Sea islander than those of an elephant seal calf, or even to grasp their general meaning. We recorded those which were commonly repeated. They sounded like: "vue e e" or "kfa kfa hu hu" or "uo u o eee", or like a good-natured short "u o". I also find in my notes "hu hu hu hu hu" and "u a a a" and many other stereotyped sounds, but I do not plan to discuss their language any farther since clearly none of my readers will be able to use it later in life.

If we uttered the sounds even approximately, as they have been recorded here, especially those listed first, we could be sure that one of the animals would assume that one of his playmates was nearby and would head in the direction of the noise. In this fashion we lured many a seal pup, so that it inquisitively covered the 20 or 30 m to the entrance of our tent. If one was unable to sleep at night one could converse by means of the sounds we had learned, with a neighbour out in the snow on the other side of the tent wall, instead of just chasing one's own thoughts around in circles. One would promptly receive an answer to one's call, much more reliably than in a telephone booth. Generally the conversation would not last very long and, as one might expect, was soon exhausted. Usually the elephant seal would want to resume its slumbers then too. If, during that last moment between waking and sleeping, the scientist got the upper hand and it was calm, one could time the heavy breathing without seeing the animal, by holding one's luminous watch; the respiration rate was 18 breaths per minute.

On the morning of 1 December we had been carrying out cartographic work from Penguin Hill and Shoemaker Hill, taking rock samples from various sites and collecting mosses and lichens. My wife had undertaken this task almost exclusively. At noon I still wanted to work from an old moraine hill in front of Grace Glacier but a cold southwest wind was constantly shaking my tripod; when it finally capsized I had to abandon my plan. I was then quite pleased to find a few spiders beneath the smooth, polished boulders.

Somewhat later, near the beach, we happened to spot a penguin that was new to us; it had caught our attention by its somewhat smaller size (length from head to tail 61 cm). Its back was a dense black, its neck white and bill black, while a narrow stripe ran across the white expanse of the head like a dark collar. Its movements were more jerky and busy and hence we named it Ikey, although science has endowed it with the name *Pygoscelis antarctica* [chinstrap penguin].

No matter how much we hoped to find a rookery of this bird, which was new, or at least rare, on South Georgia we never encountered more than just individuals, and rarely at that, or two birds at most. This always occurred on this same spot, close to both the gentoo and king penguins.

On 2 December, once again in the evening, the world became more blue-grey by the minute after a comfortless

19. From our tents we could see the ice cliff of the Brunnonia Glacier

20. Young elephant seals in captivity

21. A gentoo penguin with its chick

22. Sheltered by an ice wall we felt more secure in our abode

day of heavy rain; everything in the bay which was dear and familiar to us disappeared. We had come home from three different directions as if summoned by a bell. Benitz had had a bad day; it was no weather for filming. After some initial disagreements between him and myself he had happily abandoned people and artificial dramatic effects. All he needed now was sunshine. Now that he knew the environment and the fauna, he knew that we did not need artificial effects and aimed at doing our own way, taking advantage of our model, nature, the greatest artist of all. We do not need any gripping action, although we will certainly be reproached for the lack of it back in Berlin. We will also be reproached for the lack of people and of the trashy action with which a number of film companies has been nauseating the patient public. No: let them carp and complain. We are filming what we see; we are letting the animals provide the action. Like the sea waves, not even the most skilful Berlin director can have any impact on them.

In the evening the barometer reading revealed that it had dropped from 748.5 to 727.5 over the past twelve hours. There was still no wind playing in the guys and we could still hear the noises of the animals with unusual clarity and purity, almost uncannily, as if they were being trapped by the wall of the tent as if on a record. It was misty, fog-drenched weather. Then at 2.00 a.m., as was clearly legible on the brightly glowing dial on the tent pole, the tent unexpectedly bellied inwards with the first strong gust. A squall out of the southwest blasted over our tent from Grace Glacier. We started up, mentally reviewing all our property: sledges, skis, provisions. There followed a second and a third gust: a metal tent peg was torn out of the deep snow in which we had buried it. Gusts now came chasing each other, one after the other. There was a noticeable brightness around us. Early December is midsummer in the south and the nights pass shyly and briefly; hence dawn breaks over the island at 3.00 a.m. The thought of our Klepper boat, lying overturned in front of the tent drove me outside into the grey, stormy morning, even although we had buried it under the snow. I crawled out of the tent sleeve but could not stand up; the storm hurled me down onto the snow like some insignificant object. I was able to cover the 4 m to the boat only by crawling on all fours. Then I shovelled more snow onto it so that it would not be blown out into the bay. We needed it so pressingly.

Since I was outside anyhow I threw some more snow against the side of the tent to protect us and to increase our security, although three days before we had built up our snow wall to a height of 1.5 m. Totally soaked I crawled back into the tent as I had emerged, on all fours.

From this early hour onwards we did not have a single peaceful moment. We could not even replace the torn guys since we could not stand upright outside. We sat beneath the depressed tent roof and battled the storm to the best of our abilities. We wrapped around the triple-braced tent pole all the spare clothing we could rustle up, all our bandages, everything we had, so that if it splintered we would at least be protected from the shattered ends. Two of us braced the tent pole, leaning firmly into it against the southwest wind while the third person, like Atlas supporting the sky, supported the straining tent canvas, which was billowing like a sail. There was not a single pause; the raging of the gale dominated us, demoniacal and menacing, elemental and ponderous. We developed a list; the tent pole was leaning. If only this would end! We had to go out again since this could not continue like this. It was too hazardous. We finally succeeded in throwing a loop around the weak point at the tip of the tent pole, like a lasso, and securing it to a peg in the snow. We now felt somewhat safer and one brave soul even thought of attempting to brew some coffee in order to combat our fatigue. It was my wife who achieved this feat of skill; throughout she sat ready to grab the knob which turns off the vaporiser, yet we risked it. This manoeuvre was successful and we faced the day with more hope.

It blew for exactly 12 hours, until 3.00 p.m., then some short pauses occurred; the gusts rattled and battered the tent less frequently. Towards evening a fairly long pause occurred and we were amazed at the sudden silence. One of us said to another: "You don't need to shout; I can hear you perfectly!" Throughout the storm our voices had had to overcome the roar of the gale in order to be understood.

Around suppertime we were able to emerge from the tent. Our boxes and the Klepper boat had disappeared beneath the snow; everything was buried. Only the tip of a ski and the ridge of the tent protruded into the greyness. Elephant seals lay huddled close together, having instinctively found the safest spot. The sea to the north was like a grey shroud from which spray was continually being torn. Over in Rosita Harbour we could see two whaling vessels which had reached safety just in time.

Then suddenly a gleam of sun broke through the low-hanging clouds; a pale-blue glow raced across the front of Grace Glacier, which otherwise remained dead and grey. The demoniac ferocity of the island was slumbering again, that island around which cruises the whale, for the sake of which men travel from north to south amidst danger and through both deliberate and inflicted adventures.

During the first days of December we noticed that the young elephant seals were gradually wandering down to the beach, and over the next few days we encountered the liveliest activity there. It was as if they had recognized their real element and had for the first time gravitated closer to it.

The black, woolly pup's coat had been shed; the animals now began to practise swimming. We were unable to observe any guidance from the adult animals in this activity. The pups certainly see the adults entering the water and hence have enough models, but swimming seems to be an inherited ability which requires no coaching, even right from the first strokes.

The animals are barely 6–7 weeks old now but they

have grown enormously. Their circumference behind the flippers is almost 1 m; their average length is 1.6 m but in individual cases this may rise to 2 m. If we annoy one of them its little nasal swelling will already expand; from this we can recognize the bulls, the future knights.

They feel most comfortable among wind and waves; small, bloody scratches tell of innocent play-fights and when the glow of the evening sun strikes the water and their smooth bodies, they gleam mechanically. One would like to be an artist, in order to preserve this restless, intricate picture in plastic form.

One of them is taking a prolonged bath in a rock basin. Beneath the calm water, amongst the ghostly kelp, we can see him constantly swaying his body. Blissfully he snuggles against the rocks, rubbing and brushing as if he were covered with vermin. For a moment his full-moon face protrudes above the water then, just as he is caught by the camera, he turns to flee.

Tired with fighting and playing others lie motionless at full stretch on the beach, like little boats which have been pulled ashore. Others now are just beginning their lives; they slip into the smooth sea and leave a bright wake behind them before disappearing into the depths.

After these lighter aspects of an elephant seal's life I now come to an adverse aspect of their youth, one which confronted us when we left the beach and walked across the solid snow cover.

Here we encountered small, round pits in which one or more animals lay dead; we flushed giant petrels and skuas out of these pits where they were gorging themselves. We walked on, disgusted by their blood-covered bills, and encountered a row of different pits. They looked as if they had been cut with a punch and concealed live animals which were trying to haul themselves up the walls to reach freedom. They were captives, young animals cheated out of their youthful pleasures, confined by the unpropitious nature of their birthplace.

It was the fate of these pups that they had been born on a deep snow pack; if I condense all our observations, the sequence of events, which we were able to follow in all its stages, appears to be as follows. After a pup has been born on a deep snow pack mother and pup lie on a confined space which they never leave. During the suckling period the mother never leaves the pup; the latter's radius of movement is equally small, focussing constantly on the source of food, i.e. the mother's nipples. Now the snow beneath them melts, primarily due to body heat but perhaps also due to their dark pelts under the influence of the sun. One may often observe that the pup, with its little body has already thawed a hole for itself, into which it is threatening to disappear while the mother, lying sideways across the hole continues to suckle the pup.

Both the sealers' and our own observations confirm that the mother cares for the pup for only 3–4 weeks; even in the abnormal situation where the pup disappears, she then leaves it. The pup continues its downward journey, producing pits of every size and every stage, the distinguishing feature of the beach at Bay of Isles.

If the snow cover is shallow the situation ends happily. In a short time, with the advancing season the walls of the prison become lower and one fine day the animal will be out again with the friends who have never seen him and about which it knows nothing. It will live in a sociable group again and this first tough period of its life will soon be forgotten.

Since we have established that after feeding for about four weeks even the pups born on a stable, unalterable surface live and flourish until the ninth or tenth week without food, the animals in "captivity" are in no danger as long as that captivity does not last too long. But it is probable that the mother will often be obliged to abandon the pup earlier, since from our own observations she never descends into the pit along with the pup. Hence at Bay of Isles we found many dead animals in the holes along with many live ones which were waiting to be liberated. We ourselves assisted many incarcerated animals to freedom by digging them out in good time.

One day, after the first pause for breath during a violent storm, I was walking across the snowfield to the beach when I noticed a circular hole several handbreadths across. As I bent over it I could hear heavy breathing. There could be no doubt that it came from an elephant seal pup and I mobilized my companions in order to get to the bottom of this peculiar phenomenon.

It took us many hours of work to get to the bottom of the shaft. A narrow pit led down vertically for 3.5 m; the animal was still alive, lying in a pool of water standing on a sandy bottom and almost an ice-axe-length deep. Only its dark head stared out of this snowy prison, as if out of a Spanish collar. The pup was fat and differed in no way from those which had grown up in freedom.

Often accidents of birth and place had resulted in a pup starting life on the snow-covered ice of a stream. Here, too, it would disappear one day down a funnel-shaped hole, an event which could turn out in various ways. The drop into the water is quite harmless if it is into a quiet, shallow stream with a free outlet or into a pool. In these situations one can see the animals lying in the shallow water, with the jagged edges of the hole in the ice above them. However, if the stream is full of eddies and boulders the life of the elephant seal pup usually ends when it falls.

We estimated the number of animals at Bay of Isles who died in this fashion at 5%. By contrast the number which die from illness is infinitesimally small. Thus only once did we find a large abscess on the rear flipper of a young elephant seal, and found it dead soon afterwards. The number which died was a relatively small percentage when one recalls that in the small area around our tent we counted 420 pups.

Everything I have said about elephant seals thus far, both in terms of their habits and their relationship to their natural environment, applies to undisturbed surroundings. No sealers intruded on the quiet scenes of life and death which we watched, and hence they unfolded undisturbed before us.

One often reads and hears quite varied assessments as to the dangerous nature of elephant seals. The attitude of adults towards men may become vicious during the mating season, while for the rest of the year the animal's subdued, slow temperament is scarcely to be feared at all, or only in the event of an accident. There are defensive posturings, intimated by the animal rearing up and baring its teeth. The fact that as a result an inexperienced sealer whom adventure and the numerous strange animals had lured straight from South America, once left the seat of his pants lying on the ground should be ascribed more to the carelessness of the man concerned than to the aggressiveness of the animal.

One finds that there is a pronounced irascibility in both sexes during the mating season. In the case of the cows the irascibility and hostile attitude toward man seemed to us to extend over the pupping and mating period, and I shall now relate an incident which in the case of both man and animal was as typical as it was comical.

It was on 6 December; we were sitting together, waiting for good weather when a powerful roar from nearby indicated that an adult animal was near the tent. I immediately thought of our Klepper boat. We had placed it ready, right way up in a snow gully near the tent and as a precaution against the wind had lashed it down with ropes and pegs. Benitz was already on the move in his tent when a blow from a rear flipper struck the canvas. I heard him shout that a large elephant seal was endangering his tent. When I got outside I was greeted by a scene which really should have delighted me. A large female seal, a good 3.5 m in length, was lying on the Klepper boat and was scratching its scabby skin on it. As a human, outraged at the thought of possible material damage, i.e. by purely external factors, I leaped unthinkingly towards the animal, yelling and shouting and thinking only of the boat with which we were to carry out our marine investigations in February. If I had thought about the entire situation for even a moment and had given the animal some time the matter would probably have resolved itself more peacefully. However, I punched the animal in the mouth and immediately felt it bite the little finger on my right hand; it split the nail and, as far as a little finger can bleed, it started to bleed profusely. The wound had been inflicted by a short, jerky lunge of the head.

After the elephant seal's victory over man, it retreated, humping away; before I went back into the tent I checked the boat. I turned it over with my sound hand and was amazed to find that the weight and movement of an animal weighing many centners had not even damaged a single rib of the frame. The neat vessel lay spruce and intact before me; no better involuntary testimonial could have been devised than this accident had provided.

How does one treat an injured finger like this in a tent? Holding the scissors in one's left hand one cuts away the nail completely, then dunks it for a long time in 96% alcohol; in so doing one simultaneously atones for quite a few sins and can grant oneself absolution for a year without the consolation of a priest. This bath has to be repeated daily. I did this at least because the saliva from an elephant seal's jaws has a foul stench and because I had no experience of handling bites of such an exotic origin.

The wound took a long time to heal; it took the nail months to grow back to the extent that I could work with the finger uncovered. While attending my injury, then quite often thereafter our companion Benitz would recite a verse to which one could not take objection, namely: "Much worse than the kiss from a woman's lips is that from an elephant seal."

During my enforced inactivity following these events I realized that it was not just an inflamed vein which was throbbing, but to an even greater degree the vast loneliness of the sea and this world of ice, of which I now became more aware. One's heart becomes aroused by the surrounding scenes and disturbed by scenes from the past, when one cannot use one's hand. Everything crowds in more directly, like shadows, and one can cut through the thousand threads again by a decision to take an untrodden, obstacle-strewn route.

Thus I endured with difficulty the days which followed and which confined me to the tent, although they passed somewhat more easily in that the weather was foul and unpredictable. "Rained almost the whole day on 5 December; gale on 9 December; brightened somewhat in the afternoon. ": I wrote in my diary.

My wife and Benitz used this opportunity to go back to the king penguin rookery and when they came home they told me so enthusiastically that I might almost have experienced the day with them. They brought back a young bird for the collection, one in the brown plumage which gives them such a bear-like appearance.

They reported that the young penguins now looked just like vagabonds. Their adult plumage was now largely complete; their backs were already greyish black, their breasts white, even brighter than those of the adults, and their necks glowed lemon yellow. However, some still wore remnants of their juvenile plumage: one bird might be wearing a shawl, another an apron, some had the ruff of a priest's vestments and others again long stockings.

When I heard the whish of skis near the tent that day it seemed to me that my two interlocutors also differed little from vagabonds. Their pockets were stuffed full of rocks and eggs and they had been soaked by drizzling rain. Benitz was carrying a pole over his shoulder like a trade's boy, from which hung two brown birds' skins. They looked like fox pelts, since in order to lighten his load he had already skinned the birds in the rookery.

He found many small stones in the stomachs of the young birds, as we had frequently determined in the case of the adults earlier. In one adult we had recently found 32 little stones.

10 December. Storms and still more storms, which never seem to want to abate! For a moment we even admit to ourselves that a fourth-class train trip from Berlin to Frankfurt is more pleasant than the continuing battering and drumming of the storm.

Once again the tent is flapping around us, as if the devil had a hand in the game. The bay, the glacier and the foreland are shrouded in a white smoke. I know my friends so well that I am sure there are 30 or 40 male penguins sitting in the lee again, letting the females worry about keeping the nests warm.

In incalculable fashion, typical of South Georgia, the island had assumed a white attire today; there were numerous patches of blue sky above. At 2 o'clock, since the view to the south-southwest was clear we quickly decided to visit the Grace Glacier; its geographical characteristics are as follows. Above the frontal cliffs this extensive glacier rises moderately steeply (at about 15°) then levels off and is commonly slightly undulating, until just below the pass at a height of 357 m one is faced by a steep pitch; we overcame it in half an hour via an easy marginal crevasse. The pass is saddle-shaped and lies at a height of 518 m; beyond this the surface continues level then begins to drop gently, then after 2 km, without any break in the ice surface, it drops away. Due to the limited visibility we could distinguish for only a few seconds a multi-peaked ridge which bounds King Haakon Bay1 on the south.*

---

*A later visit to King Haakon Bay revealed that unbroken ice extends from the pass right to King Haakon Bay, so that one is justified in speaking of a continuous glacier system extending between the north and south coasts of the island, between Bay of Isles and King Haakon Bay.

Grace Glacier is cradled between two mountain chains. The eastern one separates the Lucas Glacier from Grace Glacier and runs southwestwards towards the pass at a height of 600–700 m. The western one is aligned from northwest to southeast. Its lee side reveals an almost complete, or certainly very extensive glacier cover, whereas the windward side is almost glacier-free, in places revealing vertical rock faces in which almost horizontal schists outcrop. Here it was possible to identify an indistinct lateral moraine whereas, understandably, the almost totally ice-covered western side of the mountain chain made moraine formation impossible. On the way up, without packs, it took us 3½ hours to climb the Grace Glacier.

Apart from storm petrels and fairy terns which never left us, even beyond the pass, one remarkable phenomenon which we observed on this hike, about 10 km above the glacier snout, was an elephant seal pup, born this year. At first we took it for a rock and headed for it excited, because we all differed in our opinions as to the nature of this lonely foundling. None of us was able to identify this dark point in the white desert correctly.

It was in good condition, although God knows what had driven it here all on its own. We pushed it until it faced towards the Bay of Isles, in order that it was at least pointing in the right direction.

Although one is tempted to talk repeatedly about the animals which lay closest, namely the penguins and elephant seals, I must not overlook a bird which deserves especially to be included, namely the black-backed gull [Dominican gull].

If we walked through the penguin rookery towards the beach the gulls would immediately give warning with their excited *be be be beh*, so that the penguins were alerted and began uttering their alarm calls. Frequently robbed by the skuas and often threatened by man, no bird takes such conspicuous care of its light grey eggs as this gull.

If one came close to the nest, which usually lay on a

tussac hummock or a projecting rock rib, one could be sure that this shy, timid bird would long since have left the nest. It would already be sitting in a different spot to decoy us, calling and crying. In a flash all its kinsfolk would have gathered around the threatened spot; they are well organized and the first cry would have alarmed them. An excited hubbub fills the air, becoming even more penetrating when a skua circles over the threatened nest. The bay, usually so quiet, is in an uproar, and if things become too hectic even the elephant seals raise their heads and become more alert.

If we humans know the position of the nest exactly (and we know many of them) for the sake of the gull and to spite the skuas, we walk past it in a wide detour; if we are patient and hide behind a rock we will later see the gull resume incubation on its abandoned nest.

But today we must learn what has happened to the three eggs in one of their nests. It lies so exposed on a little nose that from this high lookout point one has a commanding view over the little bay. A rock pinnacle projects boldly above a steep snow gully on Shoemaker Hill and from it a flight of steps drops away steeply. Taking a long, careful stride and stretching a little to make the manoeuvre, we manage to get a glimpse into the little nest.

We have truly arrived just at the right moment. There is a little grey ball lying in the nest, speckled with black and white spots, a darling little fellow. We have to take him in our hands for a brief moment to detect that he is alive.

And the second egg? The bird's bill is already projecting from it like a little thorn, and a crack extends from an angular hole in the shell. One can already see the slight heaving of the little body which, scrunched together, is trying obstinately to attain the outside world.

In the case of the third egg we can see neither the bird's bill nor the rhythm of life, but only a fine, little crack. But if one puts one's ear carefully to the edge of the nest, one can hear a faint peeping.

By accident we had run across the gull's nest in this three-part stage, presenting a charming picture. The bunches of tussac grass waved like standards around the young, awakening life and a pleasant day had kept the nest free of snow. While at other stages of incubation the bird is less devoted to its domain, to the extent that we often wondered how late it flew back to the nest, this time it remained hovering excitedly above us and repeatedly dived energetically at us.

Curiosity led us back to this nest quite often and we had an excellent opportunity of watching the young birds develop. The last egg, which had displayed only a faint crack, took 36 hours before it finally yielded to the heaving of the little bird. Thereafter a further little clump of feathers lay in the nest, its down still stuck together.

But we looked in vain for the two other little balls and began cursing those robbers the skuas, who we assumed had done their work here again, just as excitedly as the birds above us. But this was not the case. We could not pin anything on the skuas this time. But chance led our eyes to the surroundings of the nest where we spotted first one then soon another little creature lying absolutely motionless in the tussac grass. Only 48 hours old, they were already on their feet. But no matter how long we kept our eyes on them, all life seemed to have ebbed from them. If one were to walk quickly past this spot one would never have distinguished the little creatures from one of the grey lichen-covered rocks, of which there was an abundance in the area around the nest.

Nor was our experience confined to isolated observations of this type at Bay of Isles. My wife brought back similar observations from a short trip she made. She had discovered an empty nest; only a few pastel shell fragments lay in it, but alerted by the clamour of the parents she found a little chick near the nest. A few hours later she went back again and found two young birds. They had pressed themselves so tightly against the rock face outside the nest, hiding under some grass at the same time, as motionless as two rocks, that she had to take them in her hand to convince herself that they were alive.

She also told us of another nest where again she found the nestlings, barely two days old, about half a metre from the nest, only after a long search. Since the nest lay above a steep rock face and since my wife was afraid that the helpless little things might tumble down it, she placed them back in the nest. But, unable to understand this kindness they scampered over the edge of the nest into the nearby tussac grass.

Only somebody who has stood at a window or on the quayside watching for a plume of smoke on the horizon which is bringing his bride, a youthful friend or an important decision, will understand our tension and excitement on 14 December. Our optical nerves were working overtime; on such days our six eyes do the work of twelve.

Early in the morning we spotted a boat which rounded Cape Wilson and came closer and closer, heading for our camp. We could see the fine-lined vessel and its plume of smoke; we saw it less distinctly as it passed the dark, snow free rocks at the foot of the mountain near the cape. When the significance and objective of the ship seemed clear we quickly ate breakfast so as to lose no time; in so doing, naturally, we lost sight of the ship, but soon we were all out in front of the tent again, lying in wait. But there was no longer any ship in sight.

It was 11 o'clock; a whole range of hypotheses came to mind. Had it run into Beckmann Fiord? Was it picking up eggs for the Christmas celebrations?

Still excited, we stared in the hope of seeing smoke again, although there was always the chance that what we were seeing was just snow slopes, or the flying spray at the cape itself, until a benevolent grey veil of snow hid all our fantasies and interpretations. It restored our disturbed rest and forced us to pull out the cards again, that pastime which more than any other game or entertainment can quickly drive pointless ponderings or hopes from one's mind.

Twelve o'clock came; two o'clock came; and still no ship arrived. Hence we let the ship do what it liked, packed up our things and stowed our sledges in order to tackle our long-anticipated reconnaissance trip towards King Haakon Bay1. We hoped to hike the length of Lucas Glacier and thereafter to find out whether one could make one's way to Stromness Bay or Cumberland Bay by that route.

11

Further Difficulties: Our Second Sledge Journey, 16–20 December

IT WAS LATE AFTERNOON when we started off with heavy sledges across the ice-crusted level foreland, which extends between Grace and Lucas glaciers. Nothing could have prevented us from trying our luck at exploring the island again.

After a strenuous hour's hauling we reached the king penguin rookery but found Lucas Glacier shrouded in thick fog. Thus we were left hanging here among the penguins and derived quiet pleasure from pitching our camp right amongst this restless assembly, whose offspring had made significant progress in the past few weeks. Only occasionally could we detect the piping of the latest age group, while the birds' wing-beats betrayed high spirits and joie-de-vivre.

On 17 December it rained from 3 p.m. until 10.00 a.m. Despite the wretched weather we broke camp at 12 o'clock. We travelled past isolated groups of king penguins which were moving around, apart from the rest, on the fairly steep slope of the Lucas Glacier. We climbed in tedious zigzags, just as tedious as rolling rocks up a steep slope. We had no view ahead of us: just the fog and a gentle westerly wind. All that was visible was the limited section of route which we had just covered, and the penguins, which steadily dwindled in size. Occasionally we caught glimpses of conspicuous coastal landmarks such as Cape Wilson and Cape Buller. Despite this, using the compass we continued our march in a southerly direction. Since the route was so free of crevasses, we hoped that it would continue to remain so. Nonetheless travelling on glaciers which have never been seen by humans before is an uncanny business and even minor irregularities can be terrifying in the fog.

By 1.30 p.m. we assumed that we had reached the ridge of the glacier since at a height of 152 m it levelled off, although we were certain of this only by feel rather than by sight. The fog was even thicker; we could hear the thunder of ice avalanches and during the quiet spells we could still hear the waves breaking in the bay.

It was mainly because we were chilly rather than any prospect of an improvement in the weather that made us continue travelling until, surrounded by thick, wet fog, we pitched our second camp at 3 o'clock at a height of 218 m. The temperature was hovering around the freezing point. Before midnight it began raining and continued all night.

18 December. Spent a restless night. The tent, our body heat and the rain had carved troughs in the coarse-grained snow surface so that we were lying on ridges and valleys. As a result our sleep was broken and quite fitful, especially in my case due to my aching finger. Are these the delights of summer on South Georgia?

If things proceeded as slowly as this it would not just be the snow under our tent which melted but, with equal rapidity, the provisions we had brought with us. At 2.00 p.m. the rain stopped but the fog remained thick. We had to lie and wait even longer.

At 4.00 o'clock the wind began to gust violently and in a few moments a terrible hurricane had developed. In front of the tent the metal tent peg was torn out by the assault of the gale, the entrance to the tent was ripped open as a result, and the tent and our sleeping bags filled with snow. Benitz, who was just in the process of changing his clothes, leaped out in his underwear, drove the peg back into the snow and shovelled firn on top of it, while the rest of us had to hang onto the tent with all our strength.

Through the canvas we could watch the drifting snow as it piled up on the outside, rather like reading a tide gauge, and we were thankful to see it rising rapidly since it gave us more security.

We kept our clothes and boots on; crawling out of our sleeping bags again we squatted around since we did not trust the situation. We spent a sleepless night of storm, extremely concerned about the situation. In the morning there were some short pauses. We stayed, waiting, in our damp bags. Shortly before 12 o'clock it had stopped snowing and the storm gusts were less frequent. Towards the sea we had clear visibility but otherwise we could make out only a pyramid-shaped peak on a mountain chain to the west.

Around noon we broke camp and headed south; after we had covered the first few ski-lengths we realized that this glacier too was bounded on both sides by mountain chains of about the same height and the same character as in the case of the Grace Glacier. They, too, were aligned mainly north–south. In the case of the eastern ridge its windward side displayed minor ice accumulations only on its upper south-facing slopes, whereas the western range was almost completely ice-covered.

As we passed an ice-filled cirque-shaped hollow on the western chain shortly after 1 o'clock the visibility to the south became worse, with falling snow, and we had to pitch camp at a height of 354 m beneath a saddle-shaped pass.

Having learned from the previous night which had given us so many problems, today before pitching the tent we dug a hole 1 m deep in the coarse firn which appeared icy and granular, like fish spawn. Thereby we left only the tent ridge exposed to the southwest wind while the bulk of the tent was sheltered.

There were no summits visible; only to the southwest could we see a hanging ice-wall which was far enough away to be able to threaten us with calving ice-blocks. In the evening we melted snow over the primus. We sat on our rolled-up sleeping bags like cushions.

But is there any significance in the fact that we took four days to cover the ludicrously short distance of 17 km? Can it be true that we will be celebrating Christmas in five days? And finally is it really necessary to report on our final day of travel and on the great disappointment which it produced?

The night was relatively calm and we slept superbly after the problems of the previous few nights. We would have slept well even on pointed rocks. But with a temperature of −2° the morning brought a light snowfall; only occasionally was the pass above us visible; it formed a saddle (422 m) between the two bounding mountain chains at the head of the glacier.

Heading south-southeast we climbed to this pass by a much gentler slope than in the case of the Grace Glacier. Also in common with the Grace Glacier it possessed a marginal crevasse running along the glacier. In a rare happy mood we travelled southeastwards across almost level terrain where only a little bare ice showed through the snow, and soon were treated to an overwhelming view down into King Haakon Bay which lay below us.

From our high vantage point we could see innumerable peaks in the mountain range on the south side of King Haakon Bay, between which a total of eight glaciers pushed downwards; of these four reached the sea. Calved icebergs drifted in the quiet fiord, originating from a glacier which almost completely filled the inner part of the bay. The north side of this glacier, which we named the Shackleton Gap in honour of the English polar explorer, Sir Ernest Shackleton, rose slowly and almost crevasse-free to a wide plateau which appeared at least to be level and extended a long distance to the east, unbroken by any peaks or mountain chains.

It would be superb if, by continuing our present eastward course, we could manage to reach that surface or even if we could succeed in first making the descent to King Haakon

Bay; we knew that from there Shackleton and two companions, blessed by superb weather had attempted and successfully executed the crossing to Possession Bay and Stromness Bay in 1916.

Full of hope we travelled east for a good half hour; the sledges slid behind us at a lively pace although they had a tendency to slide increasingly down the slope. We thus became distinctly aware that we were at the start of a gentle descent.

We were still singing vigorously and happily when, totally unexpectedly we found ourselves faced by a steep icefall and any hope of proceeding farther was eliminated at a stroke. Here where isolation excluded any possibility of human support, the island had again rebuffed us; we could not defy or resist this rebuff although the wide, unconstrained ice surface, for the sake of which we ultimately had set out from home, still lay so enticingly in front of us.

There is nothing to report on our return trip back to camp. We travelled by watch and compass through blizzard conditions with zero visibility. Our tracks were no longer discernible. We covered the entire distance in one lap; as a result that same evening we were again camping among the penguins and seals, from which we had set out five days before with such high hopes.

12

Waiting for a Ship

WE WERE SITTING around our tent at the edge of the tussac grass, 50 m from the beach; we had moved camp closer to the bay after we returned home. Around us, a few metres away, the tussac grass is sprouting from round cushions which stand as if on pillars of earth; the foam of the sea shimmers through the tussac spikes.

We have to live here in order to keep an eye on the bay. A ship may arrive at any hour. It is Christmas time and presumably not all three whaling stations will forget us on Christmas Day. Probably one of them will send a message; a ship will probably bring us mail and some surprise or other. It will soon be Christmas after all.

Tired and full of the disappointments which the difficulties of the island and the weather had created for us, we sat on little tussac-grass seats. Around us lay a heap of driftwood which we had collected along the beach. The wide bay accumulates it during northeast gales. Every piece has a history and could tell a story: the wedges come from hatches; the curved planks from lifeboats; the little tree trunks from the loneliness of the Patagonian coast. All these finds and the distant darkness of their origins stimulate thoughts which in turn spin webs somewhere between dreams and reality. We can see the beech woods of a harsh coast and experience the privations of shipwrecked sailors.

We put the first plank on the fire. The smoke rises slowly, grey and blue against a clear, clean sky. Elephant seals are lying only 3 m from the blazing fire; they do not retreat even a metre, as if they were unacquainted with flames and do not sense any danger. King penguins, inquisitive and stiff, trot by. A silver gleam lies across Sunset Fiord; clouds interrupt it and make it shimmer.

This is indeed a paradise in which we are living. Say what you like, friends! Forget the tough hours and days and remember this magnificent day when sea and sky, animals and man, flame and ashes meld into unity!

The fire blazing in front of us represents our Christmas tree; in the sparks which shoot up we can identify the lights on the tree and the gleams in the eyes of our children as they dance around the tree.

The years come back to us from the past: Freinacht in Lapland, where Aslak Olsen Elvemund stirred up the fire in the cold arctic night in order to keep us alive, and innumerable campfires on the steppes. The brown body of the young maiden, Rules, danced bewitchingly in our minds, to the point where we were ready to jump up and rush headlong to join the people of the South Seas islands.

Next day that happy, colourful evening was far behind us; each day dragged through the same grey course, confining us to the tent. Certainly we saw much that was new and noteworthy: the first of the young gentoo penguins which subsequently shot up out of the nests like flowers on a spring day. Their little heads still hung shyly and limply on their breasts, and they stuck to the warm brood patch, leaving it only to beg their mothers for their first food. The latter was regurgitated into their bills in small doses.

In our conscientious desire to record the annual cycle of the seals we also paid full attention to developments in the elephant seal colony. Near our tents was a gathering point or assembly point for all the adult males in the surrounding area. Their number grew to 120 animals; we had never seen such a concentration before. All were moulting and now lay pressed close together. There were only a few adult females lying in the bay, which now belonged to the young, glossy pups; their youthful days would soon be behind them and each day they became quieter and less vociferous. Their ranks steadily thinned as many wandered to other parts of the large bay.

Christmas Eve itself brought snow and we unpacked the best of the things our friends had sent with us from the cases. There was a full moon in the north and once the snow clouds had emptied themselves it and a few stars represented our Christmas tree.

Is there a different Christmas celebration going on at home? Apart from a few children's eyes and joyful radiance? Apart from a good meal?

We were restless and became more restless with every passing day spent watching the waters of the bay in vain for a ship which would rescue us. Not a day passed during the last few days of the year when we did not sit on the eastern slope of Shoemaker Hill, keeping watch.

The tussac grass was pushing up vigorous shoots which, with our voracious appetites, we avidly consumed. Since they were the thickness of young asparagus this is what we called them, and valued them for their refreshing, nutty taste.

One concentrates on everything on the horizon when one is watching for a ship. A shadow lies across an iceberg, drifting away out there. Its face looks like a ship heading in towards the coast. Out there at the cape there is a reef which rises and falls depending on the lighting.

One person suggests: "Can't you see the breaking waves which make the ship heave upwards? I bet my last cigarette that it is heading for here." But we soon realize that he has gambled away his cigarette, but we let him keep it before he starts smoking tussac grass, something which he tried once before.

Thus the days until New Year's kept us captive. Not once did we enjoy unrestrained freedom. But on one day we walked across the Lucas Glacier again. We crossed its outer third on skis in half an hour, then walked across a stream and past two lakes across a hilly isthmus to the west side of Sea Leopard Fiord.

This bay, too, is bordered at its head by a glacier, although it no longer reaches the sea. There are in fact two glaciers: a larger one to the west, which rises moderately steeply and displays severe crevassing in its middle part, the crevasses being arranged very irregularly, and a smaller, steeper glacier to the east. Between the two a rock ridge with horizontal bedding projected. It should also be mentioned that in the innermost part of the bay a small, low island gave evidence of the shallowness of the bay-head.

Our excursion to Sea Leopard Fiord proceeded in haste and anxiety. Involuntarily we were thinking that it was risky to leave our camp for several hours, that a ship might arrive in the interim, and that if we missed it we would be subjected to the storms and privations for another unspecified period.

On New Year's the appearance of the natural landscape around us was terribly depressing. Just as the burghers at home draw up a balance sheet for the past year, so we compiled one here too. Ultimately it was not a satisfying exercise, even though we had experienced and seen much and had worked as much as possible. The final rebuff above King Haakon Bay still ran through our minds; the environment of the island had humbled us. But we refused to be depressed. On this last day, no matter how leaden and suffocating it was, we wanted to forget our disappointments and to tackle the day with a new project tomorrow.

If the ship finally arrived we wanted to make one more sortie into the mountains from a new starting point, to travel across the expanses of ice, and to try to find out what secrets and difficulties this untrodden land still concealed.

A calm, windless day of falling snow ushered in the New Year. We reassembled the folding boat and selected quite a sedate task, that of sounding the area of the bay in front of the Grace Glacier. First, using the Klepper boat, we had to free the dinghy; it had been filled to the gunwhales with water by the westerly winds of the past few days, and since it had become entangled in the kelp could not be hauled ashore. This achieved, we rowed towards the glacier, rocked by the swell. Some 250 m from the snout the kelp thickened into a meadow and we stuck to the few clear passages through it so that the oars would be less encumbered. Today Benitz was sounding; my wife was recording everything, entering the data in a sketchbook; I was the oarsman, and like the others, derived new pleasure and a very good appetite from my task which made one forget time and our situation.

As we had already been able to establish from shore by the pattern of breakers the sea is very shallow and exceeds a depth of 9 m only in the middle of the little bay. After we had finished our job we started fishing; our provisions were running low and we urgently needed something to eat. We had always counted on seeing a ship arrive by Christmas at the latest and hence our fishing, which earlier had been more for the purpose of collecting, now had a practical significance.

After we had caught eleven fish, mainly so-called crocodile fish, but also three with a flat, wide-mouthed head with a bright yellow colour on the lower jaw, we headed towards land and our tents. We threw the crocodile fish to the skuas; during this rare event of being fed they approached so close that they ate the pieces almost out of our hands. Since they had a substantial amount of flesh we retained the three other fish with the bright yellow colouring for our own use.

We are down to our last can of butter; when we open our breadbox it reveals a repulsive mould; salt, pepper and a remnant of sugar now represent items of significant value. Yes, today we are really going to eat our fill, especially since our tobacco is exhausted and we have had to fall back on Lappish senna grass, which we prefer to tussac grass. The fish tasted superb but the meal left a bitter after-taste. Half an hour after the last bite had disappeared one of us began laughing without the slightest provocation.

This was Benitz and he was soon in a better mood than I have ever seen him. He was humming out loud but at the same time complained of a violent headache and pounding heart, and looked flushed, like somebody who has recently finished off a bottle. This lasted for only a few seconds, then the rest of us felt ourselves in the same elated mood. I felt like I have done in the autumn when I have been drinking new wine in the village, but with the only difference that here I could already feel an iron band around my head, whereas during my excursions in the village this usually did not begin to develop until next morning.

No matter how much we tried to control ourselves we were all laughing with all our strength. We were unable to stop laughing. During one of these severe fits of laughter our heads ached so that every movement doubled the pain. This lasted for a good ten minutes until the headache and a vast languor were dominant and there was nothing left of the hilarity.

After this jovial start, next morning we were all sick, with absolutely no strength in our bones. We all blamed yesterday's meal of fish for the poisoning; it must certainly have been the three fish with the firm flesh and the flat, almost round heads.

What else do I have to report as to how those final days crawled past? They crawled past filled with hunger and conversation. They passed in hypotheses and judgements on men and whaling. Finally they all flew away; like everything unpleasant on earth they finally had to end. The bay provided us with many more fish; and we were forced to catch many of our penguin friends. We caught the recluses and the idlers and many of these were fried in their own fat. Only the good, brave husbands which even now stood watch over mothers and children, were safe from us.

On 7 January a light fall of new snow lay on the mountains again, while the glare of the sun lay across the bay; the little islands protruded from it like dark inlays in a bright silver platter. On one such magnificent day the ship *Diaz* arrived to take us back among people at Grytviken for the first time in almost 3½ months.

13

Back with the Whalers at Grytviken

THE SCENERY AROUND King Edward Cove and around Grytviken was quite spring like as compared to the landscape in which our tents had stood until now. The old moraine deposits were snow free; the grasses stretched up to the sun and played in the wind. The *Acaena* was in reddish bloom and moss cushions glowed green and yellow from damp depressions.

But despite the harsh greeting of the southern summer the landscape was now becoming softer. At any season or time of day even the area surrounding this peaceful bay is severe and oppressive. One has only to climb 100 m uphill to see the remnants of glaciers, the sea, icebergs, steep rock faces, moraine ridges, steep passes and, in the cirques, lingering snow beds.

But the severity of the landscape and the remoteness of the island were never felt as much as on the afternoon of 12 January when we followed the coffin of a seaman who belonged to the crew of the full-rigged ship *Tijuca* to his grave. The mountains and the cliffs of the bay were never so oppressive and severe as on that snowy day, as the grave was being dug in the meagre, peaty soil. It may well be that the impact strikes more heavily on such a day when death unexpectedly strikes among a group of men far from everything that is dear to them.

The wreath which my wife wove together consisted of tussac grass blades and a few geraniums, separated by cushions of *Colobanthus* of a lively green colour. Six seamen carried the coffin; an old alcoholic wept; otherwise everything proceeded just as at home. The dead man was buried in the same patch of peat in which Sir Ernest Shackleton rests, only 2 m from him.

At Grytviken everyone is in a good mood when there is a good catch. Everybody lives in a continual state of excitement, like a card player who always holds a good hand. Here life is brought to a state of excitement by something real, namely whales. When the vast carcasses are hauled up the plan so that cables and men's arms never rest, and one catcher after another delivers its valuable haul, there is scarcely any room for unhappiness.

When a plume of smoke is spotted out in the bay one hears the shout: "Does *Miles* have any whales and how many?" The whale catcher *Miles* is named after Don Miles, an Argentinean personality, who is perhaps even a minister. "Yes, a blue and two fin whales."

One man shouts to another: "According to last report *Orca* has two blue whales and *Skua* three."

Orca and *Skua* are also the names of two whale catchers, and their names could not be more appropriate. *Orcinus orca* is the killer whale, which tears the blubber from the bodies of blue and fin whales and expedites seals to the next world. And we have come to know the skua as the robber of the avifauna of South Georgia.

This is life, real life. Six blue whales and two fin whales: with that one could acquire a mansion in Oslo! With the share which a seaman or stoker and every single one of the station workers will receive he could buy a Tenerife dress for his girl. One can achieve so much with the money which inevitably accumulates here, simply because one cannot fritter it away.

Hence for every single man the whale means money, joy and a happy future, and one should not be so surprised that each evening everybody knows the total of barrels of oil which the day has produced. In every crew's room one can find a scrap of paper on the wall with the lucky numbers carefully recorded for every day.

14

Hunting the Whale

A WHALE HUNT IN 1929 gave rise to totally different impressions from those in 1911 when I went whaling for the first time in my life. Then, too, it was a grey day and the surf was breaking with the same implacable rage against the little rounded islands, the Right Whale Rocks, which guard the entrance to Cumberland East Bay. Just as today the sea would change its mood from one moment to the next and snow squalls could quickly throw a white mantle around the little whaling ship. But two things have changed since then.

What has become of the little ship aboard which we went whaling in 1911? What has become of the humpbacked whales which we hunted 19 years ago and which could be easily and reliably found in small, unwary schools in the immediate coastal zone?

There are no whalers pursuing humpbacked whales in southern seas nowadays. As compared to blue whales they are scarcely worth more than mackerel in the eyes of the whalers. Their blubber, and hence their oil yield, is minuscule as compared to the abundant thick layers which await the whalers beneath the skin of the blue and fin whales. Moreover it is only extremely rarely that one spots the spout of a humpback, and in recent years the British have left it in peace. One can hunt them for only one week of the whaling season off the coast of South Georgia, so that one fine day the small stocks may recover to a productive source of revenue.

And the old ships? In the optimum case, given their

23. A school of fin whales promised a rich haul

24. Fast to a whale!

25. The Three Brothers closed the head of the König Glacier

26. The final flurry of a blue whale

speed of 6–7 knots they are still hauling cargo and natives on some river in South America.

Today's whaling ship is of a different design. With her broad bows she ploughs the heavy seas of the southerly latitudes, slicing them in half, so that it is only rarely that the harpooner and his gun, both positioned on the forward deck, have to worry about heavy seas when they are at work.

And the most important feature of all: this modern whaling vessel can steam at 14 knots, and her task is to tire the whale by pursuing it constantly. Nowadays when the whale is only too familiar with man, ships and the noise of engines, the speed of the vessel is of critical importance.

Captain Fredriksen and I were sitting over a good Norwegian breakfast in the spacious mess of the catcher *Skua*. We were recounting to each other what the island meant to us: he was telling about whaling and his life, I about our experiences and our tent life on South Georgia. We were agreed on one point: that there is probably no place on earth where the weather and gales are such a pain in the neck to us humans.

Just as he was telling me that yesterday he had killed his 210th whale, with an understandable pride and with visible delight at the profit which this successful hunt would bring him, a burly, blue-eyed seaman came into the room and announced that there were whales in sight. Whales? The word "whales" can electrify a Norwegian captain anew, even if yesterday he had already taken his 210th whale.

He quickly laid aside the pipe which he had just lit and raced to the bridge in order to survey the situation. Whales so close to the coast? After we had just sighted the steep mountain chain which stretches to the northwest above Royal Bay in a giant, icy range, close enough to touch? Recently the catchers have had to travel 80–90 nautical miles from Grytviken harbour before they encountered whales.

Then he pointed with an arm to the west and described a small angle in order to delimit the area where numerous spouts were to be seen. They were fin whales and he added in explanation that their spouts were not so powerful as those of blue whales, but more bushy and compact.

No ordinary mortal can identify the spout of a whale when it is still thousands of metres away. While the tears ran down my cheeks from straining to focus my eyes, I heard a rapid alternation of commands: "Starboard!" then "Full ahead!" and no longer had any doubts that the animals and their spouts would soon become visible to me too.

I looked at the seaman in the barrel. His fur-clad form stood out dark against the fine, bright clouds. Thereafter I watched how he relayed all the necessary changes of course to the helmsman by quiet hand signals. Everyone was moving at a run, as if directed by a single will. Without any shouting or commotion the ship, the captain, who is also the gunner, and the crew, formed a single unit.

We may well have run on for another half mile when, without having to have it pointed out to me again, I spotted three columns of water rising almost simultaneously out of the rough seas 500 m ahead of us, above a minor wave crest.

This rare, impressive sight lasted only an instant. For a while longer a few gulls, dove prions and cape pigeons, which often follow whales, continued to indicate the spot where I had just seen the whales, in an almost dreamlike fashion. In my initial happy excitement I may have hoped for a minor rest pause but from then on I scarcely had a chance to catch a breath.

Orders and commands followed in rapid succession. Steaming at full speed, one moment we would swing hard to starboard, then next moment back hard to port. During these almost right-angle course changes the ship heeled so much that one automatically grabbed for the nearest stanchion to prevent being hurled over the rail.

A few moments before the deck had been empty but now seamen and stokers were standing around watching. They had crawled quickly out of their bunks because they were off duty, and those who were on duty now participated with all their hearts. Now, with a long, sure stride the captain moved down the narrow catwalk which on modern catchers links the bridge with the bow. Barely 50 m ahead of us the back of a whale was again visible.

With wonderful calm and sureness the captain seized the handle of the gun, which can swing in any direction, and before one even expected it in the excitement of the moment, with a sharp, hard roar the 70 kg harpoon with its explosive head shot into the crest of a small wave, just as the words "Fast whale!" flew from mouth to mouth. For a moment there was deathly silence. Involuntarily one wondered what the outcome was to be. One thought of the horror stories of earlier days about smashed boats and men missing in churning seas.

But the captain calmly walked the short distance back to the bridge; his job was done and he chatted again about the past and the future, as if absolutely nothing had happened. Understandably I was much too distracted to be an attentive listener. Meanwhile the line was running quickly and elastically off the winch drum. A great length of line was paid out so that the animal, a fin whale almost 22 m long, would not free itself at the last minute by a powerful jerk, whereby the sea would reclaim this valuable prize.

The line, thick as one's wrist and stretched taut, connected the whale to the ship. Then its angle became steeper; a long body appeared, shadow-like, then broke the surface. We could see the wide back and a last, exhausted spout, weakened and faint. It was no longer a clear spout but a bloodshot gush, indicating that the whale was mortally wounded.

Now we just wanted a quick end for the animal and breathed with relief when a sudden, steep upswing of its flukes, followed by violent strokes indicated the animal's death flurry. But then it became still again; only the cape pigeons and gulls fluttered excitedly and greedily above the dead whale.

Those of us who were totally unconnected with the whaling industry were proud and ashamed at the same time. Proud, because our technology had succeeded in killing the largest living creature on earth so surely and quickly. But we were proud for only a moment. Then we had to think of how a single stroke of its flukes would be enough to transport a dozen little humans even more quickly from life to death. We were ashamed, on realizing that due to our technology this animal would soon be represented only by skeletons in museums if its persecution were not soon moderated.

Why does the protection of international law not come into play at this point? Why does whaling provoke an immoderate thoroughness, an insatiable ever-growing hunger for profits? Why not adopt a quota system?

What follows the actual whale hunt is simply mechanical operations, invariably repeated each time a whale is killed. First the whale is hauled alongside and air is pumped into the carcass to prevent it from sinking and being lost; the cumbersome tail flukes are amputated so that they will not reduce the towing speed. If the weather permits and if further whales are sighted the whale is often marked with a flag then abandoned, to be picked up again on the homeward voyage.

But tomorrow is a holiday, and we are homeward bound. Hence everyone is content with one whale, and is not so avaricious as usual.

It is only 1.00 p.m. and the preparatory work has taken only half an hour. Then I notice that we are cruising eastwards past Royal Bay and that there is a seaman perched in the barrel again, scouring the horizon.

As I sit on a tarpaulin gazing at the now sunlit coast, looking like part of the Alps, or into the sea where the little petrels are fishing for little crabs on the masses of kelp which have been torn loose, I can hear the little song which the helmsman is singing to himself. Out of habit and custom a lookout is still being kept for whales. One might still cross our path.

But tomorrow is a rest day for the whalers. They do not need to crawl out of their bunks when the watch-officer shouts. They can play cards until diamonds and spades are dancing in front of their eyes, and in the evening they can watch an old American film, with millionaires and painted ladies and an improbable plot. If they are lucky somewhere an unexpected source of brandy will be tapped and their happiness will be complete.

15

Whales and Whalers

During the last decade no large animal has attracted such attention as those giants of the earth, the whales. Reports and calculations have appeared repeatedly in the press of the northern lands. It is not so much the scientific aspects, not even the migrations of the whales which are of interest, but economic questions which more concern the calculating merchant.

Hand in hand with this, questions are also raised by discerning individuals concerning effective protection for the animals, since despite all the present profits the word extermination is repeatedly being uttered as a menacing harbinger of the future.

On this point there are two opposing camps. One side says that the southern seas shelter an inconceivably large number of whales and that it is ludicrous to talk of the extermination of these animals. It is the entrepreneurs at home who support this view, those who are counting on immediate gain and who are attempting to ward off any shadow from their booming business.

Others, practical thinking whalers, whose judgement is uninfluenced by any employer, believe that the catch is already declining somewhat year by year and that the prospects are serious. No unbiased person can ignore the views of these men.

No matter how much the cargoes which the ships bring home every year would appear to defy any decrease in the population or any threat of extermination, one still has to admit that these large catches do not always have to be solely the result of abundance or even of increasing whale stocks, but of a rapidly improving technology which is more efficient and productive than that of 20 or 30 years ago. In fact at the moment the whales are being assaulted with the greatest lack of consideration, and in no other area are all the bad qualities peculiar to man revealed so shrilly and unrestrainedly as when his only goal is rapid profit and ownership. Many little flags, fluttering in the wind, would be necessary to camouflage this drive for profit.

At present whaling is pursued not only from land stations, as is the case on South Georgia. As a result of the enormous development of the so-called pelagic fishery, which now produces a greater proportion of the catch than the land stations, one is totally independent of harbours and coasts. Large tankers, some of them of tonnages in excess of 20 000 tons, besiege the pack-ice belt around the Antarctic Ice Cap, penetrate into the Ross Sea, the most southerly sea in the world, and hunt at the edge of the Weddell Sea or around Bouvet Island. In 1923–24 Captain C. A. Larsen was the first to push through the pack-ice belt of the Ross Sea with an ordinary freighter. On that significant voyage the whales had to be flensed alongside the ship. But during later enterprises the whalers have mastered this unpleasant aspect of pelagic whaling. Now, in almost any weather, using special equipment the dead whale can be hauled on deck and just as at the land stations the carcass can be processed under safe conditions, right down to production of the finished oil. As far as I know Lars Christensen of Sandefjord was the first to use an aircraft in whaling operations and the cargo of his factory ship, *Kosmos*, set an unexpected world record.

To cite yet another aspect of the increased use of technology, successful attempts have been made at killing whales electrically, in order to counter the accusations of cruelty to animals so often directed at whaling. But if one prefers not to apply the term "cruelty to animals" to the hunting of deer or seals or of the many species which are beneficial to man and to his economy, then neither can one apply it to the shooting of whales. Killing them with an explosive harpoon is really effective. No, I would suggest that the use of electric harpoons is not so much a matter of kindness to animals; rather the aim is to reduce the time involved in actual hunting so that the operation can be finished more quickly and that the catcher can be ready faster, in case more whales appear over the horizon. However that may be, a merciless war has been proclaimed against the whales of the southern seas, and everybody should welcome the demands for effective protection for the whales, no matter from which camp or which country the stimulus comes.

The island of South Georgia has a good reputation in Norway but not because of its scenic qualities. The latter represent the modest privilege of just a few travellers. The island owes its reputation to the wide seas around it, which offer profitable activity for Norwegian capital.

Nowadays the seas around South Georgia supply mainly blue, fin and sei whales. In 1904 it was principally humpbacked and right whales which were hunted. With the available technology the humpbacked whale was the easiest to kill. It travels in fairly large schools and since it stays near the coast no time needed to be lost in long cruises.

But by 1914 this whale, whose stocks had been greatly reduced, had to be protected and by the time of our expedition the humpback whale could be pursued by the whalers for only one week. The right whale is now an even rarer phenomenon, and it is completely protected.

Due to its size and productivity the blue whale is the most sought-after of all the whales. Towards the end of the season, in March and April, it appears less frequently so that fin and sei whales have to bear the brunt then. At this time one may also happen to see a sperm whale, which is a toothed whale, on the flensing plan.

On South Georgia every whale which is killed is towed

back to the catcher's home port and is hauled up out of the water by machinery and steel cables onto the gently inclined flensing plan where men are invariably standing ready to strip it of its blubber. Once this is done it is the turn of the meat, bones and tongue; in short every last part of the massive animal is handled in turn, so that after 90 minutes there is nothing left of a 25 m blue whale. The operation is as thorough and as rational as that.

The head of the major Vestfold Company, Mr. Thoralf Sørlle, who was so favourably inclined towards our expedition, once took the trouble, quite apart from the normal tempo of his work, to weigh a small blue whale, 20 m in length. He managed this by cutting up the individual organs and musculature. This operation revealed a net weight of 48,903 kg. The blubber alone weighed 9,116 kg; the meat 25,940 kg and the bones 9,433 kg. Even more astounding is the fact that the heart of this small blue whale weighed 329 kg (even the biggest München beer-swiller's heart is nothing compared to this). Its stomach weighed 200 kg and its kidneys 220 kg. I myself needed the help of three men and a block and tackle to stow a whale's heart in a barrel for the Senckenberg Museum. The small whale which was weighed produced a total of 63.5 barrels of oil, a barrel being equivalent to 170 kg.

If properly utilized larger animals may yield up to 250 barrels of oil. If whales are abundant 10 to 14 whales may be processed by the personnel of the Grytviken station in one day. Next morning the work area will again be clean and tidy.

Is whaling profitable? The Argentinean company, Pesca, which has its base at Grytviken, operates four whale catchers which in 1928–29 killed 809 whales during a season lasting barely more than six months. The results from the four other land stations on South Georgia were similar.

The value of a blue whale varies between 15,000 and 20,000 marks. If one assumes that only 3000 whales were taken from the coastal waters around South Georgia during the year of our expedition, and if one also considers that in the Southern Ocean a total of approximately 200 whale catchers is constantly available to hunt whales, each of them achieving similar or better results than those from South Georgia, one gains some idea of what a profitable industry modern whaling is.

Reports in the Norwegian press revealed that in 1928–29 alone the Norwegian companies recorded a take of 1 million barrels of oil, worth 100 million marks.

If one is not a whaler and is judging the entire industry more as an outsider, of all the whalers those manning the whale catchers are the most attractive. Because theirs is a life of struggle and effort. Because their work and their lifestyle still bear the last gleam of romance, even although it is decreasing with every new innovation.

Even the workers at the land stations and aboard the large floating factories are generally referred to as whalers. But they are nothing more than industrial workers working in the fresh air, seamen for whom machinery has made life very much easier.

The alternation of poverty and riches, the rapid oscillation between longing for home and the yearning for distant places, restlessness and an inclination for tension and excitement, in the wider sense of these attributes all whalers have retained something unique.

But one cannot describe as whalers those who are associated with whaling back home. They are good merchants and good managers. These, too, are important positions and many important threads run through their hands. But they are only whalers as long as they are down south, or to the extent that they once were. They accumulate the money and redistribute it; they are accountants, belonging to a mercantile intelligentsia; they are professionals just as in industry or other branches of commercial activity.

The heads of operations on the island form another group, all on its own. They have all come up through the ranks, and one has to doff one's hat to them. They were once harpooners, sealers and seamen and one is always forced to admire their climb to responsible positions which encompass a great deal and which are associated with large salaries.

In a review of the wildlife film "Roah-Roah" in a München newspaper I was reproached for the fact that in my book *Zur grossen Eismauer des Südpols* [To the great ice barrier of the South Pole] I represented the whalers as big children, i.e. as adults with children's hearts, and yet as being involved in the operations of whaling which, for so many people, conceals such cruelties. To this I would respond that even among soldiers at the front there were many men with children's hearts, even although they had to turn their rifles on other men.

But nobody would claim that places like Grytviken shelter a human elite. There are unsullied men there, who come from the forests and lonely places on the coast, who purposefully take a grasp on life. They play the major role in whaling and sealing. However there are also men who have taken refuge at Grytviken, directly from Buenos Aires, and who had ended up on the beach there after a life of failure. Men of every type and class. One may see Russian counts working alongside the sons of bishops.

For a while it was the practice of a previous station head, with the intention of being humane, to employ men at Grytviken who had experienced some misfortune at home and who wanted to expunge it in southern surroundings.

But the island turned out to be an inappropriate location for reforming people. The experiments with alcoholics and other psychopaths were not very successful. The former used every subterfuge in order to acquire their poison; the latter were generally unaccustomed to work and were a failure in more than one sense. The isolation demanded a certain fairly strong, mentally balanced type.

Hence the history of South Georgia is not free of human tragedies which reached their denouement there. How could a banker or an attorney suddenly become a whaler, or the spoiled son of a millionaire or of a high-ranking government official feel at home amongst blubber and filth? How could a mentally ill person find the appropriate place of asylum amid the gloomy landscape of South Georgia and how would his damaged soul display any inclination to recover here?

16

Our Trip Inland

A WEEK QUICKLY PASSED among the manifold impressions of the variegated crowd of workers with its multinational composition, among Norwegians, Swedes, Danes, Argentineans, Spaniards, Russians, Germans and Basques. We enjoyed the enormous hospitality of the Argentinean station in rich measure and with great gratitude.

But as these things happen we were now looking forward again to the camp life which so appealed to us, no matter how hard it could be at times. We were again nostalgic to get back from this full life to the simplicity of our tents, to the lonely glaciers and the unbounded spaces. While we could not always understand our friends' thrust and drive to make money they could not understand why we would want to grapple with the rough climate and the wilderness. But everything in life must have an aim, and since the aim of the majority was gold, something we could understand although it was not our own goal, there developed a certain divergence of opinion which could never be completely bridged.

Since we had a film camera with us, an item of equipment which nowadays practically every expedition has, suspicions fell on it; some individuals could not conceal their feelings and remarked, with barely suppressed envy, that we would make a lot of money. But when they saw us filming the simple grey and white gulls or the surf, they could not understand it, especially since we placed no emphasis on filming the sealing operation which in their eyes must inevitably represent a particularly saleable topic.

"Oh, the poor whales!" was my involuntary thought as we steamed through the bloody waters of Cumberland Bay aboard the little Norwegian steamer *Fleurus* on 16 January. One could not but be saddened for a moment on seeing that great, dark area of bloodstained water.

Then the ship's mate came up to me, a loquacious, critical, or perhaps just dissatisfied customer, who felt he could briefly dismiss the whaling industry: "The entire whaling industry is no more than the torture of animals; and what about the life led by the men who work on the island? That's not a life; it's simply vegetating!"

Our vessel, which was to take us to Husvik in Stromness Bay, was a ship of several hundred tons. She sails from Montevideo or Buenos Aires to the Falkland Islands, bringing the farmers news and also fresh faces and goods, then continues on from the Falklands to South Georgia with mail and cargo. But this route is not fixed and is determined by the nature of the cargo.

This time the little ship was certainly carrying a strange cargo. Everyone had to take a look in the hold where steers and sheep were standing, packed close together; they were destined for Husvik and after the stormy crossing from South America were in a wretched condition. "Yes, we're really a unique vessel," the mate again addressed me. "At home in Norway it would be impossible to transport animals in such a cruel fashion. That too is animal-torture, just like whaling. On one trip we are carrying the Governor, his wife and his mail; the next trip cattle and sheep. My God, this ship is likely to be hauling anything!"

Since I suspected that in the effusive mate I had found a born grumbler who wanted to get his story off his chest but was unable to find anybody to believe his generalizations I was glad when we reached Husvik after a voyage of 90 minutes. At least to the layman's eye the station looked the same as Grytviken; here too whaling had put its stamp on the facilities and the settlement.

When one left the vicinity of the station and examined the terrain to the southwest the route which we should take on our first ascent appeared clearly indicated by the topography. It could scarcely lie anywhere else but towards a level area of foreland via a stepped valley. To the west-southwest this was terminated by a trough-shaped saddle almost identical in shape to saddles we had observed at other locations on the island.

Would we, or at least the lady, like to sleep under a solid roof again tonight? The tough times would arrive soon enough, suggested Andersen, the head of the whaling station.

But we declined with thanks since having been frequently constrained by bad weather conditions we felt we were behind with our work. We looked around for a campsite and found it above the first step in the valley, at a height of 49 m. A small lake and a few shallow ponds lay here, surrounded by moraine ridges.

On the first day, 17 January, we did nothing but act as porters, such as one finds carrying loads in the valleys of the Alps. Since the first part of the valley was snow free we had to carry every item of baggage and even the sledges individually on our shoulders. We repeatedly tramped the same route, in a mind-numbing, slavish operation.

But that first evening we could not complain about a sleepless night; nor the next day, 18 January, when we found time in the afternoon to make a reconnaissance sortie to the head of the valley. Technically, reaching the pass was an easy task, even if rather tedious, with endless relaying. Only in a few places would some little remnants of snow have made it possible to use the sledges.

Hence that same afternoon we hauled a large part of our baggage up valley to the edge of another small lake which lay just below the pass at 203 m. 19 January was our first real travel day. By noon drifting snow had forced us to take a rest by a round lake which even at this late season was still covered with bearing ice. We impatiently tolerated this interruption inside our little tent which we had quickly pitched. For when one is heading into the complete unknown and every day and every hour ahead is a matter of uncertainty one cannot take life and every passing hour as calmly as we had done when we had been lying near the coast among the penguins and the elephant seals.

Hence when the sun broke through after a brief snowfall, revealing the pass lying above us like a sickle above some vertical rocks, the tent was quickly struck and packed away. We had to cover the route from the emergency camp to the pass via a flight of 200 steps, six times back and forth. One had to step carefully since for the last stretch the route led across a steep snow slope which rose above the lake in an almost vertical drop. We pitched the tent on a level, almost snow free ridge 200 m west of the pass at 6 o'clock.

The evening was one of the most beautiful we had spent on South Georgia. Only a gentle wind played on the tent and when we went outside we had a double view. We were overlooking our entire ascent route, Husvik Bay and all its snow free coasts and mountain ranges. Over everything lay an almost warm glow, which even the remains of winter, i.e. the snow banks in channels and gullies, could not diminish. But one needed only to glance westwards to perceive eternal winter at its most grisly. Above a glacier, which we named the König Glacier after the Austrian polar traveller, Felix König, rose a massive hill-chain, like the pinnacles of an alpine range, although its peaks barely exceeded 500–600 m in height. It ran from north-northeast to south-southwest and we were able to count nine more-or-less independent peaks and the same number of glaciers. While the upper parts of the peaks commonly consisted of rock, they were all separated by massive glaciers, so that in the over-all impression of the mountain chain the ice-cover was dominant.

They all represented branches of the König Glacier and all debouched into it; however it is now so reduced that its snout no longer reaches the sea. We named the western

27. A heavily glaciated chain west of the König Glacier

28. To the east from this desolation one could see the gleam of Cumberland Bay

29. Out in the Klepper boat on Cumberland Bay

mountain chain the Wilckens Peaks after the Bonn geologist, Otto Wilckens who, as the greatest expert on the Mesozoic of South America, had undertaken to analyse our geological finds.

But it was not just the summery view towards Stromness Bay, or the eternal winter to the west, nor even the iceberg in the bay which had stranded here due to the indeterminable laws of wind and current which put us in such a holiday mood. It was rather the feeling that from now on each day and each hour must remove something of the veil which had lain over this inaccessible island since the first days of creation. We still did not know all the vicissitudes which awaited us.

Another thought which probably put us in such a good mood was that over there, in 1916, Sir Ernest Shackleton travelled down one of the side glaciers, the first to do so before us. He was in desperation and total uncertainty until a favourable wind brought him the sound of the siren at the Stromness station, and it in turn led him to his goal and safety.

20 January. Magnificent weather. Departure delayed by taking photographs and bearings. Shortly before noon, as we were descending to the König Glacier, a steep snow couloir blocked our route. If we had not had heavily laden sledges we could easily have avoided it, but for the sledges it represented the only route. We had to rope them down individually, a task which Benitz and I tackled. One of us stood in the couloir with a rope running around an ice-axe belay while the other provided the necessary braking action with a rope from the talus slope off to one side.

After we had overcome the difficult couloir we took a rest on some old lateral moraines which were very clayey. Where little seepages and meltwater streams trickled down mosses had already established themselves along the courses of the rivulets and enlivened the talus and the moraines with their vibrant colours.

While we were resting we were able to establish how easily misinterpreted phenomena can give rise to mysteries on this island. In 1911 we had been told that there must be hot springs on South Georgia and specifically at Bay of Isles, since steam had frequently been seen rising from out at sea. From here we too could now see smoke on the foreland of the König Glacier. As we recalled the observations reported to us earlier by sailors we again thought of hot springs, until we spotted smoke rising from quite a variety of locations, even quite close to our campsite. We could now see clearly that it was rising from the very dry, clayey moraines; little whirlwinds were picking up the dust and whirling it into the air.

As we set off from our confined, secluded little corner and headed over hilly lateral moraines and later across the imperceptibly rising König Glacier, which was totally crevasse-free, towards its centre, it was easier to get an overview of our wider surroundings. We established that here also two mountain chains bounded the glacier. As in the case of the glaciers at Bay of Isles the windward side of the eastern chain was bare, as compared to the Wilckens Peaks with its numerous glaciers and ice slopes. Although there were no actual lateral moraine formations visible on the east side of the König Glacier, it displayed a dirty colour as a result of dust and small rock particles. But after we had headed south-southwest for a few minutes the glacier assumed a pure white colour and, encountering no obstacles, we travelled until 7.00 p.m. Around this time a healthy fatigue which demanded that we find a campsite, along with a gusty southwest wind, caused us to veer more to the west. We headed for a wide rock face, adorned by a hanging glacier. The height of our campsite was 285 m.

Once we had got the tent well dug in, light snow began falling. It went through my mind that evening that our Tyrolean and Swiss mountains may in many ways be more magnificent, more terrific in form and closer to the ideal of alpine beauty due to their meadows and forests but that here where the sea lapping the island is almost always in sight the contrasts are more staggering. Moreover the environment is more undisturbed, more secluded and more hostile. On that first night and on each following one I thought of how we were tackling every obstacle without any modern advantages, without dogs and without motors, almost as in years of yore. We were basically simple travellers; although we often wished for one invention which is still lacking, namely storm masks which one could wear like oxygen masks.

Despite everything we lay like princes in our tent; everything we gazed upon belonged to us, even to the glacier surfaces and the sea outside. The stained-glass windows of the church were replaced by the wide horizon; everything seemed more futile in this mountain wilderness; even the word "glory" was robbed of its nimbus. It seemed to us almost like a commercial commodity, devoid of content, possessing only shimmer and sparkle but otherwise having no significance.

But perhaps the well-wishing old gentleman who spoke to me in confidence, yet confident, prior to our departure from the capital, was right. "Success when one is travelling? It does not come from work or from whether you are lying in the tent freezing and starving. No, nowadays one has to be lost at least once, or even better several times. Only then will the press and the movies pick up the cause of the alleged dead person in unequalled fashion." Besieged by such memories from the past I was unable to sleep and listened as the wind began blowing around the tent again, at first modestly, but then importantly and insolently, in short bursts. It seemed to be constantly scolding me that we could be so stupid as to be lying here on frozen ice streams when there were roses and other delights and glories elsewhere in the world.

21 January. A cold, clear, cloudless sky lay over the glacier. We took photos and bearings, and it is now 11 o'clock although we were out of our sleeping bags when the first light touched the steep ice slope to the southwest, allowing

us to distinguish all the details which till then had been generalized and anonymous.

A clear morning flooded over this mountain landscape. All the clouds which previously had clung so stubbornly around the peaks, and all the disturbances in the air had been swept away by the sun's triumphant progress. At first we could not believe this sudden miracle and wanted to examine everything; between working and gaping a morning can quickly disappear. Hence we felt extremely happy when we then set off with our wide-runnered sledges across the hard firn of the glacier. It rose almost imperceptibly. As we maintained our south-southwesterly course of yesterday everything proceeded well and easily.

What now struck us as we travelled up the König Glacier, in contrast to those we had travelled earlier around Bay of Isles, was that there was no valley-head and no saddle. The ice extended directly up to the main chain of the island which was visible in the south in the form of three particularly cloud free summits (the Three Brothers) about 1500 m in height.

As we passed a side glacier on the Wilckens Peaks we were struck by the fact that it merged into a wide area of ice to the south. One could no longer talk in terms of independent peaks; the highest points more resembled nunataks which projected scarcely more than 50–100 m above the glacier.

Climbing moderately we proceeded southwards towards the main range, which cradled two cirques; one was completely filled with ice, the other revealed only a little ice.

In some places at a height of 390 m there was a reddish tinge to the firn, caused by snow algae; we had often observed it in the coastal area. This vivid red and the occasional flight of a fairy tern represented the last life to accompany us this far. Shortly before 2 o'clock we found ourselves about 4–5 km from the foot of the main range, having attained a height of 428 m.

Here we established the following points. The two mountain chains which confine the König Glacier do not continue right to the main range of the island and have no connection with it. Both swing around, the eastern chain towards Cumberland Bay, the Wilckens chain towards the west. Forming a western continuation between it and the main range of the island there runs an ice-stream about 7 km wide, bounded on the south by the main range and climbing slowly towards the west. Having calved off the König Glacier it sends its ice eastwards towards Cumberland Bay in the form of the Neumayer Glacier. No surficial moraines were visible at all, just a few slight lateral moraine formations at the foot of the central main range.

At 3 o'clock we set off on a westerly bearing; due to transverse crevasses up to 100 m long we had to rope up and make a number of detours which delayed us somewhat. In addition, from now on we had to battle for every step against a vicious southwest gale. Although the view to the west was totally obscured by dense drifting snow, to the east one could make out a gleaming surface which had to be Cumberland Bay itself, especially since we could recognize a round skerry.

Judging by the aneroid this continuation of our march towards the west led upwards in a slow, steady climb. We pitched camp that day somewhat closer to the main range, from which a badly dissected ice-wall discharged towards the glacier.

We had just pitched the tent when the storm's first heavy assaults began. It was less of a southwesterly gale than katabatic squalls which hit the tent in isolated gusts. Our camp was at a height of 556 m. As we shovelled away the snow cover from the glacier we first encountered a loose powder layer, which was somewhat crusted towards the surface, then there followed a severely glazed firn layer. At depth we ran into wet, coarsely crystalline firn which from now on in our own camping vocabulary we referred to as "cement" because it was very suitable for caulking the gaps in the snow wall which we built around the tent and which provided good protection, since it was several degrees below zero.

Once we had finished digging in only a dark strip protruded from the white of the glacier, the ridge of our tent. As we huddled around the primus Benitz commented: "I really feel at home here and I prefer to be in this little tent than in that big house at Grytviken."

Our skins glowed as if from the effects of young wine, since we had just experienced a sunny, windy day alternating with squalls. What marvels one can see in the blue sky on such a day! Globular clouds like big, white balls, sailing across the sky; flags, faces, and prehistoric animals.

22 January. The weather is uncertain but when the visibility increased to several hundred metres to the west, with a temperature of −3°C, we felt that we had to try our luck and decided to make a foray on skis with provisions for two days.

Still hesitating because of the uncertain weather situation, we did not get under way until 8 o'clock. We could see our route heading west, free of obstacles and climbing slowly over gentle waves. Our route was bounded to the south by the main range and to the north by six low hills, projecting 100–150 m above the ice. They were interconnected by ice and were themselves largely covered with ice.

We were able to record that shortly before 10 o'clock we had reached a height of 779 m; from here the terrain ahead was almost level and we could continue our advance. But just a few minutes after this encouraging stop we could again see nothing but ourselves and even that only with difficulty. We were enveloped in the thickest blizzard and had to retreat at a crazy pace. At first we were able to follow the safety line of our outgoing tracks; later, once they had been eliminated, we travelled by compass. Thank God that after an absence of six hours we managed to find the ridge of our tent again! How we yearned to find this little, grey speck as we wandered through the milky desolation!

No, on South Georgia one should never be separated

from tent and sleeping bag, the most important items of one's equipment. For travelling here is not like hiking at home; the area is portrayed on no maps and the laws of the weather are less stable than at any other point on earth.

We are lying in our bags again, suffering the direct onslaught of the mountain wind. We are glowing from the driving snow and have applied glacier cream to our faces. This has the great disadvantage that by morning the areas so treated are hung with reindeer hair like a rag smeared with lime for catching insects, so that one would think one had developed a second beard. Everything in the tent is covered with hair, like coal dust in a factory. At 6.00 p.m. we were startled by two ice avalanches from the mountain face south of our tent.

23 January. We are thankful that after a good breakfast we were able to set off shortly before 10 o'clock. Just as one gives horses double rations before a particularly hard day, especially if one is unsure as to its nature or duration, so we fed ourselves well. A bank of cloud lay over the peaks of the main range. But at least the route ahead of us was clear and shortly after 1 o'clock we reached the top of the plateau after a difficult, tedious climb through deep snow and with a temperature of $-3°C$. It took us almost 3½ hours to cover this short distance.

The weather was clear and we were greeted by a unique sight. A continuous ice cover, uninterrupted by any mountains stretched to the west. It was an almost circular ice plain, if one ignores the minor height differences revealed by height measurements with the aneroid. Shortly before this plateau the main range of the island swung away to the southwest. The ice plain extended almost level to the north as well; its northern boundary was formed by a semi-circular row of small, totally ice-covered elevations. Individual saddles and notches made them appear more distinct and we assumed that one of the passes represented the access route to Antarctic Bay.

Until almost 4 o'clock we made heavy, exhausting progress with our loads, which dragged as if we were pulling them over sand and rocks. Around this time we sighted the sea to the south. This was Jossac Bight; the ice plateau extended towards it, its powerful ice masses flowing down at first at a moderate gradient, but then more steeply. We recorded seven height readings along the way: 743, 761, 770, 772, 764, 743 and 797 m. Since it began to snow again we pitched our tent in an unprotected location at a height of 779 m.

Once we had pitched our airy camp nightfall brought with it a very violent snowstorm. But since we were dug in particularly deeply we could to some degree lie securely and calmly in our bags.

24 January. It is 10.30 a.m.; my two companions are still sleeping although from time to time I have to bang away with my fist at the canvas above their heads in order to shake off the load of snow. Weighing several centners [1 centner = 50 kg] it threatens the tent and is progressively constricting our space. They are still sleeping, tired by the heavy going yesterday and it is almost a shame to wake them. All day long the wind blew continually at full strength and hence we had to stay lying in the tent. Even the most essential of trips outside to get to our provisions, was impossible.

We are lying here hoping by the hour that things will improve. We anxiously watch the steady rise of the dark line on the canvas which indicates the height of the snow outside. How uncannily quickly that line can rise. It is as if we were living in a snow chamber. A few drops drip from the tent roof and cool our glowing, wind-burned skins. These are little snow crystals which have formed from our breath during the night and which are now melting again. We no longer dare to open the tent; we prefer to stay dry and satisfy ourselves with hardtack and a few lumps of sugar which we have found in the tent.

Around 6 o'clock the wind was blowing at its most violent. The tent is buried in more than 1.5 m of drifted snow. The situation is bleak; we have been lying in our sleeping bags for two hours already. A vicious gale. The weather on this island makes one tired and depressed, and in the future we will make no comment about people who reach for the bottle in desperation.

The moon is waxing. We have often determined this from the calendar but I have nothing much to report about the magic of such nights on glaciers, firn fields or bays, a magic which at other locations on earth can be of such overpowering magnificence. I can remember only one night during our expedition, at Grytviken, when the moonlight lay soft and gleaming over rock pinnacles and ice hummocks. There is absolutely no clearly evident, conventional beauty here. Beauty is invariably associated with storms and clouds, with which one is in constant conflict.

25 January. Huddled together on the same spot, and subjected to hopelessly stormy weather. The gale is from the southwest or perhaps somewhat more from the south today.

The trench which we dug for our tent perhaps has the great disadvantage that it exerts a strong attraction for drifting snow. Last night we had to crawl out to free the canvas of the heavy load of snow. By 8 o'clock today a load of several centners was again bearing down on us. It will soon be Benitz' turn to crawl out of his warm bag and slither into his wet clothes in order to defend our position again. But we hope that like the Klepper boat at Bay of Isles our tent, which has been so well tested thus far, will stand this snow-loading test.

We have to go out every three hours. Once we managed to dig one side of the canvas completely clear, the other side was loaded down again. Until now, during these two days of storm, we have not been able to light the primus and are living on hardtack, snow, butter and chocolate. It has never been so clear to me before how little water a large, round snowball produces; indeed it almost aggravates one's thirst.

We now fully understand the whalers who demand good food when they are at work and value good service highly. Both commodities, which at one time had seemed quite contemptible to us, as seen from the perspective of our tent had acquired previously unsuspected value.

26 January. Just as a soldier at the front catches his breath again after an enemy attack once the guns fall silent, and looks around him with love, so we too woke as if from a stupor once the storm had blown itself out. We crawled out of the tent, and to the west, almost close enough to touch we could see two little ice summits which had served as our most reliable landmarks on the last lap of our trek. They were embedded in the plateau but presented no obstacle to the continuation of our journey. Since there was clear weather prevailing with an unusually high temperature of 3.5°C, shortly after 5 o'clock we set off in a due westerly direction from our tent, with sledges and sleeping bags, and after half an hour reached an elevated wave on the plateau, which one might perhaps also describe as a pass from its shape.

We calculated its height at 837 m. From here our route at first led gently downhill, almost perceptibly undulating in long waves; if one were not checking the aneroid it was only the lesser resistance of the sledges and the easier gliding of one's skis which gave any indication of the minor variations in height. Thus at 6 o'clock we were at a height of 779 m; 15 minutes later at 726 m; then, after a further 15 minutes of slow climbing, at 776 m.

We could now see Queen Maud Bay and the skerries lying off it close at hand, and could see the descent from the plateau to the bay, especially its severely crevassed upper section. Ahead of us too rose the range which bounds King Haakon Bay on the south, while to the northwest we could see the coastal mountains of Bay of Isles near Cape Buller.

Hence by the end of this day we could state the following. In the central part of the island of South Georgia there exists a continuous glacier connection between the northeast and southwest coasts, between Jossac Bight and Queen Maud Bay on the one hand and Cumberland West Bay via the Neumayer Glacier on the other. The main range of the island, running from southeast to northwest swings round to the southwest just before the ice plateau and, as far as we could tell, forms the eastern boundary of the glacier which descends to the Jossac Bight.

On the day of our last advance there was a gentle north wind, a rare wind on South Georgia, and already by 8 o'clock we were enveloped in fog, so that we had to sit waiting on our sledges for an hour. The fog became thicker and thicker around us. An unusually mild temperature of 4°C brought the first raindrops and somewhat later an impenetrably thick fog which forced us to retreat, diligently following our tracks, although it was not always easy to detect them.

But once again gales and snow were to assault us in that weird desolation in which we were encamped. It began with heavy rain, which drummed on the tent, something quite unusual in this world of ice. A gale out of the northeast played its throbbing song, then when it had become too strong, it swung into the southwest and brought another fall of snow. Despite great care, with this mild weather we found ourselves carrying snow into the tent, and as a result we had a pool of water inside. The insides of our sleeping bags readily soaked up the moisture so that one had the feeling that one's body was embedded in a king-size wet bandage.

We are eating sparingly from our remaining supplies. We smoke in a calculated fashion, keeping an eye on our shrinking reserves of tobacco.

But during the change of weather we became acquainted with yet another unexpected danger. It was around 3.00 a.m. when I woke feeling restless. Since I could not get back to sleep I took my matches from a metal box which I carried on my person in order to light my pipe in my accustomed fashion. But I struck the matches against the dry surface in vain, although the matches themselves were quite dry. I took some cotton soaked in 96% alcohol. It, too, refused to burn. Fully awake now, I crawled out of the tent which was completely encased in ice. There was new snow lying on top of an ice layer. I shovelled for almost an hour. I had really earned a hot coffee and a pipe! Again I struck a match angrily on the striking surface. Although these were the same matches the flame flared up this time without delay. Then I realized that the problem with the matches had been caused by lack of oxygen and I was very thankful for the dream which had made me wake up during the night.

27 January was an overcast day with little to recommend it, except for many thoughts which drifted into one's mind inopportunely. Everything seemed even more hostile than previously. Had the sky disappeared from sight forever?

It was not until 9.00 in the evening that it grew a little calmer; we crawled out of our bags one after the other and somewhat later three hungry people were sitting around a pot in which large lumps of snow were slowly melting. Every successive move in the cooking operation was watched carefully; four hungry eyes observed my wife's movements as she shook one Maggi cube after another into the water. On sledge journeys or on expeditions generally Maggi products are deserving of very special praise. They belong among the iron rations on every trip and in every camp kitchen.

Immediately after the meal was over one of us fell asleep immediately and the others soon followed. The candle still burned sparingly, scattering sparkling crystals around us in the half-dark; we were sleeping in a magic palace in the white realm of glacier ice.

On the morning of 28 January I crawled out of the tent at 4.00 a.m. As I walked around the corner of a snowdrift a gust of wind threw me to the ground. But there was a cold, clear sky to the east, with a violent westerly wind; there were already clouds towering far to the west. Should we let that wind blow on our backs, speeding our journey back to the König Glacier with our lightened sledges? The temperature was 4°C. We could not trust this brief break in the weather.

Since our remaining supplies would not permit us any further adventures, after taking a few bearings and shooting some film footage with the hand camera, we decided to start on our homeward march. This time we took a somewhat more northerly route but it produced no new observations, apart from the fact that the plateau displayed an almost imperceptible rise towards the north.

Again the clouds were building behind us. We mustered the remains of our strength for a final effort. Our progress developed into a break-neck retreat, as if the devil were on our heels.

Thus it happened that by 2 o'clock we were again pitching the tent at the eastern margin of the König Glacier at the foot of some high, grey, moraine hills which previously had represented the end of all life for us. Now their every trickle of water and every cushion of moss represented renewed life for us. Behind us clouds raced over the main range from the southwest while we were encamped in sunshine. We ran around barefoot on the boulders of the moraine. In sheltered spots they were almost hot from the day's meagre sun's rays. The squabbling of the gulls again wafted up from the bay and out beyond the bay an Antarctic iceberg drifted like a large floating castle.

Next day, 29 January, we had reached our base camp at Husvik again after the exhausting ordeal of packing all our things over the pass I described at the outset. If one walked over to the stream in the evening and gazed at the föhn clouds which lay restlessly over the wide bay, with the hurried rushing of the water one might recall an evening in the village with a babbling spring and old-fashioned gables casting their shadows.

One could compose a song about the hospitality of Husvik and about Captain Andersen's warm reception in his house. He was the first to welcome us and, worrying about our return, had been quite anxious for us.

During the next few days we visited the two other stations in Stromness Bay, namely Stromness and Leith, where we received an equally hearty welcome from the whalers.

17

Fossils, Penguins and Lakes

EVERYTHING IN THIS WORLD comes to an end. The first festive meals after our return will remain permanently in our memories as wonderful interludes from the region of ice. But once these were behind us we began to get restless again. No matter how pleasant our stay at Husvik our time had been so badly reduced by the inclemency of the South Georgia weather that we could not let a single day slip by unused.

When stormy weather prevailed, as was the case on 3 and 4 February, we had more rest and justification for enjoying life to the full, passing the day away in conversation and relaxation. Men who have lived for a decade or more in the South Georgia environment, as was commonly the case, always have something interesting to say and could supplement and correct our own observations.

We often derived much more reliable information on the whale and its biology from the leaders of the expeditions firsthand, than from books. And when we sat around the stations with the men we soon realized that they were all very much at home with the history of polar expeditions and with many scientific areas.

What particularly pleased us there was the praise and recognition which everybody extended to German research efforts in the Antarctic. Apart from the First German Expedition to South Georgia in 1882–83 it was especially the *Meteor* expedition about which most admiration was expressed.

Not a day passed but engineer Fred Heyerdal and Dr. Will, the doctor for these stations, drew my attention to this or that feature of the immediate vicinity which was so familiar to them. They scrutinized the mountains and glaciers around them with attentive and trained eyes. Thus engineer Heyerdal pointed out to me a terrace of cobbles lying 200 m from the present beach, which had been discovered during the establishment of the little graveyard at Stromness. He brought me rock samples from the immediate vicinity which had caught his eye, and valuable prepared zoological specimens, including the embryo of a humpbacked whale (*Megaptera novæ-angliae*). Later he brought me a parasite from the same species; indeed he not only gave it to me but told me its correct name, *Conchoderma aurilium*, and classified it correctly among the Cirripedia.

Dr. Will, who was as competent a doctor as he was a natural scientist, drew my attention to a terrace at Leith Harbour which ran from northwest to southeast and where, he alleged, an English geologist had found plant fossils. Intrigued by this and grateful for the information I worked away in the rain at this exposure on the west side of Leith Harbour, whose outermost point is named Hansen Point after the head of the Leith station. When I was unsuccessful in finding any of the alleged fossils because the horizontally bedded shale turned out to be unusually hard, Mr. Sørlle and Mr. Hansen provided me with a man with a chisel and dynamite. In offering this assistance Hansen accompanied it with the hope that I would not take the entire headland back to Germany with me since otherwise he would have nothing else in the world to which he could attach his name so easily. Once the slabs with fossils had been located and recovered I could sit quietly drinking coffee and smoking my pipe, sure in the knowledge that Captain Sørlle would in the meantime have my treasures properly packed. If we came back unexpectedly from a trip the table would suddenly be expanded; the simple meal of the day would become a festive spread, and instead of water some cocktail would appear in the glasses. Suddenly one places great value on all this when one is feeling starved and can still remember the desolation and one's empty stomach, but is made to feel at home in this remote southern oasis of culture and civilization.

Then one day Sørlle remarked to me directly: "You shouldn't go rushing back to Grytviken when you are here with all your tents and equipment. As soon as the fine weather returns I'll take you to see the penguins on the north coast and pick you up again when you've finished your work."

When something as useful and beneficial as this is proposed one cannot decline and hence our next objective became a large macaroni penguin colony which supposedly had its rookery at "Sand Bay". Apart from the prospect of getting to know some new animal friends quite well, I was particularly attracted by the opportunity of searching neighbouring areas for fossils, especially since such finds would be of very great significance to geology and to the problem of land connections in the southern hemisphere.

On 5 February the storm with its racing clouds and furious seas had finally abated after two days. A whaling vessel commanded by Captain Evesen and followed by Captain Sørlle was to take us to "Sand Bay", a small bay between Stromness Bay and Fortuna Bay.

As we passed a small island, named Grass Island on the chart, Sørlle pointed out to me how burned up its slopes appeared. And indeed the fresh green of the tussac grass was totally missing from this rocky island; its limited level spots looked dried-out, almost rusty-brown. When I asked for an explanation Sørlle suggested that the tussac grass cannot stand sheep. He had put a few sheep on the island a few years before as a source of food and since then the tussac grass had died out.

When I told him that releasing some sheep could not have such a drastic effect he would not accept my explanation.

What I told him was that the constant emissions from his station, carried out over the bay month after month by the southwest wind, were much more likely to be the culprit.

Although there was scarcely a breath of air that morning the sea was still restless after several days of storm. As we swung round out of the large bay and headed along the coast it was suggested to us that a landing at "Sand Bay" would probably be impossible. But we wanted to try it. Then after a further forty minutes we could see the short stretch of beach in the bay, access to which was via a steadily narrowing entrance channel. In this quiet corner isolated macaroni penguins rocketed out of the surf and hopped up over the rocks on either side.

No matter how feasible a landing manoeuvre appeared to our unaccustomed eyes, after a few minutes the dinghy which had been sent in returned. Evesen reported that he could probably put the three of us ashore, although we would not have a dry stitch of clothing on us, but that he would not be able to get our things ashore. The surf was very powerful and the stretch of beach was being pounded by heavy breakers.

Rather than return to Stromness we ran into a quiet bay on the way home, which ran from east-northeast to west-southwest. The Norwegians called this little cleft in the mass of the island "Herkulesodden" [Hercules Bay] because the whaling vessel *Herkules* had once sought shelter here in foul weather. The little bay, about 400 m long, was the first inlet recorded on the chart between Stromness Bay and Fortuna Bay. It might almost be termed a fiord since steep cliffs bounded its quiet waters.

Here in the interior of the bay where the water lapped quietly and peacefully against the rocks, there was no great problem in getting ashore. On the first trip with the dinghy we took part of our baggage, and after a few strokes we slid through the kelp to the rocks. A second boatload brought the rest of our baggage as well as Benitz and my wife. Our thanks and a last greeting, and we were alone on this paradisiacal spot, as we saw it.

In terms of the choice of this new location – thanks to the wild surf at "Sand Bay" – we had hit the nail on the head as far as fossils were concerned. In a sort of fossil fever, which is related to antique fever but more harmless and less expensive once one is on the spot, I first searched the slaty, almost vertically dipping rocks. The first slab which I pulled from its position revealed a surprising similarity to the pieces I had found at Leith. The fossils in the schist, on the first inspection of the collection, were essentially identified as worm tracks and wormholes.

We pitched our tent some 50 m from the site of this find but on hard shingle since on the landward side the beach was immediately bounded by a rock step and there was not much room. There was an area of rock reef lying off and if one walked out onto it at low tide, one could see that the bottom dropped away very steeply and abruptly since the water was clear.

Here, indeed we were to enjoy the peaceful, undisturbed isolation of a comfortable Robinson [Crusoe] life, which matched so well the fantasies and expectations of youth and without the whims of winter or bad weather. A little stream which trickled down from under a melting snow bank provided us with water only a few steps away. Admittedly we found no driftwood for lighting an open fire but dry tussac grass and a few planks sufficed at a pinch. Perhaps there were fish on the bank off the rocks; if so we would soon have them cooking over the primus.

Sørlle had given us a fishing rod, a few hooks and lines and had suggested that it might be worth trying to fish from shore. I roughly baited a brand-new hook with some meat and within a few seconds we had enough fish for a meal. It was the same fish (*Notothenia larseni*) which we had caught earlier, and which is extremely common on South Georgia.

When we had ten fish logic told us that we should stop, even if our fingers were still itching. Once we realized from this unexpectedly rapid haul how inexperienced these fish were, we wanted to test their intelligence even further. I bet Benitz that the fish could be caught on a bare hook without any bait. Scarcely had the lead sinker been tossed with a splash into the pale blue water when there was a twitching and tugging at the line again and the rod was bending; we succeeded in pulling the hungry or sleepy fish out onto the beach in almost endless succession.

While I was pursuing this entertaining sport some quite large rocks tumbled down from the rock face above our camp. Another was hanging so menacingly above the tent, ready to fall, that one would have preferred to remove it before going to sleep for the night, in view of the mild weather. Since we failed to do this, towards evening we moved camp down slope towards the sea, although it was inconvenient and time-consuming. For even though the sea were to rise, and old tidemarks did not exclude this possibility, the danger from that source was preferable to a continued incalculable threat from the loose boulders above.

As it grew dark, and since we had already collected a whole box of fossil specimens, a friendly peace and beauty lay over the bay. Towards its head four elephant seals lay on the beach, leaving scarcely any room at all. In keeping with our own unhurried mood one of us expressed the thought: "Oh, they have a pleasant time; they're truly getting something out of life!"

On the second day we planned to visit the macaroni penguins (*Cataractis chrysocoma* [= *Eudyptes chrysolophus*]) which nested on the north coast. Since the heavy seas had prevented access yesterday we now had to try to reach them overland. We travelled along the north side of the bay over rocks which were still wet and slippery from kelp and the high tide. Trickles of water ran down across the slabs, and a little waterfall poured over some damming rocks. To our right the kelp played sinuously around the sharp, steep rock face. It was *Durvillaea*, a very rare kelp on the island, which is always in motion even if the sea is only breathing very gently. Although it was generally dark and black, a sunbeam bounced a silvery reflection off it, moving around with the waves and the clouds.

Unexpectedly a harmless little stream channel, in which some hard, firn-like snow still survived, led us uphill out of the bay, and after a few minutes we saw ahead of us to the north a saddle barely more than 120 m high. Carrying the heavy bags containing the camera, tripod and photographic equipment we chose the bare rocks, which gave a more secure foothold, rather than a snow slope to the left.

Soon we had an open view of the sea again; then the wing-beats of a skua whizzed close past my head. On the next swoop its wings grazed me. Perhaps at that moment, as we put on our snow goggles, we were thinking of that little, dead elephant seal whose eyes the bird had first pecked out. At any rate we felt safer once we had protected our eyes, even just in our imaginations, since a raptor will scarcely ever attack a man's eyes.

Once this adventure was behind us, our route westwards involved a continued progress across tussac-grass slopes which in places ended in a steep cliff dropping to the sea. But one could walk between the grass hummocks as safely as through solid brush, the stalks shot so high and strong into the air. It waved in the wind like fields of grain. Narrow, vegetation-free channels between the tussacs gave one a more secure, reliable foothold.

But there is something wonderful about slopes which lie inclined between sea and sky. We moved along as if detached, with the surface of the sea lying like an abandoned world or desert beneath us. The sun appeared from behind the clouds and with this brightening in the weather our nailed boots moved more easily, with a more elastic step. As we grabbed automatically, almost convulsively for the tussac stems because of the steepness, the surface suddenly became almost horizontal again, almost as if we were on a wide road, and our expectant ears were surprised by the first quarrelling sounds of the macaroni penguins. Below us we could see a small bay, running north-south. In order to reach it we had to traverse steep, slippery slopes and boggy channels, all occupied by penguins. It was like a progress through a madhouse. Beaks constantly pecked at our calves. We clenched our teeth and finally reached the upper edge of the rim of the bay, consisting of obliquely dipping slabs, where we were presented with an indescribably beautiful view.

But peace and quiet are two words which the visitor can forget from now on. It would also be advisable to eliminate one's sense of smell while one is in the midst of this environment. Only then will the impact be undisturbed and powerful.

First of all one has to admire the head of the bay. The rock slabs, inclined at 10°, rise directly out of the sea; there is no beach, no rocks or shallows to constrain the fury of the seas. Even today when the sea lies so quiet and peaceful when seen from above, the water hurls itself in a wild assault against the rocks. But it is not simply water. Every wave spits out several dozen birds; thrown onto the slanting rocks they brace themselves, straighten up, and having landed safely, they flee out of reach of the sea. For them the day's journey is over. Stuffed with fish and crabs, the penguins' stomachs are stretched tight. Happily they hop or waddle inland. They tackle little rock faces in an agile leap, even if they are a metre high. But some of them are neurasthenics and possess inhibitions. Before they decide to make a leap one can see them running irresolutely to and fro a few times. Many of them finally risk it; an equal number take the back stairs where the rock step can be overcome more easily.

Again and again the sea disgorges more groups onto the slanting slabs, which form the most natural landing site and provide the entranceway which leads to the realm of the penguins. The slabby rocks gleam snow-white. Guano, weathering and the surf have given them this gleaming colour. Those who have just arrived rush away. There is a constant coming and going. Everything proceeds in an orderly fashion. If we follow individual groups we can see them trotting up the slopes. Each one knows the wide, common access routes; each one knows the side streets which will lead it to its young, to its family.

Beyond a brief level area, a steep slope of tussac grass begins. The last nests lie on a slope with a gradient of a good 30–40°, 150 m above the sea. It was a long, steep trek up to these highest nests, one which demanded good muscles, even if the birds had to make it uphill only once per day.

We now watched a bird who was heading diligently homewards; it disappeared into a channel from which a little stream of water emerged, looking on this sunny day like a thread of silver. He now found time for a brief pause for a quick freshwater bath and a spot of preening. The yellow feather adornments which during the mating season stand out sideways, now lay smoothed flat against its head. Then it went hopping on again until halfway up it turned off and found its mate and young beneath the swaying grass.

Then came the greeting ritual, which never fails. The heads swing low to left and right in short, energetic arcs, the neck stretched somewhat backwards, while a call is uttered which is very difficult to imitate. This procedure, which is repeated several times in a row, is so peculiar that in one's astonishment one almost fails to hear the accompanying noise.

The individual images are full of fine detail. Almost invariably the young birds stick close together, generally in groups of five or six. One commonly sees two adults standing with them.

Today there are many young birds lying flat on their bellies with wings outstretched in the warm sunshine; even their heads are flat on the earth. They are enjoying life just as a sunbather does in our society. They blissfully allow the mother bird to preen their downy heads with her bill. She makes almost snapping movements as if trying to catch agile parasites.

On other occasions the mother administers blows at her offspring, pecking powerfully at its neck, whose stretching movements reveal that the insatiable young bird also needs food to maintain its body. Varying between 20 and 40 cm in height depending on its stage of development, the swollen little belly is the most prominent part of the anatomy of the young bird.

This subspecies of the penguin realm also reveals some peculiarities. With young life prevailing everywhere and the young birds stretching their bodies towards the source of life, two late arrivals are still sitting on their nest, as if they felt themselves at a disadvantage but diligently wanted to catch up with their peers. Elsewhere an accident revealed that in the case of one penguin the iris, which is usually entirely reddish-brown, was bi-coloured, with a brownish-grey ring surrounding the normally coloured centre. But these are just subtleties, equally insignificant and ultimately irrelevant to both penguins and man.

Having watched the sheathbills which also reside here in the rookery, searching through the excrement for still edible components, with short, hurried steps, we climbed somewhat higher to a vantage point. Again we could see the white bodies in the distance; again we could get an overview of the flood of life, the constantly repeated rush of birds after each breaking wave, and over everything the restless sky from which the first snowflakes were now drifting down.

Before the entire scene had a chance to disappear we had to assemble some numbers and start estimating. First we tried to count the birds on the slabs and quickly reached several thousand. Since we were unable to reach a total despite prolonged counting and adding, we began estimating, even although the total calculation thereby became somewhat more problematical. In so doing we also remembered that on the rare years when the weather permitted a landing the head of the Leith station was able to gather eggs here for his Christmas cakes, with the permission of the British administration. They were cheap eggs since the cost for 20,000 eggs was only a few shillings.

When we looked again at the vast rookery, bearing this number in mind, and began counting again from one corner or another, we soon realized that an estimate of 50 or 60,000 would not be too high for the total number of adult birds.

We left this idyllic summer place on 7 February almost reluctantly. It was like a summer resort. While the nights were colder, and indeed they invariably produced ice on the freshwater ponds, during the day a temperature of a few degrees, combined with calm conditions, was sufficient to make the day comfortable in sheltered corners. We again went fishing with bare hooks; we again searched the rocks for fossils; and we even went to visit the little "stinkers" who in their light-coloured plumage at this juvenile stage resemble young albatrosses.

As prearranged, on the evening of 7 February Captain Sørlle took us back to Stromness in a little motorboat, and new tasks quickly pushed this unharassed period of our island life into the background.

In front of me, in a scientific institute on the Bodensee, I can see almost a hundred bottles standing in rank and file. I have seen them several times and with every visit their number has increased as new ones have appeared in the rows. Professor Dr Schmalz of Konstanz has arranged them, bringing loving order into the chaos of our limnological material from South Georgia. Her formalin solutions contain plankton material wrested from the lakes lying on the coastal plain along the northeast coast. It is very satisfying when one sees these shiny bottles standing there, and one forgets the three weeks which we devoted to this task.

I do not want to say anything about what they

individually contain in terms of plants and animals, copepods and cladoceans, mites and other finds, but will leave that to the specialized researchers who are experts on such things. But I want to say something about the lakes themselves and the landscape which surrounds them, about our camps and the gypsy life which developed by itself. For no matter how organized and submissive everything appears on the table in front of us, none of the many lakes and ponds came to us. We had to find all of them first, sound them, haul a boat to them, camp and, in addition, struggle with the gusty winds and the inhospitable summer.

While we had observed our first lakes at Stromness on the headland between Stromness and Husvik and had made some minor collections of water samples earlier at Coal Harbour and Bay of Isles, our real work only began after our return home from Stromness.

In the vicinity of Grytviken there are two lakes above Maiviken which were sounded and investigated by the Swedes in 1902. The researcher, Dr. Sven Eckmann, analysed the results at Uppsala. But what made our work so different from that of the Swedes was that they carried out their investigations in May, i.e. in late autumn or winter in South Georgia terms. As they reported, the small ponds they investigated already had an ice cover. Our investigations occurred at the height of the southern summer, and hence one might assume that they would provide a clearer picture of the planktonic life. We had also been equipped by the Institute for Bodensee Research at Staad, near Konstanz, with a plankton net, and if the water depths permitted we planned to make hauls from different depths, probably the first time this had been tried on the island.

The most important item, completing our lake equipment, was an elegant Klepper boat which had already given us excellent service in the bays. But it would come fully into operation here for the first time. All our investigations would stand or fall with this boat.

As we climbed the hills north of Grytviken with the wind at our backs on 10 February, we were well aware that we were carrying a priceless load. It did not even seem heavy to us since there was a strong wind blowing against our packs, as if into a sail.

Reaching the high, wide saddle at 169 m, in view of the unaccustomed temperature of 13°C we were thankful that there was now a fresh wind blowing out of the north. We dropped our packs and hiked unladen up a hill in order to get an overview of the entire scene. We could look over the tub-shaped Maiviken and, to the north and north-northwest, the 400–500 m snow free mountains of Cumberland West Bay; and if one turned around one could see the icy chain of the main range. In front of us our attention was caught by the red coloration of the snow patches. On many moderately steep slopes we spotted peculiar arrangements of the debris: a marked parallel arrangement as if a gardener had separated ridges from furrows with little stones (patterned ground).

If one walked down valley again, past some distinctive dry cracks, one soon reached a large lake, which we had suspected existed for a long time, but which was hidden by the slopes around it.

We camped on a scrap of beach, covered with *Acaena*, at the southwest corner of the lake by a rushing stream which hurried past us into the lake. For hours on end we enjoyed the South Georgian summer. The water surface was slightly rippled and a green tinge on the slopes announced the sun's victory. Terns and dove-petrels poked diligently in the moss for little worms.

In the area between Grytviken and Maiviken one can find two fairly large lakes, but also innumerable smaller water bodies, ponds and narrow, branching water channels should be mentioned. However, this is perhaps not a permanent situation; their number, shape and size may change according to the amount of precipitation that year.

Once we had assembled our boat, after a few minutes

we were paddling across the empty lake which at first glance was devoid of all life. The only thing we had been able to find under rocks along the shore was some small water beetles.

The lake lay at a height of 79 m; it was 660 m long from north to south and 420 m wide. We measured the maximum depth in the middle of the lake at 49 m.

Once we had sounded the lake and made vertical profiles and associated collections at various depths, as well as some dredge hauls, tasks which took two days, we could see life forms crowding our bottles which previously had been hidden from our eyes. Fiery red little crustaceans flitted excitedly around the jars, along with transparent ones, and if one had enough patience and favourable light one could vaguely see the intestinal tracts of these little creatures, their sexual organs, and the shimmering movements of their paddles.

We found the temperature of the lake to be 3°C, with an air temperature of 4.25°C. Carrying the assembled boat on our shoulders we next walked to the second, smaller lake which lies southwest of the first one at a height of 125 m.

The two lakes are connected by the lively falls of a stream which one simply has to follow in order to reach the sea. Some very violent gusts forced us to take a little rest. In an unguarded moment we saw the boat whirled into the air by the powerful wind; but fortunately it landed in the outlet from the lake and hence we were able to fish it out undamaged. Once the wind gusts became a little weaker we launched the boat again and despite the waves and spray felt quite safe in it.

As we worked we felt almost safer yet when we sounded the maximum depth in the lake at only 5.5 m, and although one can drown just as well in 3 m as in 500 m we experienced something of the impact that numbers can make on a person.

Everything proceeded as nearly as we had hoped and in the last gleams of twilight we were lacing up our bundles. We were able to return to the whalers' house that very same evening.

It is 9.00 p.m. on 13 February and I am lying alone in the tent at Hestesletten. I've pitched it behind a low ridge of tussac grass which protects me from the surf and makes the camp invisible, although it lies at the edge of a plain. I am waiting for Benitz who has been taking care of some whale specimens and who promised to get here this evening. Since some large, heavy drops were falling on the tent and since it is getting dark I have lit the primus and thus brought some light into the lonely hours. A pair of elephant seals nearby in the grass are my only living companions and they are bellowing loudly in the night. The surf breathes heavily and throbbingly; gulls and skuas are tearing at a lump of meat which the current has drifted here from the remains of a whale.

Then I hear a shout and a couple of whistles and know that Benitz is looking for my camp. Soon, guided by my answering shouts he comes stumbling over the tussacs to the tent and what I had planned to be an early night turns into a long evening of conversation.

We've certainly turned over a new leaf in terms of expedition living. When one is camping only 5 km away from human habitation, totally without snow and glaciers, one can forget about hardships. One lies on soft moss cushions as if on soft beds; the wide stream beside us, almost a river, provides us with pure water effortlessly, and it is now a matter of total indifference if the wind now threatens our tent. We would simply pack up our bundles and move camp to behind a nearby rock pinnacle where we could lie dry and more sheltered. It is a carefree period. If the stream were to provide us with salmon there would be nothing more to wish for.

We are located at the edge of a level plain which is a good 2 km wide and extends 7–8 km south without any perceptible rise. At its head the Hamberg Glacier has left behind two lakes during its retreat and it is because of them that we are camped here. Ultimately, too, we can thank the glacier for the rushing stream along the northwest side of the plain and which runs across it in numerous sinuous bends. Ultimately, too, we can thank the glacier for the fact that instead of lying on ice we are lying on green cushions of moss and on the *Acaena* which clambers around the cushions and in places winds around them in its vitality as if trying to strangle them.

It was another bright morning with magnificent sunshine when we set off. The dew was glistening freshly; the modest vegetation in the land areas between the lakes and ponds spread out with the colour of fresh spruce shoots. Last night's rain had made the tussacs heavy and wet and when we had to walk through stagnant water channels we sank unexpectedly and emerged from this treacherous cover again with wet feet. Shoots of *Acaena* sprouted up, a pale red.

But all these meagre delights of colour yield before the brick-red colour of some ponds and quiet stream channels. Never before have we seen algae of such a gaudy colour.

Once we had reached the first lake after numerous detours, we quickly completed the work. It was only 2.5 m deep and its shores were reminiscent of a swamp, partially submerged and overflowing with water with no clear boundary. Only on the west shore where it was hemmed in by rocks was the shoreline distinctly demarcated. The water temperature was 9°C; the air temperature was a summery 15°C.

Our homeward journey was completely different. This time we did not have to cope with treacherous slime on a yielding bottom, or with wet feet. Everything was loaded aboard our little boat: two men, nets, dredges and containers. Then we shoved off into the stream and let the racing current take us. The overhanging banks flew past us; shingly shallows alternated with roaring, whirling rapids.

Although this was our first river trip in a Klepper boat we had no difficulty in navigating the sharp bends by alternating use of the paddles. Even when we ran aground on gravel due to our deep draft, often all that was needed was a slight change of position in order to get our boat afloat again.

Back home again we were never bored; even when one wandered idly to the beach without a specific goal, one could spend an hour studying whale anatomy from the stranded whalebones.

Towards evening the steep mountainside of Mt Duse, the landmark of Cumberland Bay, would stretch its shadow towards the sea. This was the start of our relaxation period. The sparks would fly up from the wet driftwood; the tobacco would hang over the edge of one's pipe like little, glowing worms, and on a peaceful, quiet evening one's thoughts would wander away from their usual constrained paths, as if they too were enjoying a holiday, and as if there was not a single corner of the world or a single heart which they could not touch.

Next morning the previous day's work was continued. Apart from other activities we measured the temperature of the stream near the bank; it was 11°C and the air temperature 15°C. We told ourselves that if the temperatures rose any higher we would be able to take a voluntary bath after all the involuntary ones we had experienced.

Benitz paddled to the opposite bank while I remained on the same side as our tent. Then having rove a line through a ring at the bow we pulled the boat effortlessly upstream.

As we reached the lake we had investigated yesterday we were struck by a violent squall which blasted down from the summit of the Sugarloaf. With the boat we hugged the eastern shore of the lake and reached its head despite the storm; there an earth ridge separated us from a second major lake.

Our gaze was now drawn to the nearby Hamberg Glacier; we could see that its lower, recently formed tongue was covered with detritus. In front of it lay a transverse rock-step consisting of two rock knobs and a number of smaller ridges, which had already been colonized by *Rostkovia* rushes.

We were soon able to proceed with sounding the lake; the deepest point was only 5.5 m. A quick survey of the plankton hauls revealed that they differed not at all from those from the lower lake. Again we had a merry homeward trip, without any incidents. Much more confident today, we doubled our speed by energetic use of the paddles. Although we were not making the 25 knots of a warship, we were making 5 knots. We revelled in the fact that today, when everyone is striving for speed and rush we lived in such a quiet corner, and that while speed is becoming essential in trade and work, motors and the other excessive marvels of speed had not penetrated here and were not even usable here. On quiet stretches of our rapid journey we could look back in leisurely fashion to the severe world of the glacier, at the rock face which divided the glacier, and over which five strands of water hung like silver fingers.

The campfire and, towards evening, racing turbulent clouds over the bay. No phenomena on earth can have such a quick, exciting impact on restless people as scudding, rushing clouds. Fortunately at least to the southeast a vastly large, agate-red cloud lay quietly over the main range and reigned over the middle of the island like a sovereign.

17 February was a Sunday. On that day, unless there has been a heavy catch the whale factories at Grytviken take a holiday and then the normally lonely beach becomes more active, even busy. On that day workers and clerks run around in little groups and individuals even appeared near our camp, although they stopped and turned back at the swollen stream. When we saw one of a group of three men wading through the swollen waters, getting wet almost to his hips we offered to ferry the other two hesitating members across in our boat so that they could continue their walk to a projecting nose.

When they came back the coffee pot was already hanging over the fire. We invited two of the young lads, one 29 years old and the other a few years younger, to stay. The elder of the two had been whaling since he was 19. He came from Stokke in southern Norway; he was fair-haired, with a powerful, gnarled physique, and Frederick the Great would have allowed him to enlist in his regiment without any hesitation. It was he who had defiantly tackled the swollen stream and had waded through in his Sunday outfit without turning a hair. I asked him if he were still wet.

"It doesn't do one any harm to be wet; we sealers are wet all day long. If I get wet in the morning I never change my boots and stockings until evening."

I asked him if he were happy with his work down here. Yes: having 3000 kroner in one's pocket in ready cash at the end of the whaling season every year was worth all the work and effort. Yes, one could save it and it would quickly appreciate, but once one got home there was soon nothing left of it. With whalers it goes faster than it comes. A brand-new suit, treating one's friends to party after party, driving around in one's car: activities like these would have eliminated the three zeros of that large sum by the end of a Norwegian summer.

But you could go a little easier back home, I interjected. Yes. This time he had decided to start acting differently and he planned to set it all aside. Two cows and some land were his goal, and apart from that he wanted to go courting when he got home- "Komm weit mit mir in den Wald, Jenta (Mädchen), wir wollen dort eine Hütte bauen" [Come away to the woods with me, *jenta* (maiden) and we'll build a hut there]. This was the approximate gist of the song that he sang cheerfully and cleverly, as he faced out to sea.

Yes, he repeated; things would be serious now. But by God, a *jenta* such as he needed was not easy to find. We agreed that for whalers, seamen and adventurers it was not easy to find the *jenta* who could fulfil a restless soul.

We were unable to prevent these two modest men from hefting this or that bundle on their shoulders. Hence our transport back home became a simple, easy matter, and if we had had the inclination we could have spent the evening at the cinema in Grytviken, as indeed most of the men did.

There followed another three days of rain and storm. New snow, the first sign of winter, lay on the mountains, and the catchers which came into the harbour reported ferocious gales off the coast. The whales, too, were less common; there were no longer any blue whales to be seen and one was lucky if one encountered a school of fin or sei whales.

Due to this stormy weather our limnological work was postponed until 21 February when the seas in King Edward Cove were calmer.

Our next objective was the Nordenskjöld Glacier in Cumberland East Bay, i.e. we wanted to camp near it. Accompanied by two sealers, a Russian and a Norwegian, the landing proceeded smoothly. Since the bay was full of bergy bits we had to proceed along its edge but finally, 5 km from the glacier snout, we were able to risk a landing. Even now the last remnants of the heavy swell made things difficult.

Soon after noon we were slowly climbing over hilly, gently rising terrain, heading eastwards with a stream on our left, in search of more lakes. After 20 minutes we camped by a shallow pond, lying at a height of 99 m.

From this extremely shallow lake the U-shaped valley continued east and after a brief level section ended at a height of 117 m, closed by a ridge aligned north-south. Near a pass lying northeast of the valley head we could see the remains of a glacier; it formed a steep-sided saddle and undoubtedly provided a link with Ocean Harbour.

While my two companions were engaged in plankton collecting and dredging and everything associated with that work and later were collecting insects, I had already examined the south side of the valley with great interest. Here I was struck by the three terraces which immediately reminded me of the scene which Gunnar Andersson had described from Moraine Fiord.

30. The 23 m-high ice cliff of the Nordenskjöld Glacier

31. The Sugarloaf seen from Hestesletten

32. Every breaker hurled dozens of penguins onto the rock slabs

After half an hour of stiff climbing I had reached the third level and had measured all the heights with the aneroid. The third one lay at 278 m; the middle one at 174 m; and the lowest at 158 m. All three descended gently from east to west, and near the uppermost one the rocks displayed the most distinctive whalebacks. All this indicated that the little glacier remnant above the head of the valley must once have filled the entire valley. One could not but be amazed at the changes which South Georgia's environment so clearly reveals, especially when one could see some *Acaena* battling for its stunted but aggressive existence in cracks in the whalebacks at a height of 278 m. Nothing can remind us humans more of our own brief course and of the puzzling "from wheres" and "to wheres" of life, than nature's vast stretches of time and the traces which they have left in the rock and in the landscape.

As compared to what we had just been looking at, the reindeer antlers which we found in this lonely valley, and which we had been hoping to find for some time seemed very recent and yet very appropriate. For we knew that Captain C. A. Larsen and his brother, who were always dreaming up new plans, had brought a dozen reindeer to the island from Lapland in 1908 and had released them in the most suitable area for the purpose, namely between Cumberland Bay and Hound Bay. The result was an unprecedented success. Some 400–500 animals now roamed the valleys and hills, even although some were shot every year. In this area we had not only seen their tracks but had repeatedly seen the animals themselves. They are not even particularly wary and find everything they need here to maintain their normal, free life: a strong growth of their favourite tussac grass, *Acaena* and lichens, which are related to those in Lapland. The animals we had seen at the station, killed by hunters, were amazingly large, much larger than I had ever seen in Lapland. We were told that they might weigh up to 130 kg and, as we were able to confirm ourselves, their antlers were of amazing proportions.

The biological aspects of this artificial transplanting of these animals are particularly noteworthy in that they reveal a rapid, almost immediate adaptation to the reversed seasons of the southern hemisphere. Whereas in Lapland the calves are born at the start of the northern summer, i.e. at the end of April, on South Georgia they have to be born at the start of the southern summer, i.e. in November, otherwise their lives will be at risk. What makes Larsen's experiment so remarkable and interesting is this almost immediate adjustment of a complicated biological procedure, i.e. this adaptation to the temporally different climatic conditions in the south.

From our camp we can see to the north-northeast the 23 m ice cliffs of the Nordenskjöld Glacier which is 2000 m wide at its snout. We can see this steep front and can hear its powerful, almost incessant, thunderous roars. We waited almost an entire afternoon for a clear spell, so that we could see more than just one end of the snout. But clouds rolled endlessly across the glacier and only once did an icy summit stick up clear against the sky.

Since the cloud cover did not disperse the next day either we continued our work on the lakes under overcast skies in order to finish it as quickly as possible. By now it had become a mechanical task to determine the size of the lakes, their shape and height above sea level, and to carry out soundings, dredgings, and the preservation of the haul. The only variety was that we had to change our location of operations each time we finished with one area. But since on 23 February the temperature was hovering around zero, handling wet nets was an unpleasant task. We stopped frequently to restore some life in our fingers, in the icy wind and falling snow.

Thus since we were not tempted to take a rest, one day's work produced sufficient material that we could take an exhaustive impression of the limnology back home with us for the scientists. The area between Cumberland East Bay and Hound Bay, which can be reached without much trouble via a plain-like divide at about 120 m, conceals a large number of larger and smaller shallow lakes as well as vast numbers of ponds, so that once we had finished one lake we would soon see the surface of another glinting as we walked along.

On the afternoon of 24 February, after having been delayed long enough by the fog and northwest winds, I was finally sitting in the lee of a rock pinnacle which adorns the shore in front of the ice cliffs of the Nordenskjöld Glacier. Severe weathering provided evidence of the continued erosion by the southwest wind. Lichens and mosses sat in their niches as if in little nests. If one looked at the entire formation from the side, even without bringing any fanciful imagination into play, it resembled a robber knight, who owed his sharp profile to the work of the wind. Beard, a large nose and an energetic mouth were all complete; the whim of nature had placed a watchman in front of the approaches to the glacier.

But our wrapt attention was immediately distracted from it when one of the most magnificent scenes on earth emerged from the swirling clouds and fog. The peak of Tenerife, like all peaks which tower from the sea, may provoke an overpowering impression when seen from sea level, but this is even more the case here on South Georgia where eternal ice casts its mantle over the chain which extends as a ridge from southeast to northwest and reaches its maximum elevation in Mt Paget at a height of 3000 m. Our field of vision was bounded to the south by an unnamed peak which now lay clear before us for the first time. If one excludes two small portions its ridge was completely ice-covered. It was followed by the long ridge of Mt Paget with its three summits, on which a high wall of ice rested.

As one traced the course of the ridge on to the Sugarloaf this impressive scene was heightened even more by a further summit which was displaced somewhat to the north and gave the impression that the main range itself curved round somewhat to the north.

In this untouched realm of eternal ice nature had placed between the main summit and subsidiary summits of Mt Paget a steep rock wall which was almost ice-free, and as seen from our viewpoint gave the impression of a massive cirque. Eight ridges, all ice-free with the exception of minor ice slopes and remnants of glaciers, extended down from the main range and provided the Nordenskjöld Glacier with its surficial and lateral moraines which ran down the glacier like roads.

As we examined all these details, our gaze wandering from glacier to glacier and from ridge to ridge, a prolonged thunder forced us to look back at the ice cliff of the glacier. Calving ice was tumbling almost ceaselessly into the water and today's northwest winds were driving the waves right up to the glacier cliff; as a result the turmoil in this ice-cauldron was intensified.

Then we were struck by the severe rocking movements of a disintegrating Antarctic iceberg which the waves had also driven into the bay. We watched it capsizing amidst a vast upheaval and soon afterwards saw its effects as a rushing wave set the drifting bay ice into a lively uproar and threw large floes onto the beach.

Even here at the edge of the perpetual ice we found nests of the giant petrel with their little whitish-grey young, on a rock knob beside the glacier. As we walked steeply uphill towards the east we were struck by the clamour of the terns, and after a long search we discovered their little nestlings hidden among slabs of rock at a height of 150–200 m. In the vicinity of our camp Dominican gulls rocked on ice slabs, along with their young, now fully capable of flight; meanwhile the slim body of a leopard seal slid from a rectangular ice block which was threatening to become stranded on the shingly shore.

Since the primus was on strike that evening, filling the tent with smoke, we again built a little rock stove near the tent, although today we would have preferred to stay quietly inside, since it was beginning to snow gently. We stoked the stove methodically, having laid in a store of wood, with which the beach is abundantly blessed. We had found a chest wrapped in bast. The thin tropical wood burned quickly and easily even if it were not as heat-productive as hearts of South American trees. The coffee tasted of tussac grass or elephant seals. We argued over which it was, and before we reached unanimity the coffee pot was empty.

It is 25 February and our last day, according to our arrangement with the whalers. But we are still not sure that a boat will come from Grytviken since the northerly winds, the swell and the close-packed ice might prevent a landing from a dinghy. But the day still has 12 hours and many things may change.

We searched the slaty coastal rocks in vain for fossils, then we selected a small, circumscribed area. We overturned a slab of rock and observed what was to be seen and found beneath it.

At first, our eyes still dazzled, we could see nothing at all as we glanced at the dark, almost subterranean location. But do you think that there is no life here? At the root hairs of the *Acaena*, which are light-coloured at their ends, there are little, light-coloured formations and when we look at them carefully we notice some minute movements which can barely be distinguished from the pale roots. They are little worms, which love the damp. Once we have dropped them into the formalin solution and look back at the small dark location which we have disturbed, the shiny back of a beetle is just disappearing; it is trying to escape among the root hairs as a hiding place, thus hoping to become invisible.

But its life is not as secure as its size might indicate. Where otherwise did the numerous little chitin armour plates come from, which lie under the stone like old, abandoned armour in a lumber-room? It clearly is in great danger from all the black spiders which, confused by our assault, now rush across the damp surface beneath the rock slab. When a ray of sun strikes the body of one of them, it gleams like a shiny, black stone. No animal can withstand its delusion; it will lose first its head, then its armour, i.e. its hard chitin plates.

If we are lucky and patient we will find even more under the same rock: little white sachets, as if made of cotton wool, containing a clutch of three pale, often yellowish eggs. Or yellow or scarlet lice, as well as pale ones, which are probably just a juvenile form.

The entire realm is in uproar because human hands have raised the protective stone roof. The walls of the little dwelling place are moist; carpets of moss lie in the corners; rock debris which lies on the plaster floor reveals pale green colours, other rocks reveal whitish-grey patterns as if composed of little circles. These are lichens which need dim light and darkness in order to live.

Absorbed in this work, marvelling and watching, to the extent that the entire world around us might disappear without us noticing, I heard the noise of a propeller throbbing offshore and even before we had got back to the tent the whaling vessel was lying among the restless ice, come to liberate us from our quiet life once again.

18

Lonely Annenkov Island is Our Next Goal

On 1 March the sealing ship *Diaz* was to begin the autumn seal hunt. Not even the foulest weather can persuade the energetic Captain Johanesson to remain an extra hour in King Edward Cove once the date has arrived on which, according to British law, the season for shooting elephant seals begins again.

"You must be on board on time," he told us on the afternoon of 28 February: "we'll be leaving at 5 o'clock in the morning."

It was vicious weather; the rain poured in torrents and the wind was blowing undecidedly from every direction as Benitz and I headed out around the old sailing ship *Luise* [*Louise*], against whose coal-blackened sides *Diaz* was lying bunkering. The barometer stood at the uncannily low figure of 715.00, with a temperature of 6° and the little sealing ship was rolling in the northeast swell in King Edward Cove as if she were in the open sea.

And indeed we set off at around 5 o'clock. Johanesson, a Swede, is a diligent captain and a zealous hunter of seals. As we sailed only the foot of Cumberland Bay was visible as a grey strip as we headed along the northeast coast. The only landmarks for maintaining a correct course were the rocks and the kelp, and after about 90 minutes we swung into Hound Bay in order to anchor for the night.

By law sealing could begin and it was this fact alone which made Captain Johanesson weigh anchor again at 5.00 next morning, although the dubious weather conditions still almost turned day to night. But no, he wanted to reach his sealing grounds on the southwest coast without fail, and without delay.

I woke up shivering on the hard ship's bench which had to be our accommodation in a ship where space and comfort do not have very high priority. We were putting to sea on a totally grey morning. At the mouth of Royal Bay where it always blows, according to seamen's tradition, the weather of South Georgia overwhelmed us unrestrainedly, so that it was almost impossible to go on deck. I could see Captain Johanesson standing at the helm himself; near him stood a ten-shilling clock, and since there were absolutely no landmarks he was navigating by the clock. Something like a chronometer was an unknown, or at least unused, luxury here. Hence we were all the more surprised to see that Johanesson had a mental picture or a feeling for every rock and every strip of kelp. Even the best chart would have been of no help here, where one could distinguish neither the coast nor the rocks just off it.

Shortly before 11.00 a.m., to top everything, a very thick snow squall began. We had to proceed at half speed on a hesitating, searching course, estimating that we must be off the mouth of Drygalski Fiord.

"Yes," said Johannesson with relief, "there's the steep rock cliff over there. Now we'll soon find Larsen Harbour and then it will be quiet and peaceful."

Shortly afterwards we swung out of the wide fiord, where a steep cliff meant that we could maintain a sure course, through a narrow strait into the small Larsen Harbour, which is a favourite harbour for whaling vessels in bad weather. As if at a word of command the gale and the sea fell quiet here, and we breathed with relief to be safe again.

Five whaling vessels were already moored here, one beside the other, and we could see some whales already secured to special buoys, waiting for transport at the first improvement in the weather.

Given the foul weather, since one could not even see across the little bay, the best thing would have been to lie back on the bench like the sailors, smoke one's pipe, and play whist with the captain and the mate. But it has become a habit, or passion, of mine, one I have in common with many Englishmen, to drop a fishing line over the side in any harbour to find out if there is any life in the water.

There was an extraordinary amount of life in that little bay. I pulled out one fish after another, and after two hours I had enough for many meals for our entire ship's complement. I was totally soaked by the driving snow but one can stand that on board ship. For below in the mess there was a little iron stove which was stoked constantly so that one could sit on the sleeping bench in one's shirt-sleeves.

In the evening as I lay on one side of the table on my bench and Benitz at the other, gazing at the light which, for some unknown reason, burned all night, I pondered over when, after this stop-and-go voyage, we would ever reach Annenkov Island, to which, according to our arrangement with Esbensen, the captain was to transport us. In fair weather one could be off the rocks of Annenkov in twelve hours after a straight run from Grytviken, but we had already been drifting around the harbours of the northeast coast for two nights of storm and foul weather.

At 4.00 a.m. on 2 March, in pitch darkness, the anchor chains were again rattling. What restlessness the elephant seal can arouse in men, that they can leave such a peaceful haven in this foul weather!

We steamed past Esbensen and Doubtful bays and passed through a strait about 800 m wide which separates the southeast corner of the main island from a small group of islands and reefs known as the Green Island. This is probably simply because it is one of the first islands in spring to display the green of the tussac grass, or because in its green mantle it makes such a friendly impression on the sailor, when he has passed the row of glaciers on the southwest coast and now sees the contrastingly green island.

Shortly before 7 o'clock, with a westerly wind blowing, one heavy sea after another swept the deck. Soon afterwards I recorded in my diary: "I just hope that the frames and plates can withstand these impacts with the sea!" Soon after 9 o'clock we passed the wide Novosilski Glacier which extends from south-southwest to north-northeast; it rises slowly, suggesting that it connects with the glaciers of Royal Bay.

While I was standing near the wheel which was in the captain's safe hands, he pointed to the west in order to show me the Pickersgill Islands as they surfaced and disappeared in the form of small, round domes, according to whether our ship was in a trough or was heaved up onto a wave crest. Then during a slight brightening he pointed more to the northwest where our goal, Annenkov Island, rose from the sea as a double summit covered with new snow.

But both visions quickly disappeared and we hugged the coast more closely; shortly before Undine South Harbour it revealed no further glaciers until around 10 o'clock the ice-cliff of a large, matt-white glacier came into view in the northwest corner of the bay. But according to Johanesson one could not see the main glacier in the bay from our ship's position; it lay in the southeastern bay and was aligned in the same direction as the Novosilski Glacier.

The ship was pitching so heavily that it took us 90 minutes to cross the mouth of Undine South Harbour. The coast between here and Jacobsen Bight, which came next, displayed two massive glaciers, unnamed like so many things on the island, and reaching the sea in steep ice-cliffs. From their position they must originate in the Paget massif; the captain confirmed this deduction.

From then on we did not see much more of coast or sea that day. Heavy seas and driving snow placed severe limits on any observations. Again we were navigating by compass and clock and had to be thankful that we could at least catch a momentary glimpse of the row of reefs which links Cape Darnley and Annenkov Island. Often, depending on the ship's position, a castellated rock would tower out of the grey of the sea; often just a pinnacle, which could be used either as a warning or as a landmark in order to adjust our course.

Around 3 o'clock the Swede's abundant experience and dash brought the ship past some ghostly skerries to an anchorage in front of an awe-inspiring glacier snout, and I learned from the steward who had just run shivering across the deck, that we were now in Holmestrand.

Such is the life of a sealer on South Georgia! They do not know in the morning where their little sealing vessel will be lying that evening. They set off in high spirits and with great hopes, and have to seek shelter in the nearest harbour. As in our case they may have to flee from harbour to harbour for 2½ days or 60 hours without once seeing a *Mirounga* or elephant seal, i.e. the quarry for which they have left their homes in Norway, Russia, Germany, or a slum in Buenos Aires.

That evening I felt an urge to leave our overheated quarters and go on deck; for a moment I almost thought we were lying among south polar ice. Ice blocks from the constantly active glacier were rubbing the whole time against the ship's iron hull. We were completely beset among the close-packed ice and hence I went back to sleep after a fruitless day: fruitless both for the sealers who were itching to harvest elephant seals and also fruitless for us, since we wanted to get to Annenkov Island.

On Sunday 3 March we were still no more successful in attaining our goals of elephant seals or Annenkov Island, but lay quietly in King Haakon Bay, to where the swell and the ice had again driven us from Holmestrand Bay. But on this leg of the voyage I was at least able to determine that the stretch of coast from Holmestrand to Cape Nuñez displays no glaciers, if one excludes a glacier remnant which we observed half an hour out of Holmestrand Bay and which, bounded above by rock, hangs over a saddle.

Hence, despite their wishes, the sealers' muscles have an easy time of it. No duties are imposed on them when there is nothing to be done, and this is only fair. When the beaches are accessible and the sea and the weather calm down their days will be more than full.

Apart from this it was Sunday afternoon and a deathly silence lay over the entire ship. The peace could not have been more holy in a church. Everybody on board was asleep following the past eventful days, and this protracted sleep had nothing in common with sloth.

I shall report later on the landscape of lonely King Haakon Bay, when I am discussing our voyage with the sealers around the entire island. I shall say only that repeatedly on that Sunday we gazed across at the continuous ice wall in the inner section of the bay, above which we had stood after our trek from Bay of Isles on 19 December 1928. We gazed at the steps and at the irregular crevassing, whereby longitudinal and transverse crevasses ran at right angles to each other, creating a pattern which lay on the ice like a trellis or a window grating.

Over to the west and south the sun was shining from among dark clouds. Yellow stripes fell across the sky like sheaves. Bay, mountains and ice momentarily assumed something of this fleeting magnificence. A last gleam wandered, pale pink, up across the glacier over which Shackleton began his trek into the unknown in 1916.

19

Camp Life on Annenkov Island

I SHALL SKIP OVER A DAY which began with snow squalls yet on which, despite this and because the sea was calm, 13 elephant seals had been harvested before the second breakfast. As evening fell, and as we were again lying peacefully at anchor in Holmestrand, the 53rd seal was hauled aboard with cables.

As we sat together in the evening in the mess, hashing over the day, the preceding days, and all the adversities, Captain Johannesson said that he would attempt a landing on Annenkov Island next morning. However, one could never definitely predict this ahead of time; everything would depend on the day, the hour and the state of the sea. But he thought that after all the foul weather we were due for a more favourable period.

On 5 March, gazing from the deck, I saw Annenkov Island ahead of me, snow-covered and grey. With its low, steep-to coasts, its snow-covered tussac-grass slopes, and a peak rising steeply above them the island presented a stern, remote appearance which signified the many expectations which we associated with life on an island.

Since the sea was quiet, with only a slight swell playing around the reefs, our landing in the middle of the northeast coast proceeded without incident and with dry feet. We pitched our tent 30 m from the sea among some gentoo penguins which were standing around. This was not such an easy task since after penetrating only a short distance almost every tent peg encountered rock. Since we still had respect for the southwesterly winds we relied more on the steep tussac slopes which, we hoped, would shelter us from them.

We were finally on Annenkov, which many whalers describe as a paradise, although only a few of them, who had previously been sealers, were familiar with it from fleeting visits. But they all maintained that there was always some sun on its peak when South Georgia itself lay hidden in grey clouds. We had been told enthusiastically about the many shags on the island's rocks, about the young albatrosses, and about the fish which frequented the kelp off the island. Yes, all this we were to get to know at first hand.

We also knew that a member of the *Norvegia* expedition commanded by Olaf Holtedahl, had made a brief landing on Annenkov with the sealers and had found a fragment of an ammonite on the northeast coast near a rock arch which, however, we had not yet located. We hoped that chance might land more such treasures in our hands, such as we had been lucky enough to find at other locations on the island. But above all we wanted to search for the albatross on Annenkov and to film it and its young and thereby present this magnificent bird, which is known in Germany only by name, to a wider audience. We had so much to do!

Thus, immediately after our arrival, as restless, complicated men of the twentieth century, we wandered east along the beach and encountered an abandoned gentoo penguin rookery. Most of the birds were off doing their day's fishing; only a few moulting birds and juveniles of the latest brood had stayed at home, while a 'stone collector' pattered around in a corner. The gentoo penguins were no longer maintaining nests; after the mating season they no longer stick so closely to the old nesting area.

Without delaying longer we climbed the steep slopes through the snow-heavy tussac grass in a southwesterly direction; in so doing we fell several times in the loose snow which concealed every crevice. Since each of us wanted to outpace the other in order to be the first to see every new feature we both found ourselves suffering from a premature and sudden exhaustion. All those nights at sea, which we had spent on that hard bench, were still in our bones, although a lot of strong tobacco and the good but heavy ship's fare may also have contributed their share. After a few minutes, once we had climbed the first steep rise and the terrain rose more gently ahead of us, we spotted the first adult albatrosses (*Diomedea exulans*). They were sitting on their well-sited nests which give the impression of a truncated cone, about 35 cm high on average. Composed and proud each bird sat in majestic immobility without even rising or flying off. It is a wonderful bird, not only because of its snow-white breast and its size, or because its wings may reach a span of 3–4 m. Rather because in our minds we remember it wheeling in quiet circles above the ship's wake and think of its solitary world and of how its life consists of wandering eternally over the seas. In short the albatross is a personality, a prince of the air, and dearer to me than many of my own species.

Here, on its nest, the majestic, proud composure of the albatross is in even greater contrast in that young giant petrels are behaving in such an unruly fashion nearby, spitting at us with a zeal that would make one think their life depended on it. Since we had last seen the little stinker by the Nordenskjöld Glacier the young giant petrels had grown tremendously in both length and width, but in so doing had become all the more hideous. They have now lost their white, downy coats and have acquired a dark grey plumage.

After twenty minutes we crossed a shallow stream along which, to judge by the existing but abandoned nests, a gentoo penguin rookery had been located, almost 3 km from the beach. And indeed a few dozen birds were still standing around behind a rise in the ground. Without their noticing us we sat down in the wet grass and from this concealed position repeated the noises we heard them uttering. Although we were no experts at imitating penguin calls and produced rather clumsy efforts, we observed the penguins, one after the other, moving with cautious steps towards the baffling, new sounds. I lured them from a range of 30 m away to within 30 cm, and when they began pecking at my head I was glad that I was wearing sunglasses as protection against the blinding snow glare.

When we switched back to conversing in human speech they did not retreat noticeably but continued to besiege us. The little flock of charming, trusting birds inquisitively examined every part of our clothing almost like natives who are seeing a European for the first time.

What a magnificent paradise! Thank God that no humans live here! At first glance all the penguins appeared the same. Only when a soft whistling reached our ears from time to time did we realize that there were juveniles among the crowd. These sounds now uttered by the birds were ones which we had never heard before. Perhaps it was the unperfected utterings of juveniles. At Elsehul and Bay of Isles we had heard only the calls of the adults at mating time when their lives were so intense and excited, especially during the weeks when their "Roah-Roah-i Roh" calls rang out through the evenings.

As we climbed farther up a little tussac slope towards the southwest, imperceptibly gaining height, to our delight we sighted a lake beneath us to the southwest, from the top of an elevation 86 m high, which had concealed it. It was 350–400 m long, extended to a width of 250 m, and was rectangular in shape. It lay 69 m above sea level and one could easily walk round it on its east side. While strolling along we could see the rocky main peak of the island to the northwest when it was cloud-free; we judged its height to be 500 m.

If one climbed a little farther to the southwest, from a ridge one could see the surf along the southeast coast of the island, with steep tussac slopes leading down to it; one could also overlook a good part of the eastern half of the island.

As we headed home from this first little excursion,

33. From the albatross's nest one could overlook the alpine chain of South Georgia

34. A young giant petrel in down

35. We encountered the odd isolated Weddell seal

shortly before noon we saw an albatross land and waddle to its nest with a ponderous gait. Once it has landed the bird discards all its elegance. It walked heavily and uncertainly, as if its legs might not support it on land.

For this bird air beneath its wings is as money is to so many people, if they are to reveal their most advantageous side. But we soon reconciled ourselves to its waddling gait as we watched the new arrival, which we presumed to be the male, shuffle up to the nest. He now stood on the edge of the nest, clattering with his beak and overwhelming his mate with an abundance of protestations of love, which sounded to our ears like grunts. Not satisfied with this he stroked her head, thus enhancing our respect for this *pater familias*. Once all the conventions, repeated many times, were over, the king of the air himself climbed onto the nest in order to relieve his mate from the task of incubation. In the process we caught sight of the large, white egg which must be nearly ready to hatch, if the whalers' reports about the first appearance of the young birds are correct.

During these careful observations it began to rain and since we were already soaked to above the knee as a result of sinking into bogs treacherously concealed by snow, we started back towards the tent. We had frequently been thinking with some anxiety about the tent when the wind gusted powerfully across the slopes. But we found everything in perfect order. Our hurried meal consisted of dry, air-dried mutton, coffee, bread and butter. The meal finished we changed our clothes and boots. This was all done in haste; eating was a secondary activity and on Annenkov we spared ourselves the tasks of tidying and washing since my wife was not with us. The sealing vessel did not have sufficient suitable space and hence she had had to stay at Grytviken for the first time. Hence we were bachelors again with all the related rights and freedoms.

Then we walked for a few minutes along the northeast coast towards the gentoo penguin rookery. Now, at noon, the beach was populated with homeward-bound gentoo penguins. If we stepped slowly and inconspicuously we were able to walk through them without provoking any disturbance or fear. Only sudden movements disturbed the birds' composure. I suspect that no animal likes surprises or unexpected impressions, unless they are associated with food. Hence during any animal observations and especially when filming one has to stand still for hours if one wants to be rewarded by success.

The behaviour and manner of the birds, even their gait and movements, have quietened down since the mating season and while they still hurtle out of the water with the same amazing grace their verve and bounce are no longer as energetic as at Elsehul where they had rushed up the beach to get to their nests with an extraordinary joie-de-vivre.

Today I was distracted from these scenes which I had seen so often by a rock outcrop above high water mark, which displayed horizontal bedding. Penguin excrement had whitewashed it in places. But despite this the rock invited a blow of my hammer and I felt an indescribable joy when, after several blows at promising spots, I found a fossil of a mussel. Since twilight was falling (in early fall nightfall occurs at 7 o'clock) I again turned my attention to the penguins and tucked my valuable find carefully away.

In contrast to the first fleeting impressions in the morning I now succeeded quite well in distinguishing the young penguins from their parents, despite the twilight. Apart from the fact that the juveniles are somewhat smaller and more slender, and that their bills are a lighter pink as compared to the more deeply coloured bills of the adults, now at the start of the moult the plumage of the adults shines more rust-brown in colour, whereas that of the juveniles is a deep, dark almost blue-black. Apart from all the external differences, in the evening the occasional whistling of the juveniles also helped in distinguishing them.

But the first cleavage already separates young birds

from their parents; their relationship is no longer the same as that in Bay of Isles where we could not extol highly enough the enormous care taken of the young by their parents. Many aspects already pointed to the final separation, to an attitude of "I don't want to know any more about you," at least on the part of the parents.

Over the entire period of our sojourn on Annenkov we were so often witnesses to the most intimate scenes of penguin life, yet I would not report the following situation as credible, if it had not happened every evening, so that I was able to point it out to Benitz several times.

Among birds, just as among human children, there are certainly individual examples who hang onto their parents' apron strings for as long as possible. Certain human children, just like penguins, soon realize that it is easier to keep begging food from one's parents than to earn it for oneself in the struggle for life.

Thus among a group of penguins we watched the rhythmic head movements of a young bird, aimed at the parent's bill, which are typical of the demand for food and which are continued indefatigably, with short pauses. Twice already we had watched the response of the harassed mother, namely a powerful, angry peck at the young bird's plumage. No, she did not want to have anything further to do with her offspring. The young bird was large and the neighbour's children were already catching crustaceans and little fish on their own. Suddenly we saw the mother fleeing at high speed, as if at the end of her tether, when the young bird again continued to harass her with its importunate movements. The young bird raced after her at top speed, whistling plaintively. This continued for a short while. The mother fled along the beach in a sinuous course past many other penguins. If this flight on land achieved nothing we would see her dive into the surf and disappear in front of the young bird's eyes. Helpless and complaining the little fellow would gaze out over the vast sea which had swallowed its mother. After a few seconds we would see him wandering back towards the rookery and the other groups of penguins, helpless and disappointed.

In many cases this delightful sequence of observations would be continued even farther. The mother would not stay in the water for long, in that it had simply provided a less-than-desirable refuge in extreme necessity. We would often see her come ashore again at a different spot a few dozen metres down the beach. That it was *she* and not some other penguin was quite obvious in cases where the young penguin, cheated out of its food, had headed in the same direction along the beach as the mother had taken under water, and hence accidentally ran into its surprised mother again. She would then immediately be accosted again. In many cases she would plunge back into the sea again; but in many cases, too, she would yield and would provide the little one with food by the usual technique of regurgitation.

When I looked out of the tent at 5.00 a.m. on 6 March, as it was already starting to get light, I found it practically surrounded by gentoo penguins. Some of them were stumbling over the guys but all were getting ready for their daily fishing trip and were heading out to sea in groups. Although after the stormy night the early morning spread a glow of softness and beauty over the beach and the crowds of birds and for a moment the sun gilded the reefs and surf, this early period of glory quickly ended. South Georgia soon lay embedded in clouds again, while heavy rain rattled on the beach and the tent, giving us plenty of reasons to approach the grey day with equanimity and to crawl back into our bags.

It was not until 8 o'clock that we set out for the southeast coast of the island which we had seen yesterday from a ridge above the lake in the interior. The entire trip took an hour, and every journey was filled with the strangest impressions. Naturally one really needed longer than this. We would stop again at the gentoo penguins; watch the little pipit (*Anthus antarcticus*) which flitted across our path, because we still did not have a specimen in our collection; and finally spent some time with the albatrosses. We also devoted some time to establishing where the boundary between slates and volcanic rocks lay, since we had determined that it occurred on the island. Once we had walked around the lake and sighted the southeast coast beneath us, a macaroni penguin rookery, almost rectangular in shape, emerged clearly ahead of us on a short, fairly level part of the slope.

One could no longer recognize individual nests in the dense rookery. Life was proceeding at a more moderate pace than during the mating season. One could walk through the rookery of birds, previously so irascible and excited, without receiving any bruises worth mentioning. Once they had got over the excitement caused by the movements of us humans each bird would move to a specific spot. The stir would die down and finally it would become quite peaceful again, with each bird standing on the same few stones which, by habit, had become identified as its special location since nesting time.

We now walked right down onto the rocks and encountered an unusually resistant volcanic rock; only with great effort was I able to knock loose a few chunks with my hammer. As far as it was accessible to us the entire southeast coast revealed the same rock structure.

Down on the rocks we lay under the overhang of a cave; we needed only a little fire to make this cold, rainy day more bearable. But there was no driftwood to be found. The sea was getting rougher than ever before; the wind was lashing the waves so that the sea was a single expanse of spume.

The storm's rage made us think of our tent. Hence we stirred ourselves, although we could not have found another rainproof spot like this cave on the whole island. Heavily laden with rock samples we battled against a howling northwest wind in order to make our way back home.

Apart from the fact that the storm had torn some tent pegs out and given the tent a list, it was at least still standing on the same spot. Inside we were so warm that we sat on our bags practically naked. We were soaked to the skin but left our underwear on since we had both learned that in such wet weather one's body dries wet clothes fastest.

Just as one can get a sick horse back on its feet by a change of diet - barley instead of oats - under certain circumstances, even to the point that one can no longer recognize the animal and thinks that one has seen a miracle, so we filled our eternally stinking primus with petrol, which it digested more readily, instead of paraffin. We were now spared the clouds of smoke which it had emitted previously. Also our clothes dried faster when the primus began radiating tropical heat waves.

The beauties of the day were still running through my head: the snow-white albatrosses; spume and spray over the sea; the little city of macaroni penguins. Or we recalled how we had lain under the rock overhang and lured the cunning white sheathbills with their crafty faces by imitating a short "Rue-rue," from a distance of 10 m to within 1 m. The sheathbill certainly has a roguish expression. I will go even farther and say that in the case of many animals the physionomy and the head make us think of then variously, according to the type of life they lead. Hence one can speak of the cunning head of a skua and the roguish head of a sheathbill. I would interpret majesty and purity in the head of an albatross, and I would associate the mediocrity of a bourgeois with that of a gentoo penguin.

It is only 9.00 p.m.; I force myself to crawl out once again to check the tent and the guys. It is a black, impenetrable night around me and the breaking waves are running up to almost within 3 m of our tent. There are many on whom I would wish the experience of such a dark night by these surf-swept rocks. Every human vanity would disperse like the wave crests which are breaking, white and gleaming on the coastal reefs and certainly here many people would find ridiculous and insignificant things which at home they had surrounded with an aurora of glory or holiness.

For my part (and I stress this) I would like to become an elephant seal in another life, lying out there in the surf amidst the gale and the wind. From the point of view of usefulness I could dispense with tent, primus, sleeping bag and all superfluous thoughts. How much more simple and uncomplicated life could be there. I would not have to collect any rock samples or execute sketches with frozen fingers; nothing could make any impression on me.

But from my experiences with the sealers there is one hitch. Assuming that I became an elephant seal bull and not, by chance, a female, I would have to locate my harem of dozens of cows on an inaccessible beach with cliffs towering all round it, or in a quite peaceful, hidden corner such as on the Pickersgill Islands, where no sealers and no rifles ever go. Yes, in that case, it would truly not be a life to be despised.

With reflections such as these, with which not every person would agree, night fell, leading me off into further mental wanderings. I fished for hours on end, just as I had been doing some time ago at Larsen Bay. But now I am back in reality in my sleeping bag, but am still fishing. I distinctly felt a bite - my God, have I gone crazy? Then I woke up and realized that it is the penguins tripping over the guys, giving me the impression in my dreams of pulling in one fish after another.

For the next two days we were tent bound due to the weather, and it was good that we were tied to our immediate surroundings instead of running over the slopes of the island and stalking birds. If the temperature is above freezing, even when it is raining and blowing it is not possible to sit quietly with one's thoughts in the tent for an entire day. Hence we would wander frequently down the little, confined section of beach, which allowed us to walk both east and west. We knew that the tent was handy and hence could risk being soaked in the evening since we could soon crawl into our sleeping bags.

Thus one day was blessed with large numbers of fossils,

especially bivalves, which I carefully hoarded like a precious treasure. Once I had found several specimens I would head into the gentoo penguin rookery and investigate the numerous boulders which lay around it in disorder. Four bull elephant seals barred my way to a slab and I had to drive them off before I could make even the first hammer stroke. When I rubbed away the penguin excrement with sand and tussac grass, little elevations, sinuous tracks and fine series of points appeared on a second slab. No, these were not weathering phenomena but rather the branching patterns of vegetation. Or could these rune-like markings be tracks of worm trails? I was not sure in my own mind, but having easily quarried the heavy slab using hammer and chisel, I took it with me and showed it to Benitz, who was quite wild about it. His scientific knowledge, or rather his imagination, made of these patterns just about anything that struck his imagination: needles, fruits and even insects. But I had to disabuse him of all this and told him that the scientists at home would certainly give this fossil its correct name.

On the second rainy day, on which one would have preferred to be sitting anywhere but in a wet tent, one fossil after another turned up along that same short stretch of coast. It was not as if they were easy to collect. One often had to search painfully for a long time, splitting rocks with the chisel, to the point that one wanted to abandon the whole project when nothing surfaced. But then, as one split open a tough joint a large, well-preserved ammonite would leap out of captivity. Thus one's hammer almost became a magic wand, which could tell of life on long-disappeared areas of the earth which were so different from those of the present.

South Georgia is a little-explored area with regard to fossils and it was a scientifically exciting discovery when in 1911 Felix König found the first ammonite on the island at Possession Bay. Although it did not fix the age of the schists exactly it placed it probably in the Mesozoic in earth history.

Thus rock samples from all over the island, and especially fossils, were useful in solving the major early land connections between South America and the Antarctic continent. Since we knew this we sacrificed many other things on Annenkov Island in favour of fossil hunting, especially since we had begun to have such positive luck in this area.

The monotonous, dreary day passed in these sorts of activities. When the first blisters began to appear on our fingers, we would grab the little Florbert (shotgun) and using the small-bore barrel would get a sheathbill for the collection. Or we would walk along the beach and watch a penguin of this year's brood standing on the beach, presumably waiting for its mother to return home. Whenever a bird emerged from the water one would see the young bird rush up to it in the hope that it was its mother. But if it were not the young bird would realize this immediately and the disappointed, betrayed bird would start complaining so helplessly and forlornly that even God must take pity on it!

Or we might have an opportunity of observing the corpulent rotundity of the elephant seals at this season if we spotted one which had just landed. After sniffing briefly, its head slightly raised, it would head towards some other seals which were lying 60 m from the beach above the penguin rookery. This involved a slight uphill slope and since the seal was so enormously fat it could scarcely make any progress and would stop for long pauses; as a result it took him a full hour to cover the 60 m.

Having taken numerous bearings on the main range of South Georgia I was lying among the bundles of tussac grass above the camp in the first morning light of 9 March. Opposite me the alpine chain from Undine South Bay to Holmestrand and Horten lay clear and pure. The beach beneath me was peaceful and empty. Almost all the penguins had already headed out to sea; only a few juveniles, late-starters or asocial elements were skulking around or standing, apathetic and freezing in the shelter of the tussacs. The white flags of the surf climbed high up a rock stack near our camp.

My eyes were glued to the high ridges of the Paget massif which is so rarely visible. Today we could see that three ridges extended to the southwest, dropping away very steeply, and with the intervening areas filled with ice. Looking over the entire main range one can say in summation that the main massif is characterized by side ridges whose flanks and crests are also more or less covered with ice. Mt Paget and the Sugarloaf appeared from my observation point to be separated by the flat saddle of an ice pass. The most massive ice streams descended between Mt Paget and the Sugarloaf.

An hour later we were again lying by the interior lake; due west above us we could see a saddle. Although, as usual, the main summit of Annenkov Island lay in fog, we still hoped for a clearing and headed steeply uphill to the west over tussac- and moss-slopes. On the steep talus slopes before the pass we determined that schists and volcanic rocks alternated; at the pass itself, at a height of 226 m, my hammer encountered only hard volcanics. But what was the reason for the numerous little fist-sized openings in the loamy soil? A few feathers lay around and we conjectured that the holes were the homes of some bird species. We hence dug out one of the holes which ran back horizontally for 50 cm at the maximum. One of us then inserted a particularly bold hand until it encountered the little, rotund body of a bird clad in its first blue-grey down.

Since we did not know what to do with the little bird we put it back in its burrow, then in order to protect it we walled up the entrance again with stones, piled earth on top and thus imitated the original state of its hiding place in rather a botched fashion.

We were more fortunate at a second hole. We found an adult bird which was still incubating and recognized it as the whalers' king auk [common diving petrel], which we had often been struck by out at sea, especially by its low, rapid flight; initially we had confused them with terns. This bird (*Pelecanoides urinatrix*) was the third species which we had encountered living in burrows on South Georgia (the others being the white-chinned petrel and the dove prion). But while the others locate their burrows in tussac slopes near the coast, the "king auk" lives well above the sea and the coast, preferring heights of almost 230 m, i.e. quite a respectable height for such a small bird. But it is amazing how this beautiful little bird of the twilight can find its little burrow entrance in the earthy slopes of Annenkov in the twilight hours.

On our way home we were given further evidence of the predatory handiwork of the skua. On a sandy stretch of beach dropping steeply to the interior lake the ground was thickly strewn with little feathers and skeletal remains. Practically fresh portions of bird carcasses also lay around, while delicate little bones lay along the entire stretch of shoreline. A good 200 skuas cruised above us. We could deduce from the bluish remains of plumage that the remains in this bird cemetery were those of the dove prion, which does not leave its nest until dusk. At that time one can see the skuas circling in vigorous, excited flight over the slopes where the nests are located.

Next day, 10 March revealed the first young albatross as we again squatted by the albatross nests. It was a greyish-white little thing, lying weak and helpless beneath its mother. We next visited other nests, approaching each of the great birds carefully from behind to avoid any blows from its bill, and lifting it from the nest like a tractable piece of luggage. In some cases a head had already emerged from one of the eggs. Others again displayed cracks and one could see convulsive movements within the now-cramped quarters. This was an ideal natural setting in which to capture all the phases with the camera.

Almost the entire day was spent at this task. Benitz had to wait for brief, meagre glimmers of sun in order to make his pictures more striking and more graphic. It seemed like an eternity of waiting. The next day and the day after that we spent hours at the nests.

The story of "plenty of albatrosses" on Annenkov Island and South Georgia disseminated by the whalers and sealers, is a major exaggeration. On Annenkov only one slope on the northeast side is occupied by them; it drops at an angle of 10° to the northeast and east. If one were to begin counting nests in the field one would not find more than 30 to 40 even if one stood on a point with an all-encompassing view.

Hence on behalf of the king of the avifauna of the South Seas I would once again make the plea that it should be protected and that eggs and young should be spared. There are vast fish resources in practically every bay; hence there is no need to exploit the albatrosses. I would ask seamen whether they have erased that moment from their sailing-ship days when they first admired the flight of the albatross, and whether they have forgotten the only true companion on their lonely voyages?

The spacing between nests is much less here than I saw on Campbell Island in 1924; commonly it barely exceeds 20–30 m.

On Campbell Island I was repeatedly told by farmers that the incubation period for the royal albatross which nests there and differs only insignificantly from the wandering albatross, is three months. But in making this calculation none of these farmers would have marked the eggs, the only procedure which can incontestably establish this point. We ourselves had many other things to do on South Georgia which we saw to be more important, and also had changed campsites and bays too often to be able to solve this ornithological question. But I can say this much: on 22 December we saw whalers from Prince Olaf Harbour taking eggs from nests on Albatross Island just off Bay of Isles; and on 10 March we saw the first beak of a hatching albatross chick emerging. In terms of climate Albatross and Annenkov islands are barely distinguishable and hence we can establish the incubation period as approximately 2½ months.

During these stormy late-autumn days which sing their song so persistently and reliably over the sub-Antarctic islands, when the waves run high, the clouds race, hurling snow across the landscape, I made an especially unique bird observation. We watched stormy mating scenes among the giant petrels and albatrosses such as I described earlier in my travel book on Campbell Island.

Then I described crazy dances by the excited males as a prelude to mating and I wondered then, when I had seen only what I was describing, whether mating and the preceding rituals might not occur in the southern autumn. Now, having formed similar impressions on South Georgia and Annenkov Island, and especially after consultation with the Swiss ornithologist Dr. Noll-Tobler I suspect that it is last year's not-yet-sexually-mature juveniles which are engaged in practice exercises in order to prepare themselves for the real thing. A sort of awakening puberty, which could scarcely lead to success, even although we did observe birds in copulation positions.

The entire performance proceeded in unusually stormy fashion, and among the giant petrels we observed birds billing and behaving as if the nesting season were beginning. But when the snowstorms sweep across the little island in the next few days, this late-autumn idyll will vanish and the young albatrosses and giant petrels will have to wait another winter before they will be seriously accepted among the ranks of the adults.

When we reached our tent on the evening of 12 March it was snowing and a strong southwesterly was blowing. We are lying in the lee and can only guess at the strength of the wind from the fact that the tussac grass nearby is being lashed about, and that we can hear the moaning of the wind as it buffets the tent. There are no waves on the sea in front of us since near the coast it is in the shelter of the island, and hence it would be a good opportunity to land in a dinghy. But since night was falling we did not need to keep a lookout for a ship, although by arrangement it should arrive almost any day.

From now on we could not leave our little stretch of beach; we were constantly gazing out over the row of reefs which extends from the northeast coast of Annenkov to the east side of Jacobsen Bight, to see whether we can spot a ship.

But during these last days which chained us to the vicinity of camp we managed to greatly augment our fossil collection; it now consisted of a good 250 fossiliferous samples. Apart from very many molluscs and well-preserved ammonites we found pieces of wood and remains of a fish. According to Professor Dr. Otto Wilckens, one slab of schist brought from Annenkov displayed worm casts and tunnel casts.

Everything superfluous was now removed from our boxes and the pieces were carefully packed. Once we had exhausted our newspaper we took dried tussac leaves and old shirts and stockings and used them to pack the rocks, to keep them undamaged and ready for transport.

On the morning of 14 March we saw a ship heading towards us. We knew that it was *Diaz* coming to pick us up and take us back to Grytviken. In our initial excitement we packed in a few minutes what would have taken us an hour under normal, leisurely circumstances. The last rocks were quickly stowed and in that first rush some were even stuck into our trouser pockets. But when, in a moment of reflection, we looked at that rough sea, our zeal abated again since it appeared impossible that a dinghy could reach land intact today.

Diaz dropped anchor about 300 m off the rocks and we could see her bow rising and falling in the heavy seas. She was lying deep in the water and we guessed that she had the blubber of numerous seals on board.

Noon came, and we were still sitting on our boxes, like

emigrants waiting on some remote coast for the sailing ship which is to take them to the Promised Land. Afternoon came and in the meantime we had resumed our activities just as if this were like any other day. I continued my search for fossils but did not find any more.

Light rain forced us to retreat to the tent which we had left standing, since we no longer believed that we would be picked up today. Not just right away, we thought. Spending another week on this little island was not part of our plans. Perhaps we told ourselves this just to be able to pass the hours more composedly. We ate the last of our very mouldy bread and drank strong coffee, as once again we gazed through the glasses at the "Flying Dutchman" just offshore. She seemed now to be riding the seas more quietly; also two reefs which flanked the narrow entrance to our landing site were submerged by the waves more regularly.

Weren't those men we could see on the fo'c's'lehead, busy with something? Then a dinghy was lowered into the water and we were sure that Captain Johannesson was about to have us picked up.

It was an exciting sight as we watched the dinghy, heaved upwards by the heavy seas, approaching our beach through the narrow cleft in the rocks. I wondered if it was all going to turn out safely as a breaker swung the boat off course, until the oarsmen suddenly dug in with their full strength and a pursuing sea hurled the boat up the beach.

Our abundant haul of specimens and the rough seas forced us to make two boat trips. Benitz went off first with the boatman and all our things; we others stood around on shore and were only truly happy when we too were aboard ship, had emptied our pockets and had stowed everything away; fossils, plankton hauls, bird skins and our own tired bodies.

Our homeward route was via Jossac Bight and Jacobsen Bight; en route we took several dozen more elephant seals. We reached Grytviken on the early morning of 16 March.

20

Around the Entire Island with the Sealers Again

On board the sealing ship all life appeared to be extinguished as I finally clambered over the rail shortly before midnight with my sea bag on my back. It was Easter Sunday, 31 March. The mountains around Grytviken lay like long, black crouching bodies above the sea. Although there were stars in the sky, which was furrowed by a föhn wind, the night was black and dense so that, following the little, narrow pathways it had been difficult to find the right ship.

Finally I was standing in front of a row of masts and bridges and clambered over three vessels. But it was still not the sealing ship *Diaz*. I discovered her only when the stench of old seal blubber assailed my nose.

Now I knew my way. I squeezed my sea bag and myself down a little chicken ladder and was again standing in the little saloon with the paraffin lamp and the benches around the oval table. I had been told that we were to put to sea at 5.00 a.m.

But apart from the captain there was nobody on board on the evening of 31 March. Nobody spends a holiday in his cramped cabin or in the fo'c's'le when there is a film showing on shore and when the sailing ship *Tijuca* has just arrived from Buenos Aires. An old friendship here; a glass of wine there; here some news; there a game of cards – this is how the night is spent. The ship will be rolling out at sea tomorrow; not till tomorrow does one have to think of the fact that the waves are the seaman's bride. Tomorrow is time enough to be moving around among blubber and filth; time enough to drink the thin shipboard coffee and to know that the old man controls one's life. But as the end of this holiday period occurred with the first light of dawn there was a tough contrast as the men made the transition directly to the start of their first watch on board.

By 7 o'clock we were already heading along the north coast past Fortuna Bay. I had already spotted from out at sea three small hanging glaciers between Stromness and Fortuna bays, one of which reached the sea.

On this circumnavigation I had to stand watch, be my own statistician, recording all the ice and glaciers I saw as well as augmenting or correcting much that I had seen before.

Just as the sealers never really understood why ice could interest me so much, it will be a matter of indifference to most readers as to how many of the island's glaciers reach the sea and where this occurs. Hence to spare the reader having to leaf over a large number of pages I have recorded my major results in a map at the end of the book. Those few who are interested in the present glacier cover of the island will there be able to see in one place what I saw and recorded.

Here and there minor errors may have crept in, especially in places where visibility was poor and there was no chance of a landing. But since there was no previous map of ice distribution on the island it seemed important to me to compile the first draft of such a map.

As I have briefly pointed out elsewhere a common feature of South Georgia is small, rounded, off-lying "holms" or skerries, which one finds in many bays and off unindented stretches of coast. Thus off the mouth of Cumberland Bay lies a rounded reef, right past which even deeply laden ships may steam; Stromness Bay possesses an identical feature. And indeed the Welcome Islands are basically nothing more than a series of such skerries. Especially on the southwest coast innumerable rounded, exposed reefs may be observed, almost none of which were marked on previous charts of South Georgia. One bay, Holmestrand, in memory of the Norwegian connection has even been named for the rounded little islands which protect or bar its entrance.

On the British map of 1920, which was at our disposal, there was a major error on the stretch of coast between Cape Buller and Elsehul in that only Right Whale Bay was marked, whereas in reality two bays bite into this section of coast. This is well known by the whalers and sealers, who in a very natural fashion have introduced two names for the two bays, namely Right Whale Bay and 'Welcome Bay'.

By 12 noon we were in well-known territory and had entered Elsehul. The slopes on which the gentoo penguin rookery had previously set up house lay before us, totally snow free in the matt green of late summer. Only a few birds now stood around on the beach. When one thought back to the frenzied life of November one would almost think it was a different place. And elephant seals? For it was they which the sealers hoped to harvest. In October there had almost always been 20 animals lying around, but today, after much searching, we could find only a single bull lying behind a rock, as motionless as the rock. But a single elephant seal was not enough.

Johannesson took the helm again and the engine began to turn over slowly. *Diaz* swung out of Elsehul in an elegant curve while I and five sealers walked across the narrow isthmus to Undine Harbour on the opposite coast where the ship was to meet us again after running through Bird Sound, which today was calm.

"See if you can find anything over there," Johannesson shouted after us. "Usually one can't expect to find anything in the bays on the west coast at this time of year."

I should now like to add something about the time aspects and legal aspects of sealing on South Georgia. On the island sealing involves only one species, namely the elephant seal, the only seal species whose stocks at the moment are in a satisfactory state. Early reports indicate that formerly South Georgia's coasts sheltered vast numbers of fur seals (*Arctocephalus tropicalis gazella*) but that in earlier decades the Americans pursued a ruthless butchery so that now it is a rare event to see a fur seal. During the entire period of our expedition we saw only a single fur seal, in Coal Harbour in October. It is easily recognizable by obvious, although quite stunted, rudimentary ears. It may be distinguished from the sea lion, which is not known on South Georgia, by its smaller size and by a fuller, darker pelt. In contrast to the elephant seals, which are classified among the true seals, eared seals have longer flippers and are much more mobile on land, where they spend a much larger portion of the year than the elephant seals.

Another seal species, the leopard seal (*Hydrurga leptonyx*) has already become quite rare on South Georgia; moreover, due to its insignificant layer of blubber it barely enters the picture in terms of the sealing industry.

In addition one should add to this rough classification the fact that an Antarctic seal, namely the Weddell seal, is occasionally encountered on South Georgia. A small herd annually frequents in particular the quiet waters of Larsen Harbour, the side-bay off Drygalski Fiord. It was here, through the good offices of Captain Johannesson that the female and two pups were collected which I was able to bring home for the Senckenberg Museum.

The Compañia Argentina de Pesca, the only whaling company operating on South Georgia, is awarded the right to kill elephant seals by the British Government. In a clever and calculating fashion the monopoly extends for only one sealing season at a time, stretching from 1 March to 1 November. But in terms of productive sealing it is mainly the period from 15 September to 1 November which is relevant. During this period the animals congregate in vast numbers to mate, especially in bays which possess a wide beach and are backed by tussac grass slopes. The seals assemble in herds and are blind to any danger from humans during mating and during the battles for females, and hence sealing is easy and profitable. One may observe that during this period rifle shots will not disrupt the circle of bulls which crowds around a harem of females, as long as the old bull of the harem has first been shot by the sealers. Even while the old bull, the owner of the numerous females, is being bloodily flensed by the sealers the other bulls will approach the females and, in so doing, the sealers with their rifles. They blunder towards danger. The scent of females is stronger in their nostrils than the smell of powder, for which they have no fear during this period of arousal.

Blow follows blow; shot follows shot; it is a magnificent time for the sealers; everything is perfect. Diligently they whet their knives; it is a happy, cheerful time, this autumn seal hunt. No unnecessary walking; all this wealth of seals is concentrated together. It is a delight to be a sealer. When the dollars are dancing in front of one's eyes, who can be sensitive enough to think of the fact that animals are dying, one after the other, soaking the sand with their blood!

Only the females are protected during the seal hunt. They are respected not out of courtesy or maudlin sentimentality but because they profitably sustain the species and are protected by law. The females watch the slaughter around them, and suffer as a result. And if somebody says that this is not so, then he has never looked into the distorted features of these animals, with horror staring from their eyes. Has never watched as their ranks start up in fear, as if the men approaching them were the most terrible thing that an elephant seal cow could conceive of in this life and this environment.

One has to thank the British government for the fact that females are protected. There was a time on the island when the elephant seal was subject to unrestricted killing, to the point where it became rare. From the reports of the German South Georgia Expedition of 1882–83 it is clear that at Royal Bay, which is now well populated by elephant seals, the species was then extremely rare.

During our present voyage in the southern autumn the seal hunt represented nothing more than a gleaning operation. We could not expect herds or masses of seals. Rather it involved the killing of individuals, since the animals were now alternating between land and sea and went ashore only on calm, sunny days and lay around singly. Moreover, to make sealing inconvenient and time-consuming they preferred to wander inland. They might lie hundreds of metres from the beach and thus gave the sealers many tedious hours. One would rather drive a stubborn donkey several miles across dry grassland than a fat elephant seal 400 m from its basking site to the beach.

Following this interjection let us wander from Elsehul to Undine Harbour. It is only a few minutes' walk. One has scarcely lost sight of the ocean on the north side when it appears again on the other side. One hikes across tussac grass and cushions of moss as if on a resilient, soft carpet, until the wide beach appears ahead. This is the beach which in November, at the end of the southern winter, had presented such a lively and alluring panorama of animal life.

Today we first encountered a few hundred gentoo penguins. They stood around looking bored; they no longer had a densely packed rookery, jammed with young birds and nests. It is a matter of indifference to them as to where they stand around during these last weeks before their great sea journey, i.e. whether it is in Elsehul, which was their home previously, or Undine Harbour.

I collected some rock samples and filled my pockets with them, and then examined a beach terrace 40–50 m from the beach and 2 m above present high tide mark; finally I was gazing at the white points on the slopes which represented albatrosses guarding their young when I was startled by a shot which struck about 100 m from me.

No, I am not sentimental. I do not equate sealing with animal torture as many do, but at that moment I started and felt myself hating all these fine lads who were just doing their job, and have to earn their bread in a tougher fashion than many others. What went through my mind was: Could this be the end of the Pasha, the capitalist with the 50 females he possessed in October? Could it be he who is staining the water red over there? The animal who helped us to bear our loneliness, who delighted us and whom we were forced to like with his autocratic manner and his boundless animal egotism, even when his great fat belly was humping over the little calves in order to repel an opponent.

At that moment a succession of thoughts went through my mind as to what this beach had meant to us in the autumn when we had lain in wait in a snowstorm and had eaten a meal over there behind the tussac grass hummocks in order to witness more of the life and love-making of these animals.

But one thing was still the same as then. The first shot had barely struck home when we saw skuas closing in, in ever decreasing circles. Even while the knives were still stripping the blubber from the seal they settled on the fresh, steaming carcass, just as greedy and quarrelsome as before, despite the fact that ten shots rang out that noontime providing ten carcasses with vast amounts of meat, enough for every skua on the west end of the island.

At 3 o'clock we continued our way eastwards towards Schlieper Bay. The coast from Coal Harbour to Schlieper Bay is free of glaciers and characterized by steep cliffs and stacks, off which lie greater or lesser numbers of reefs. Without any snow cover this coastal landscape, with its predominantly dark colours, makes a stern, repugnant impact, so that one's gaze turns repeatedly to the sea, especially since the summits themselves are hidden by cloud.

Twilight was falling and one could still just make out that in Schlieper Bay, where the men were still diligently and successfully pursuing elephant seals, two glaciers adorned both the eastern and western sides of a valley and still reached the valley bottom. That they were retreating at present was betrayed by the numerous moraine ridges in front of them. Although it was already almost completely dark a lucky blow with my hammer revealed a fossilized piece of wood, and to conclude an eventful day I stowed it away carefully.

Today is the evening of Easter Monday. It was not a holiday for us and the day's work had made the men tired. There was no sound to be heard from the fo'c's'le as I walked across the deck in the early hours of the night. An iceberg lay off the entrance to Schlieper Bay. As I paced up and down a few times with the skipper he remarked: "As you see Schlieper Bay has been provided with a light beacon which entails no cost and needs no maintenance. Yes, we've been able to rely on that iceberg throughout these past weeks. It sits as steady as a tower and even when the sun has set it still glows for a long time with a pale pink gleam."

Next day it was the turn of Ice Fiord, with its two bays 'Middle Bay' and Miles Bay; it had produced seals on *Diaz*'s last trip. However Narval Bay and the head of Ice Fiord itself were blank spots as far as sealing was concerned, and were not even visited. The coastal scenery was identical to that of yesterday, and was distinguished by stacks and cliffs behind which some snow free summits rose to 300 to 600 m.

During the day we worked from bay to bay. The ship slipped along the coast as if it were alive. Johannesson, our tireless captain, known to the seamen as *jordtramper*, i.e. the earth tramper, is never slow at taking a hand himself in anything that needs to be done, once he has taken stock of the situation from on board ship through the glass. He goes ashore with the men wherever he feels it is necessary, and then one always finds him searching diligently for more animals. He treks up slopes and down, doing a thorough job. Wilson Harbour, which we reached shortly before noon, was productive. Half a dozen elephant seals were lying sleeping at the entrance to a valley, from whose side a compact glacier tumbled, high above the present valley floor, which it did not reach. We crept up on them and they were harvested. An offshore wind, blowing from the northeast and roaring down the valley somewhat moderated the rough sea which a southwest wind had lashed up. Hence the heavy dinghy with a load of eight men was able to reach shore at least reasonably dry. With seven or eight men the work proceeded quickly. One man is the boatman; he is in charge of the boat and of the fate of its occupants, and by evening his muscles are aching from the heavy loads of pelts which he must haul aboard alone through the heavy surf. One man is the boss; he is *Diaz*'s mate. He carries the rifle and does the shooting. Two or three men, depending on requirements, carry all the accoutrements, namely curved flensing knives with long handles. They pull the blubber off over the animal's head in an instant, once it has been cut free. The rest of the gang drive the animals to the beach once they have been discovered.

Once everything is finished and there are a dozen bloody carcasses lying on the beach, previously so peaceful, with its undisturbed environment, everyone sets to in order to secure the load of pelts to lines which the boatman in the interim has led ashore from the boat. Everyone is in a hurry now; if it is snowing everyone is freezing and is longing for hot coffee or a hot meal once evening arrives. During the entire operation one hears no loud orders; everything has been drilled into these men. Every procedure is always the same even if there are eight pairs of hands at work, hence all the men and their activities are controlled by a single invisible will.

The really lively activity precedes the shots. One can hear the excited roaring of the animals as they are driven on their helpless trek from their concealed resting places to the beach. Only when they are just a few metres from the sea are the first shots heard, and by this one knows that they have not reached the sea. For these fat, unwieldy animals discovery and death are synonymous. On our entire trip around the island I did not see a single one escape. They are guided by the men who chivvy them along, hitting them on the head

Around the Entire Island with the Sealers Again · 249

and the nose with springy metal rods, thereby controlling their direction and speeding up their last journey.

But what role would I choose from this multi-facetted operation if the threads of fate had dictated that I be a sealer? By choice I would be the boatman, even if it involves strained muscles, and even if the difficult landings are nothing to laugh about. Recently, if the sealing beach is too far from the ship a little motorboat has been used. Then he has to rely on his muscles and experience only for rowing a few boat's lengths and for the landing itself, which can be difficult and dangerous enough. The boatman remains isolated from the entire operation and is only the go-between between the sealing ship and the beach. He is impartial to the highest degree and perhaps, emotionally, may even lean towards the seals.

I would have no desire to be one of the men who spot and drive the seals, since it is mind-numbing work, and I would feel sorry for the animals, which I would have to drive to their certain fate, heading in the direction which they themselves prefer, i.e. towards the water and freedom.

Flensing would be the last job in the world I would want, although I could handle the honourable job of butchering at home. I would also readily decline the job of beach-boss even if every shot meant a few kroner to me.

In summary, then, I would say of sealing, i.e. hunting elephant seals, that it is not an entertaining spectacle for animal lovers. Nobody wants to belittle the contribution of the sealing gang who do a difficult job, but neither should one cloak his or her profession in exaggerated romanticism.

But one must have respect for these fellows because a major portion of their lives is spent on the tough, stormy islands of the south in isolation, and on risky voyages, and above all because almost every landing represents an achievement of the seaman's art. One must always be amazed that usually everything turns out well, when one thinks that there are often breakers crashing over the reefs and that often only a narrow, seething passage leads between them to the strip of beach which is the goal. Of how the men have to leap hip-deep into the water, and of how they get their boat off again through the swirling eddies and the chaos of a rough sea. It often happens that a landing is possible and is safely accomplished and the men reach terra firma; but then the weather may change, the sea may rise, and they cannot get off the shore again. They have to tramp the peat for hours or even the entire night, while their warm, well-lit ship is constantly in sight, trying in vain to retrieve its sealing crew.

One is also delighted at the good relationship between all the men; their comradeship, matured by the common danger, their unity in every situation, and their mutual, unconditional sacrifice, are admirable.

Perhaps discordant relations may prevail elsewhere among sealers but on our round-trip and whenever I encountered sealers I was struck by their genuine cohesiveness. Theirs is an international society in the best sense: Germans, Russians, Norwegians, Swedes, Italians and Spaniards, *Diaz*'s crew was composed of men of all these nationalities. Yet every one of them swore by his native land and loved it even if it were small and disrupted, and had been inaccessible to him for many years.

But if one asked an individual how he liked sealing he would invariably say: "It is a terrible life." As with whaling some even said that it represented cruelty to animals.

Before I left Grytviken I was told: "You will see terrible things and frightful cruelty to animals." But if one wishes to pass a true and fair verdict the term "cruelty to animals" is totally inappropriate. No other hunt ensures that the animal will be killed as inevitably as the elephant seal hunt. The animal dies instantaneously; it drops at the very moment that it is hit by the explosive rifle bullet. During the entire trip I did not see a single miss. It is the almost effortless nature of the hunt and the guaranteed shot which not even a child could miss that strip away any romanticism. Ultimately it is a slaughtering operation, just as one would find in an abattoir.

Only if one is among those sensitive people who decry any killing of animals for man's purposes could one describe it as cruelty to animals.

Another criticism which one hears is: "Even before the animals are dead the flensers begin their work on the still-twitching body." The carcasses do indeed twitch, but these are simply muscle contractions after death, misinterpreted by the layman.

The entire process is so sober, so well organized, so efficient, without any delays, that one cannot talk of animal cruelty with regard to modern sealing, at least not with regard to the final acts of shooting and flensing.

As we passed Cape Demidov we spotted some albatross nests on the grassy hills and Johannesson told me that one could find isolated nests of both the wandering albatross and of the grey-headed albatross (*Diomedea chrysostoma*) on many grassy hills on the island. The latter prefers especially steep tussac slopes, on which its nests lie closely spaced. In contrast to the larger wandering albatross, it does not need a gradient for take-off. We also saw some nests in Elsehul and observed young birds making their first attempts at flying from little breaks in the slope. The birds would simply allow themselves to drop from a higher step to a lower one.

Once we had finished in Wilson Harbour, before running into King Haakon Bay we swung into a bay which is unnamed on the map, but to which the sealers have given the name Elephant Cove. It is distinguished by three hanging glaciers separated by rock ridges.

Even when we landed in the cove and collected rock samples we found no reason to change the name of this cove, which certainly had never been visited by scientists previously. Even if there were no adult elephant seals to be seen today but just calves, and although the name had been bestowed at the height of the sealing period, on other occasions this bay must again be full of seals, again justifying its name.

I am repeatedly amazed at how quickly our ship's crew can operate. It's as if our captain remembers every rock behind which an elephant seal can hide. Hence we are often swinging back out of little bays and corners before other mortals could have identified a single detail or distinguished a single seal from the rocks.

We spent the evening in King Haakon Bay, with the western sky glowing red. Even if it were grey and expressionless one could not imagine a single bay on earth which displays such a terrifying remoteness as King Haakon Bay. We were lying at a good anchorage in a depth of about 33 m.

To north and south we were surrounded by an almost unbroken crown of glaciers with steep ice cliffs. Even although there are ice-free areas at lower elevations between the ice cliffs, this bay with its five glaciers on the north side and four on the south side, is one of the most heavily glaciated on South Georgia. It is difficult to establish the number of glaciers since one can increase or decrease one's total depending on whether one wishes to lump certain ones together or treat them as separate glaciers. Thus in one bay, on the side of which we landed, and which has recently been named 'Long Beach Bay', three glaciers descend steeply, reaching the sea in vertical ice cliffs. They are separated by rock ridges and Johannesson suggested that they are only two. He would not count one of them because it was smaller than the others and squeezed down through a narrow valley. On the south side of King Haakon Bay one can identify four glaciers if, like Johannesson, one discounts the innermost one because it lacks a steep front.

Whist represents part of the evening life of a sealer, once things have fallen quiet. It provides some tension, luck and chance, just like the day's hunt. On rest-days, too, a chess-board is in demand, while there are some books lying above my sleeping bench. Among them I found Brehm's *Tier- und Vogelleben* [Lives of birds and animals] and Gunnar Andersson's *China und seine Kultur* [China and its culture]. I am amazed at the good taste.

But activities on board do not last long into the night. One of the first to retire is the mate, who fired many shots today and has just finished cleaning his rifle. He fills his pipe for the last time and disappears into a blank wall by pushing open a little sliding door. Above my sleeping bench there is an identical niche for the cook, who doubles as the steward. He disappears somewhat later, and once he has stowed himself away it is my turn. No preparations are necessary; one keeps one's clothes on if they are dry. Since the cold creeps through the walls towards morning I also wriggle into a thin silk sleeping bag, in order to retain my body heat better. Then, with my tired body accommodated as well as possible on the narrow, curved bench, the last melody of the day that I hear is the gnawing of the rats, who lead a peaceful and sheltered life above the ceiling of our cramped quarters. We have probably angered and annoyed them today by sticking pencils through little holes into their nest, the straw of which is visible through the holes. It was just too tempting. But in return we have to listen patiently to their activities every night; finally we set a trap in the little cupboard behind the sleeping bench. But even if we catch one every day this will not reduce their population at all.

Every morning, including the morning of 3 April in King Haakon Bay, the men in our sleeping quarters came to life according to a definite schedule. No matter how free the life of a sealer and how lenient all the procedures, in its noiseless punctuality the entire proceedings reminded me of life in barracks. Naturally this applied only on days when it was good sealing weather and everything had to proceed according to chapter and verse.

A few minutes after 5 o'clock, an early hour in the autumn in southern latitudes, the watch-keeper comes below and I hear him shout to the steward: "Sverre, it is 5.15!" This means that there is no more lolling about, even if one is tired and would like to sleep a little longer. The benches we are sleeping on are needed as seats.

If I sleep through the watch-keeper's first wake-up call and continue slumbering, which is a rare event, the steward, as he clambers out of the sliding door of his bunk, befuddled with sleep, will step on my posterior in the most amiable fashion, and then I know for sure that it is time to get up. Thus on this sealing voyage I developed a virtue born of necessity: I became an early riser and hence was always one of the first sitting at the shield-shaped table. The ghostlike, dexterous steward would conjure the first breakfast onto the table as quick as lightning. It consisted of milk-soup or porridge, bread and butter, or rather margarine. The crew's menu and that of the captain were identical at this and every other meal of the day. Everything was cooked in one pot, a practise which has a levelling and conciliating effect aboard sealing and whaling ships since even in the matter of filling their bellies the men recognize a fair equality and consider this desirable. Before the others have crawled out of their bunks I give the steward, who is keenly eager to learn new things, some instruction in German; he would hurl a few faultlessly pronounced sentences at me. Two of these I remember particularly well. He would ask: "Heiszt es nicht Eisbein mit Sauerkraut?" [Isn't this pigs' knuckles with sauerkraut?"], or "Komm, mein Schatz, wir wollen ein Likör trinken" [Come, my dear, we would like a liqueur]".

When the weather was good and hence we had no time to sit lollygagging on the benches, the first breakfast would soon be over. The men would be in a restless mood.

Thus early on the morning of 3 April the anchor chain clanked up through the hawsehole, although the weather was still uncertain. It began blowing; the mountains lay shrouded in clouds and fog and the glacier snouts were visible only as steep, grey walls.

But the weather was good enough for sealing in King Haakon Bay. We put in at four spots on the north coast, one after the other and even the reefs at the entrance to the bay were checked but the yield was a meagre one.

Only one spot, between the third and fourth glacier on the north side, if one counts the sequence of glaciers from the west, yielded eight fat animals which had difficulty in making rapid progress. Among them there were stubborn animals which – to my delight if I am honest –, despite the metal rods being wielded constantly, persistently tried to flee inland to escape instead of making for the beach. But on the other hand the persistence and patience of the drivers was even more admirable so that ultimately, after much chivvying, the seals ended up where the men wanted.

At the landing place near which this operation was proceeding, a till exposure was revealed right on the beach such as I had never seen before: it contained horizontally bedded rounded rocks. Only the lower part, about 3 m thick, displayed this stratification.

On the east side of the nearby glacier cliff a torrential, turgid, milky stream emerged a little distance inland; shortly before it reached the sea it widened into a lake where year-old elephant seals were lying and playing. As unsuspecting as if they were in a peaceful little zoo, they paid no attention to the shouts and commotion of the men as they drove the mature animals to the beach. Shots rang out but they continued their games; even when we waded through the shallow lake and had to pass quite close to them, only our strange scent interrupted them somewhat, but then they continued to spend the morning in their usual, carefree fashion.

Massive, rounded boulders with many striations lay beside the stream; along with some beautiful roches moutonnées, these indicated that the glacier had once been much wider. Just as in its upper part where the glacier now merges in an unbroken continuum with the adjacent glaciers, once all the glaciers in King Haakon Bay were contiguous right down to their snouts as well.

Shortly after noon we were in Queen Maud Bay; only

one small bay on the north side, which displayed a hanging glacier, permitted me to land. It yielded some more elephant seals but it was not a happy situation to have to hunt out one animal here and another there, without seeing the hold filling perceptibly. Heavy rain made the entire proceedings even more dreary; heavy surf frustrated any attempt at visiting any other sites in Queen Maud Bay and hence we swung in past a stranded iceberg, heading for Cape Nuñez, in order to try our luck on the southwest coast. We landed in a small bay just before Holmestrand and had another hour's sealing. This brought the final, satisfactory success of the day, namely a dozen elephant seals; thereafter, with night falling rapidly, at 7 o'clock the captain took his ship into Holmestrand itself with amazing sureness and audacity. The entrance was barred by rounded, monster-like reefs up which the surf reared before losing itself impotently in the bay itself. We found a safe holding ground in a depth of 18 m with a loamy bottom and protected from west and southwest winds.

The steep, awe-inspiring ice-cliff of the great Esmark Glacier was restless all night long; quite close to the ice cliff we could see a black rock mass which the captain pointed out as being the most natural leading mark for the run through the skerries.

But Holmestrand has one disadvantage. If the wind is onshore the ship is soon blockaded by ice and the night can become unpleasant and dangerous if at the same time heavy seas penetrate into the bay, exposing a ship to the risk of being beset or nipped.

The early morning of 4 April began with engine trouble, just when we had left the bay. Something was not quite right and we could not achieve top speed; since we had to turn back we were detained in the bay until 10 o'clock. Then we set a course for Annenkov Island and while the sealers swore by the island's individual little bays where there were always some elephant seals to be found, I was delighted to be getting back so soon to the island which had provided our geological collection with such an abundance of fossils. But our work was completed by soon after 3 o'clock. It was a poor sealing day although the sea played no nasty tricks on us during the landing; we were able to land at three points on the row of reefs which connects Annenkov with the main island – a very rare event.

But the haul was only eight seals from four different landings with all the tedious effort which this implies. Hence the day certainly did not make much of an impression on the men. When it is getting so close to the end of the sealing season numbers like this are not very encouraging. When one considers the muscular effort involved the few øre which a man earns in this fashion are hardly won.

With regard to fossils, I too returned on board with empty pockets and could have left at home the little box which I took with me with such great expectations. The only thing I determined was that both rock types, slate and a volcanic rock, occurred in juxtaposition at the three points on the row of rocky islands at which the sealers landed. These rocks were 40 m high.

When we dropped anchor in Undine South Harbour that same evening our ship, which can hold a good 250 elephant seals and which until now had harvested that number every week, was not even half-filled; her bow still towered elegantly out of the water. There was none of the festive mood which follows a successful day. Sitting protected in the little, overheated mess and yet sensing the seamen's unrest, I had the feeling of belonging, a feeling which made me feel at home in this little circle even if I was sailing around the island in pursuit of totally different objectives and aims. As the men around me told stories of things they had experienced together, of adventures at sea and on land and spasmodically, in the intervals, thought of home, of girlfriends, wives, children, or even perhaps of a loose woman who had given one or other of them a fine memory prior to sailing, the world of the men with whom I was living began to be revealed to me.

If I wanted to be entirely frank with myself I would often tell myself that if I had not avoided this or that pitfall in life through the influence of friends or due to accident or circumstances, I might have fled from school and an irritable teacher prematurely, and hence might also have become a sealer, pursuing elephant seals amidst a peculiar mixture of adventure and unrest. Or I might be pursuing the whale, standing behind a harpoon gun and aiming at a whale's back, just as I now take bearings on mountains.

Don't believe that it is only bad types who are involved in whaling or sealing, as simple seamen or flensers! One encounters students who rejected the *Anschluss* or Russians who have been driven out by the new regime.

Work and blubber make everyone equal here. This is communism controlled by life's destiny, a communism which is eternal and will always exist.

We also have a German on board: he is a Saxon, 27 years of age. He has been away from home for four years having left home penniless; he did not even have enough to get his shoes soled. Previously he had been a naval cadet. This is a profession which is not of much help to one in the outside world. Then he became a carpenter, locksmith, saddler and seaman; it is good to get some knowledge of many professions. With all these skills, in the acquisition of which the naval cadet had become submerged, he landed up in Montevideo. After one day he got a permanent job. He might still have had it today if his blood had not been so restless. But a Saxon and restless blood make a dangerous combination. He wandered from Montevideo to Buenos Aires playing the accordion, giving a spirited performance in exchange for food and lodging, and had then worked on farms in Argentina, a life which was to his liking. One didn't earn much but it was a fine, free life.

Since he was so free with details about his life I asked him whether he would go back home once the sealing season was over. Yes, he had a 68-year-old mother who was always writing to him, and for that reason alone he would head for home. Otherwise it was immaterial to him whether he was in Australia with the Bushmen, or in New Guinea.

Finally he asked me what I thought of the Amazon, with a view to learning something from me for planning his life. Up till now he had saved 10,000 marks, which was quite impressive for four years. No, sealing was not the worst thing in the world. Next day he brought me some socialist newspapers but his travels and his experiences had divorced him from that party. It was all fine and good on paper, but the reality of the world looked completely different.

The mate, Nordland, seemed to me a contrast to this restless German, who suppressed nothing and wore his heart on his tongue. They called him Nordland because he came from Norway's Norrland; as far as I am concerned his name may have been Jörgensen or Hansen. What had driven him from his beautiful home? Wasn't he homesick, like me, for the long summer nights of the North? Or for his girlfriend by the fiord?

"A girl here or a girl there, a Nordic girl, is fine, but first I have to have some money, then I'll get the girl I want. Whether I go to the spring fishery in Norrland or Finnmarken or come here sealing, the work is almost the same; both there and here one is on the sea. And I want to be where I can earn most. Then the girl will come automatically."

He was the marksman aboard the sealing ship, a goodhearted lad of twenty-five, somewhat dreamy and heavy like all Nordlanders, with many dark melodies and emotions in his heart despite the realistic views about women which he proclaimed to the world. Yet at 25, as the steward assured me, he had not looked any girl in the eye.

Thus I could take any one of these men and needed only to write down his words in order to have an eventful, varied life on paper. One of the men at the table with us possessed the restlessness and mannerisms of Per Gynt. Although he was approaching 60 he was still not content and never would be. He had lived for 10 years in tropical lands, in the West Indies, the Gold Coast and China. Here in this healthy, cold climate he hoped to cure his malaria, his blackwater fever and also to restore his moneybag. Previously it had been bulging but now one could lift it with one's little finger. He told me proudly of his beautiful racehorses and of the magnificence of his former mansion.

All that was now gone. But apart from the skipper he was the most diligent when it came to the seal harvest. But his mood varied with the number of elephant seal pelts which were daily brought aboard. This made him as restless and nervous as the owner of stocks, who twice daily checks the columns and is in a good or bad mood depending on the rate of exchange.

I will wind up my profiles with that of our cook. He began as a stoker on a whaling ship, after he had been expelled from home. There he had done everything a man can do between the ages of 20 and 40. One day, as a champion skater, he was the hero of the hour; next day a book dealer, travelling salesman, manufacturer and merchant. Now his restlessness was curbed by marriage and by whaling. He now thought more about his wife and children than about seals or his surroundings; his dark eyes came alive when he talked about them, about Helge and little Per. Yes, he was a stranger to his children when he came home every two or three years, and they would look at him suspiciously when he first arrived. But this time it would be easier; he had promised his son a little sailboat and their relationship had become more secure as a result of numerous letters in which he had referred repeatedly to the sailboat. So now, he just wanted to go home; he didn't give a hang for the money; he wanted to be with his family.

That evening a bottle of brandy stood on the table and we all imbibed from it avidly but in moderation, in view of the limited supply, after the cold, wet day. One life story after another unfolded. On this lonely day one felt comfortable among men who were totally unvarnished and who took life just as it came.

On 5 April I was a little late in coming on deck; I became aware that we were again heading northwest. The Russians were sharpening their knives on their steels and were wearing their oilskins. We were soon lying off a bay which bore the name "Rockby" in the sealers' nomenclature. It is the first bay northwest of Undine South Harbour and in its overall shape it resembles Undine South Harbour, but on a much more modest scale.

A landing in Rocky Bay was successful but we were unable to get any seals since they were lying at a spot where the sea was breaking with unusual force.

No boat could have established the connection between the elephant seal hides and the sealing ship. Captain Johannesson suggested that for such situations one should invent some sort of small harpoon which could be fired from ship to shore with the hauling line. Thus one could get access to every corner and could exploit every hiding place of the elephant seals. If a line could be thrown or fired from on board, the connection between the seals and the ship could be established and the difficulties of retrieving them eliminated.

I was glad that on our cruise this technical invention, which must be dear to the heart of every sealer, had not yet been discovered. As a layman one can easily become tired of the constant repetition of hunting and shooting, and with all one's heart one would like to ensure for the animals that vestige of safety which inaccessible locations offer them.

As if we had to take by force at least a few more elephant seals to mark the end of the season, we continued our progress north-westwards along the coast, although everyone would have much preferred it if the ship had turned back and set a course for Grytviken. Any more pelts which might be brought aboard now seemed somehow trivial and not worth the effort.

But no matter how much Captain Johannesson searched successive stretches of coast through his glass for seals, east winds and driving snow set limits to his zeal. Even in the southeastern part of Jacobsen Bight towering seas had been whipped up by more southeasterly winds so that ultimately we had to make for Undine South Harbour.

Here the captain finally got a dozen elephant seals. Here, too, I established the volcanic nature of the rocks and, more by accident, found an almost totally white giant petrel. It had been gorging itself and hence could barely get off the ground and offered an easy shot.

Although under normal circumstances one can lie securely in Undine South Harbour in a depth of 22 m, over the course of the night a strong south wind rose to hurricane force and we had to pay out 110 m of anchor chain. The engines were kept running throughout that dark night to keep us off the nearby coast which, in the driving blizzard, represented the greatest danger to us. Johannesson did not go to bed at all. We others lay at least half asleep and hence did not need to look this dangerous situation straight in the eye. Hence the crew's responsibility is never as great as that of their leader. The men could rest and sleep and that is an important thing.

With the ship's heavy rolling I felt the deficiencies of my narrow sleeping bench more than usual; it made a damnably uncomfortable bed. On nights like this one does not think much of sea voyages and sealing which, indeed, never stood very high in my eyes at any time. During the resultant sleepless hours one simply cannot understand the whole business, and especially not the idea that something like this could happen purely for the sake of money. It seems incomprehensible that one should assault the peace and beauty of nature in an organized hunting operation which ultimately simply fills the coffers of those who sit at home on soft seats, listening to the results of the hunt as they are relayed from this remote coast.

Around the Entire Island with the Sealers Again · 263

But this night passed too, and the anchor chain held; it must be made of good stuff, perhaps Swedish steel, of the same tough sort as the captain himself. Next morning we were up and about an hour earlier than usual since the residual heat of the stove had lasted barely beyond midnight and we were soon freezing, In the early hours there was ice on deck; every water container was frozen and one longed to be away from this terrible place, back to the northeast coast and the fleshpots of Grytviken.

But first we were delayed by a task which lay completely outside the realm of sealing. On one of his recent cruises Johannesson had discovered a new harbour, or more correctly he had rediscovered it.

Although whaling had been pursued on South Georgia since 1904 and sealing for almost as long a time, during the initial period activity had concentrated more on the northeast coast with its sheltered harbours. Initially no sealing occurred on the southwest coast, which was always considered the tougher and more dangerous coast for ship handling simply due to the lack of sheltered bays. As long as there were sufficient seals on the northeast coast there was no reason to exchange an easy locale for a tough one and to opt for the difficult section of coast from Jacobsen Bight to the southeast corner of the island, when it came to sealing.

It was only in the past 2½ years, since Johannesson had taken the helm and had begun repeatedly to sail this inhospitable coast that this southwest coast had become a familiar area. Even though the British charts are erroneous with regard to this area Johannesson could take a pencil and put on paper every bay, every glacier and every reef from memory. On his return to Grytviken from his last sealing cruise he had reported a new bay and had brought back the news that he had found the remains of an old camp there.

The result was that we were charged with calling at the new harbour again; I was to report to Captain Esbensen and to the British authorities about any finds and about the remains of the old camp.

Hence early on the morning of 6 April we ran out of Undine South Harbour and set a southeast course under a cheerless grey sky and with southerly winds. A striking feature along this coast is that stack formation is less marked here, although conspicuous, but low cliffs do rise from the sea in places. But the entire stretch as far as the Novosilski Glacier, indeed right to the southeast corner of the island, is marked by a very heavy glacier cover.

It may have been this that gave rise to Klutschak's less than accurate report of an extensive ice cliff here. The image of an ice cliff is erroneous, however; rather one should think more in terms of an almost continuous glacier cover. But even this is not quite correct, since all the glaciers between Undine South Harbour and the Novosilski Glacier are separated by rock ridges; only in the accumulation areas are these separations missing. Thus, in fact, one gets the impression that the stretch from Undine South Harbour to the Novosilski Glacier and indeed right to the southeast corner of the island is the most heavily glaciated part of the coast of South Georgia.

During our run towards the Novosilski Glacier we passed two glaciers which still descend to the sea and then, as we steamed along quite close to the coast we suddenly spotted a row of rounded reefs. Simultaneously we heard from the helmsman that we were approaching the new bay, which we have named in honour of Captain Johannesson. The bay [Diaz Cove] runs from northwest to southeast and we were able to make an easy landing in the lee of a small island [Kupriyanov Islands]. Behind it the ship lay in a depth of 5.5 m as if in an inland lake, at least on the day when we were there. But one can say in general that the bay is suitable for fairly small vessels, being protected from southwest winds by the skerries which ring it.

On reaching shore, one is surprised by a completely level valley bottom, 100 m wide, which extends for 800 m and is closed off by a hanging glacier, above which tower two rock peaks. First I achieved something important, in terms of something which, one might say, dropped right into my arms. I caught by hand an almost black giant petrel which was running around the beach. Then, using dynamite, I procured some good specimens of a hard, volcanic rock which contained abundant showings of pyrites. Then finally I concentrated on the matter of the former camp, as I had promised.

One had to look very closely to identify the little rectangle which people had once inhabited. But one could still see the beams of the wretched dwelling and by digging and shovelling we discovered the remains of a stove and also of an open fireplace. From the numerous bird bones and egg shells which lay in the ashes one could assess the privations of the people who had once lived here. We found clothes, shoes, hand-woven material, the remains of a telescope, a long copper tube and pipes, one of them primitively made from clay, the other from a large elephant seal tooth. Around the outline of the building lay lots of copper sheeting, which must have served as roofing material; we also found gun barrels and lead bullets. Along with the remains of a ship's planking all these finds intimated that a sealing vessel had once been wrecked here, stranding its crew on this desolate spot where they must have eked out a hard life until, after long months or years, relief arrived. But perhaps no relief came, and the centuries which have elapsed may have eliminated all traces of graves or of the men who lived in this refuge. I searched in vain for graves or skeletal remains. A fragment of a skull, which did not really appear to be that of an animal, was too small and too weathered to allow one to deduce with any certainty that a human tragedy had occurred, involving the unsung heroism of some unknown seafarers. Once we had loaded our boat with all the remains we had found, in order to take them back to Grytviken as proof of the camp here, we went back aboard. First, however, the Russians had used up all the dynamite which we had been given for blasting rocks.

"Isn't it gold?" asked one of them who had been filling his pockets with the glittering pyrites which gleamed like gold, holding a chunk of it under my nose.

"No I'm sorry for you and your hopes, but it's certainly not gold," I said. But he took all the glittering rocks with him; he would only be convinced when he was unable to dispose of his gleaming find in the market in Buenos Aires.

In rough seas we swung around between the green islands and the 800 m high rock pyramid which terminates the southeast corner of South Georgia, to reach the northeast coast. From there on we steamed across a peaceful, quiet, mirror-like surface to Larsen Harbour where we dropped anchor late in the evening in a depth of 9 m.

There is not much to say about the last day of our cruise with the sealers. Next morning as we swung out of the quiet little Larsen Harbour into Drygalski Fiord, bounded by steep rock walls, between which a gale blew at full strength, all further thoughts of sealing were forgotten. The backdrop to this fiord, which had been named by the Second German South Pole Expedition after that energetic master of south polar research, Erich von Drygalski, was formed by the steep ice-cliff of a glacier, which was quickly hidden by a veil of snow. The whalers say that the wind always blows out of this fiord and, even if he has never seen the topography the practical seaman deduces from this that there must be a pass or saddle above the glacier and that there is no mountain face to check the wind. Johannesson even asserted positively that there was an ice connection between Drygalski Fiord and Novosilski Glacier. I could not refute the existence of such a connection although at the time I suspected that a connection with Royal Bay was more likely.

From on board ship one can count a total of eight glaciers on both sides of Drygalski Fiord, if one excludes minor vestiges of glaciers from this total. They consist of four hanging glaciers and four which descend to the sea.

The remainder of the homeward voyage was very cheerful. For the sake of the shags we could not deny ourselves a little side trip around the Cooper Islands. All sealers have a strong hunting lust; moreover shags are a delicacy among seamen. And finally one can trade them at Grytviken; I heard that a dozen of the birds would secure a large, fat ham.

Just about every man had a gun in his hand and as we swung around Cooper Island loud shots rang out with gay abandon, to the point that one feared for one's life. It was a wise move to stay near the pantry. It was a very special type of hunting since it demanded a good aim and a skilled estimation of distances. The birds had to be shot above the deck, since they would be lost if they fell into the sea; we did not have time to search for them.

The shag is one of the most inquisitive birds on the whole island. It flutters around the masts and bridge and thus flies directly into range of the numerous guns which are trained on it. One shot follows another. They can be lured by whistling, which makes them even more inquisitive. The Russians stand on deck childishly swinging the dead birds like puppets, since they believe that this will lure the birds even more effectively.

By 3.00 p.m. we were again lying off Grytviken. Warm sunshine lay over the bay, as if it were a fine summer's day.

21

Farewell to Glaciers and King Penguins

WE HAD LONG INTENDED to visit our bird friends the king penguins once again before we began our homeward voyage over the deep sea. We had missed one section of their annual life cycle, namely the period from egg laying until the first few weeks of life. In particular we did not have this period on film. In addition there were still many aspects of the habits of these remarkable birds on which we had no notes.

We were in some doubt as to whether we should go to Royal Bay or St. Andrew's Bay, lying north of the former and leading off the shallow embayment marked on the British chart as Davis Bay.

No matter how much I questioned the whalers nobody could tell me why this bay was named after one of the saints of the Catholic Church, since his sphere of influence probably could never have embraced these bays and animals. At the last moment we settled on St. Andrew's Bay despite the fact that two weeks before it had refused us access. In high spirits and with all our camping gear on board we had proceeded from Grytviken past Ocean Harbour and Hound Bay, but the sea had smashed one of our life boats when we could already distinguish the little forms of the king penguins on the beach with the naked eye. An easterly wind prevailed and an attempt at landing would have been madness.

As a substitute after this first unsuccessful trip we had gone hiking around Grytviken; we had hiked over a pass, Echo Pass, to Cumberland West Bay and from the mountain above it had looked out once again over the extensive ice plateau which blankets the island. We also made a day trip to Cumberland West Bay in the sealing vessel, *Little Karl* during this period of waiting. Once we had brought back the dredge hauls we had brought up we had two days' work back at base while we organized and preserved all the organisms we had garnered from the depths.

The middle part of the month of April was distinguished by strange weather. Heavy, torrential rains such as we had not experienced all summer filled the lakes and streams without intermission and Grytviken was worried about the concrete dam which supplied the whaling station with power. It was practically the only worry the whalers had; they were beginning to lay up the whaling ships one after the other since, given the weather and the disappearance of the whales there was little prospect of more work for them. The Grytviken station had already harvested a good 800 whales that season, mostly blues and fins. Everyone was delighted at this and was already looking forward to home and all the splendours of summer.

When the rain gave way to snow on 13 April, and the mountains became enveloped in white mantles right to their feet, the worries about the dam disappeared as the water level returned to reasonable heights again. But then came more bad news! On 12 April, the day of the deluge of rain, the whaling vessel *Sky*, based at Prince Olav Harbour, had sailed from Coal Harbour to make the barely five-hour trip to Prince Olav. The vessel had reported her departure and approximate time of arrival by radio. When she did not arrive that day people began to worry but waited until the 13th before taking any action. But then people began to get really concerned when no news of her was received on the 13th either. Every whaling vessel in South Georgia began searching for her and her 12-man crew; they scoured every stretch of coast and every cove according to a systematic plan. Once the twenty ships had completed this task we knew that any further search was in vain; South Georgia's coast had recorded another tragedy and had claimed the lives of 12 young men.

At first we wondered whether Bird Sound, of which we ourselves had once experienced the treacherous side, might have been the site of the wreck; but later the catastrophe was believed to have occurred on the little Welcome Islands! Nothing of the men or the ship itself was ever found; a giant wave may have swamped her in just a few minutes. But flotsam and buoys which were found on the north coast intimated that there was no point in searching further.

After a brief snow squall on the morning of 15 April we entrusted ourselves to the old *Little Karl* and her skilful captain and headed around Barff Point in sunny weather with a north wind and light swell. Black patches on the tussac slopes on the stretch between Barff Point and Godthul at first made us think they were burned areas. But since there could not have been any people here we drew the correct conclusion: namely that it was just the black earth exposed by slope failures after the copious rainfall.

If one knew the history and age of *Little Karl* one had to thank the Creator that the weather was so fair and that no heavy seas threatened the ship. *Little Karl* had greatly exceeded the human life span and displayed one infirmity after another. To a certain degree she had been restricted to a fairly constrained retirement and was used for sealing only in nearby bays where, in view of the short distances her activities could be kept under surveillance, and hence neither the old captain nor the sealing company need be exposed to unnecessary worries. When one saw this worn-out tub lying at the pier at Grytviken, unprepossessing and almost cringing beside the proud, modern whaling ships, covered in seal blubber and filth, it was difficult to credit that this little ship had a brilliant past or, more correctly, had experienced a very feudal episode in her past. This was the ship aboard which Kaiser Wilhelm II was present during a whale hunt near

36. A glimpse into Possession Bay

37. The sea, a glacier and the main range from St. Andrew's Bay

38. King penguins on the beach at St. Andrew's Bay

39. Father, mother and child (king penguins)

Nordkapp at the end of last century. If I remember correctly a Norwegian artist has commemorated this event in an impressive painting. Later *Little Karl* exchanged the Arctic Ocean for the Southern Ocean and during the initial hunt for humpbacks rendered magnificent service. But now she had come down in the world like an alcoholic behind whose ravaged appearance one could still make out, with some difficulty, an original personality.

But the 60-year-old captain of this vessel had retained a touching love for her, because he recognized her long years of loyal service and knew all her weaknesses. The captain's name was Johannessen and he was a Norwegian. His men, who thought highly of their commander, called him Pokker, because that was his every third word in conversation or, although I cannot confirm this, because like so many seamen he had become addicted to playing poker years before. But be that as it may Johannessen handled his little vessel like a raw egg; he said himself that she consisted of nothing but rust. One got the impression that when at sea he would give way to the smallest chunk of ice, not even large enough to hold a leopard seal, and when he had to lay his little darling alongside another ship, something he was very reluctant to do, he would avoid any jolts; he even seemed to feel any hard jolts himself.

Hence what we were observing was an affectionate relationship between a man and an inanimate object. As we might fall in love with an old cupboard in a passion for antique furniture, Johannessen had fallen in love with his *Karl*. And just as we might want to rejuvenate the appearance of that article of furniture, at Grytviken we would often observe the old gentleman personally and in his spare time, running a paint brush over the vessel's cracked hull plates, trying to conceal the rust.

We had passed Hound Bay without incident or difficulty, and beyond a row of reefs which projected far out to sea we swung into a wide, curving bay. Then Pokker sent for me from the "priest's house' (*prestegaard*), as the little cabin with two benches on the starboard side was called. It was so named because during the period when there was still a clergyman on South Georgia, he stayed in this cabin during his trips to nearby stations. These simple people are never at a loss to find appropriate names. Hence the roofed wheelhouse to which I was now heading to see the captain was termed the "meat chest" because there was often a side of beef or some shags swinging on a line there.

There were gusty squalls; an offshore wind was raising a short sea and Pokker remarked weightily: "Let's see how we make out. St. Andrew's Bay and Royal Bay next door are the worst holes on this entire coast. It's always blowing here; quite close to here I once smashed my rudder on a shoal when an offshore wind hit *Karl*."

"All right," I said, "if we don't make it today we can spend the night in Hound Bay and sup our toddy there. "

But just as quickly as the squalls had begun they disappeared again. The closer we got to the bay itself, which now emerged from the coast as a separate entity, the quieter and more peaceful it became; the mate, Sarpen, whispered to me that what the old man had told me about the hazards was all nonsense, and that we would definitely get ashore to our penguins safely today.

And indeed a landing appeared possible even to my eyes, especially in the northern corner of the bay; there instead of furious seas we could see only a narrow white line of surf, which became progressively thinner and weaker behind some reefs.

All went well; we three and our entire baggage got ashore in three boatloads; we pitched our tents right by the beach on a recent ice-crusted snow cover. Here the southwest wind, which was most to be feared as it raced down the slopes could reach us only in a tempered form. There was no pass to break the line of the main range and to allow it to penetrate to us. Towards the west and northwest we were sheltered by steeply rising tussac slopes; even the east wind was restrained by a projecting rock nose and could not trouble us much. We lay fairly open only to the southeast, but this did not worry us much since this is an extremely rare wind on South Georgia.

In order to be safe against unpleasant surprises, come what may, during this transition period we removed the ice crust with an ice axe and dug away the sand to a depth of 40 cm. The upper, almost stone-free layer was already frozen, but the deeper we went the moister and heavier the sand became. After we had dug a depression for our tents, pitched them with a wall of sand around them, we then piled up even more sand, dug out tussac hummocks from the snowy slopes beside the site, and laid them like a cornice on top of the sand ridge.

Now as we again sat alone and safe in our camp we discussed the past few days at Grytviken, which now at this distance we could assess more clearly. We were full of praise for the Norwegians' hospitality and the fine support we had received from the whalers. As a disadvantage, however, we identified the monotonous, secluded life, and finally concluded that each person's idea of good fortune differs and that in this otherwise imperfect world, this was a very fine arrangement.

Lying alone in our tents, the conversation returned almost of its own volition to the wreck of the *Sky* on the Welcome Islands. Having now spent months at sea or in camp we could much more easily and painfully imagine ourselves facing the tragic, unforeseen end which had befallen those poor people. It takes so little to find oneself in trouble or in danger; a false movement of the helm; a crashing wave in these foul coastal waters, which in many places are totally uncharted.

Our first outing next morning was to the king penguin rookery; we set off southwards to look for it since as we were landing we had seen some birds trotting homewards in that direction. The weather was mild and the sun was shining, even though there were clouds billowing around the peaks of the main range. The clouds extended as far as the edges of the two glaciers which provided such a powerful backdrop to the bay. Almost 1.5 km from our camp we could see the steep ice front of a glacier, presumably the one seen by the First German South Georgia Expedition in 1882–83 during their excursions from Moltke Harbour, and named the Cook Glacier. Today we did not head for its vertical ice cliffs which, we could see, ended on dry land. Since we wanted to get to the king penguins, after walking 300 m along the sandy beach we swung west and after a further 400 m across a level foreland we reached another glacier. We kept picking up rocks and shortly after leaving the beach we repeatedly observed that there were numerous striations etched into the hard schists.

As we hiked across the foreland we encountered many shallow streams which raced, swollen and roaring from the glacier front towards the bay. As we leaped across these obstacles we often sank unexpectedly into the turgid water.

The king penguin rookery at St. Andrew's Bay contains a good 700 birds; if one counts both adults and juveniles the total is considerably larger. Erratic boulders, elongated in shape, protruded from the marshy, churned-up earth, standing out like little hillocks. Directly behind the rookery a glacier rose at an angle of 20° and this sloping ice surface continually tempted the idle king penguins to make little sorties. We watched some groups, with their important gait and often walking in single file, heading up the slopes and then, after a little while, back down again. Apart from the main rookery where the birds stood in ranks, we could also see small, separate groups; we surmised correctly that these were last year's still immature birds. But the scenes were not always peaceful; among them we saw pairs fending off a rival with violent blows of their wings. Others stood rigidly together; they were already paired even although snowstorms would sweep across the landscape in the next few days, and the stern, tough winter stood in the way of the further development of their union.

But what made this glimpse of king penguin life at St. Andrew's Bay at this late season so fascinating was that, totally counter to what we had expected, we encountered every stage from eggs to young birds many weeks old; this was an extraordinarily favourable situation in terms of filming. We found penguins which were still incubating eggs on top of their feet. Others were guarding a newly hatched chick; others again had young several weeks old. Many, already quite large, were wandering around at the edge of the rookery, unprotected by any adults, as they waited longingly for their parents. They stood, as if in rank and file, and when an adult bird trotted past and was recognized as being father or mother, the little downy jackets would come to life. The waiting had not been in vain; the next moment the young bird would be fed, with food passing between parent and young innumerable times. If the latter continued to harass its parent, and the mother herself could not produce any more food one would see the male, standing nearby, finally weaken. He too would regurgitate some food into the young bird's bill.

Since these feeding scenes did not always occur clearly or openly we had to wait very patiently, wet to above the knees, until we could get a good film sequence, one which would visually reveal the procedure better than any description.

It was not until late afternoon that we left the mass of birds because the light conditions were unfavourable and because we were frozen although, with a temperature a few degrees above zero the weather was really quite mild.

Once we had changed our boots and lined them with new senna grass from Lapland, we headed northwards from camp up steep tussac slopes to a broad ridge about 150 m high. The warm weather during the day, together with the sunshine had wakened an abundant insect life on the new snow surface between the tussacs. We collected three different species of Hymenoptera and a vast number of dark spiders which shrank into little, elongated forms and appeared to be lifeless as we approached. If one tried quickly to catch them they hid beneath miniature drifts in the fine, powdery snow. Towards evening, when it became somewhat colder and the snow hardened, the insects became stiffer and one could catch them more easily. Hence we were able to fill a small glass with these sub-Antarctic life forms which had been awakened for their brief life by a few hours of sun and calm.

On the evening of 18 April, after the rain and snow, the clouds became lighter and for the first time we saw the main range which crowned the backdrop to the glaciers. All this time practically nothing could be undertaken outside and once again we had had to patiently endure life in camp.

But ultimately the whalers were right; they could not understand why we had wanted to establish another camp at this late, unpleasant season, when the environment and the weather daily became more unpredictable. As the winter approached it indulged in one orgy after another and inside our tent, which lay in shadow all day long, it became cheerless and cold when one had to sit inactive inside it for hours.

On the evening of the 18th, when it cleared up we managed to achieve some mapping, photography and sounding in the bay so that despite all the warnings we were quite glad that our trip had not been in vain.

But these were cheerless days. The following day again brought us one of the worst storms we had experienced on the island. It was nature's final domineering act. The sea and the reefs were enveloped in spray and spume; the entire bay was seething and we could not even crawl out of the tent on all fours. The pressure was relatively high, at 742.00 and the temperature only $-2°C$.

Yes we would gladly leave if a ship were to arrive on the

first favourable day! But the island was to grant us one last dry, bright day so that we could absorb for the last time all the beauty the island hoarded, in terms of glaciers, penguins, clouds and surf. The 22nd of April, the day we forsook our life of camping and hiking, was to be that day.

We walked along the beach in a light mist; tongues from the rapidly abating surf still licked far up the sand. Gulls were standing around with their full-grown young at the mouth of the stream, just where the fresh water poured into the sea; here we swung off and headed for the penguin rookery. We could see nothing around us but the roaring stream guided our steps over the uneven glacial drift. A few gentoo penguins were standing around, doleful and still. Skuas, perched on rocks, seemed twice as large as normal and only flew off into the protecting fog when we came right up to them. Then the first sounds from the king penguin rookery, sharp and abrupt, began to penetrate the milk-white greyness. We needed only to head towards them and all of a sudden we were standing looking at the birds.

The fog became more mobile now; a gentle southwest breeze was stirring the dense mass. The surrounding slopes became clearer and already the plumage of the birds began to display a bright sheen. Then suddenly a sharp peak on the main ridge thrust its spire through the grey clouds and in a few seconds the white landscape and the cliffs of the glacier dropping sheer into the sea lay as if newborn before our delighted, searching eyes.

What would we see today? Not very much that was new, but for the last time we could again watch the varied, peaceful life of the rookery with eager eyes. We dreamed almost more than we saw.

Father and mother stood together, anxiously keeping their offspring between them. Repeatedly the mother would press her offspring close against herself with her bill. Once again her happy call would ring out like a chant proclaiming her avian happiness. After this call had rung out the bird's head would swing down like a baton. In other locations the cheerful piping of young birds, greedy for food, arose. Close by two late-nesters were still incubating. The fathers stood nearby, waiting patiently.

But the liveliest scenes that morning occurred on a steep snow slope 2 m high. This was a practise slope where birds attempted walking uphill and downhill. One bird would try to tackle the slope using its feet alone. Then, if it became unsure, it would use its wings for assistance, and if even this did not succeed, it would drive its bill into the snow and thus make its way uphill by dint of a little cheating. Once it was at the top it would flap its wings. Clearly the whole operation was an experience: this penguin's first steep slope!

"If only I could get down again," one could almost hear it thinking as it carefully felt its way down, neck outstretched, at right angles to its upper body. Or if this was too slow a method it would slide down on its webbed feet as if it were wearing triangular skis.

While I sat there, dreaming more than watching, a wall of white breasts stood behind me, and the birds' golden-yellow neck decorations glowed richly. Behind them stood a few brown juveniles. I clicked my tongue, producing a noise totally unknown in the penguins' vocabulary. One of them came right up to me and seized my bare hand in its bill. Its white tongue was covered with prickles so that in later life crustaceans and fish would adhere to it better, and it felt as if a wire brush were being passed across my hand. I pulled on a leather glove and again the bird pecked at it becoming so excited that it began sliding and tumbled down the slope.

But look at the excitement that's occurring in the middle of the rookery! One of the little urchins is running through the rookery where the parents, or at least one adult, are guarding each juvenile. Perhaps the lone little bird is trying to find its mother. But this harmless little brown fellow will suffer for daring to disturb the peace and tradition.

Dozens of pecks are aimed at him, serious blows which

are totally different and much more powerful as compared to the gentle pecking and nudging of its own mother's bill, aimed at the bird's little body when it still lay hidden beneath the mother's abdominal skin fold. This went on for a while until all the excitement subsided when a Dominican gull flew over the rookery giving its warning call. As a result the strife ended abruptly and all heads turned skywards.

I walked away from these charming scenes in bright sunshine and spotted smoke from in front of our tent, indicating that Benitz, as arranged, had lit a campfire. And so we began the last evening of our Robinson [Crusoe] life.

We sat and warmed ourselves at the dancing flames and once again absorbed the wave beat of the surf which had become a part of us, and in it we could hear the world's heart beating, and in it we could see a link between these bays of the south and the green water of our North Sea.

A weak moon cast a pale, unreal light over the glaciers, while the Milky Way, bright and glowing, shone over the bay and emphasized the infinity of space.

But as the flames blazed and the salty wood scattered sparks, all three of us knew that this bare year would mean more to us all than just a memory. We felt this strongly confirmed in our heartbeats and in our emotions. When, later, we again sit around a campfire in some other country, many images of the island will be re-embodied and will appear before us: bays, animals and glaciers.

On 23 April two boats ran into the bay. The first was a whaling vessel from Stromness which Thoralf Sørlle had sent. He wanted to check that all was well with us since during the last stormy night they had been fearful about the station buildings; the gale had whirled sheets of iron into the air like scraps of paper. Later *Little Karl* arrived; Captain Esbensen had instructed her captain to pick us up.

As pre-arranged we went aboard her and over the hours of the afternoon Captain Pokker took us back to Grytviken past familiar bays and coasts.

22

Fresh Blows the Wind for Home!

THE TIME OF THE FIRST WINTER GALES had now arrived in all seriousness; with warm air and cold air in conflict, these gales are totally unrestrained until the first complete winter snow cover lies solidly over the island.

The whaling vessels still went out day after day on the lookout for more whales, but came home empty. When they did sight a school of fin whales the weather prevented them from pursuing them or firing. As the niggardly island summer quickly drew to a close, everything associated with whaling also wound down. The men began to dismantle equipment. When one whaling captain, a real trier, killed a fin whale, the men were almost reluctant to process it. They had already abandoned all thoughts of the flensing plan, the filth and the oil – even of the money involved. Their shares would not be greatly increased by one whale whose value, in the eyes of the men, had dropped to a mere bagatelle compared to the magnitude it had assumed earlier. No! We want to go home now! To hell with whaling!

This was the sort of mood as the harbours of the northeast coast rapidly cleared; one after another the large freighters put to sea laden with valuable full cargoes and happy men. For now South Georgia's desolate winter with its long nights was about to start; already its mask was becoming sterner and more frightful with every passing day.

A small handful of men voluntarily stayed behind at each of the five land stations; perhaps the island had become something of a second home for them because they had nobody waiting for them at home. A wintering is always welcomed by some who still need a little more money to buy that little farm, that motor boat, or that scrap of land. It is impossible to squander money on the island; there is nothing to spend it on; it piles up. And hence if one does not go home until next year one's savings will have grown.

Just as the departing men went their ways, distributing themselves among the various ships, so we expedition members were also separated. Benitz began his homeward voyage on 27 April aboard the freighter *Bugen* with the film cans; since they would have travelled twice through the tropics the latter could not stand any further delay.

What remained for me to do during the last days of our sojourn on the island?

So much that I had my hands full from early morning until late at night. Over 100 boxes, of which 54 contained exclusively scientific collections, had to be prepared for travelling. Everything had to be checked one last time. It only remains for me to give further details.

No, I would prefer instead to tell you about other things! About the unusual event on 5 May when, starting at 2.00 p.m. we experienced thunder and lightning for 90 minutes, as if the world were out of joint, with a temperature of 14°C.

Or I can confess that during my last days and hours I walked around Grytviken for a last time. Just like a farmer who, when he has finished his summer's work, takes a last walk in this or that direction, to check the condition of a tree or a field which has cost him a lot of effort.

I walked to Hestesletten once again, to where we had camped in summer and sounded the lakes. Now winter had covered the margins of the little stream with ice and I had to tramp through loose, powdery snow. The *Acaena* was already buried in the new snow and its round burrs cast long, timid shadows.

I also walked once again over the hills to Cumberland

West Bay in driving snow and cold, and for a last time looked out over the white landscape with its numerous pinnacles.

On 12 May my wife and I went aboard the freighter *Harpon*, the same vessel which had brought us to the island. We were to sail for home early next morning. It was a clear, starry night and when we went out on deck we saw nothing but happy faces, longing for home.

This was our last move. Hardly the last one of our lives, but the last one on the island. We had said goodbye to sleeping bags and the hard ground and our bed was again soft and long so that we could stretch out at will. The battering of the wind on the canvas had ceased; the calls of the penguins were silenced. We no longer needed to gaze hopefully at the sky and no longer needed to pray that it would be propitious for our wishes and plans. The stinking primus could no longer poison our lungs. In short the struggles and battles, the joys and sorrows of our island life were behind us.

In a few weeks, instead of strange noises we will be struck by the thrush in the garden, and a calm lake will soon make us forget the mast-high waves which rage around the island.

On board this large ship, whose dimensions seem enormous to us, we are transported back to an organized, civilized world from a more uncurbed and vigorous one. We hear noises of which we have been long deprived. The electric light responds to the touch of a finger.

We can hear the wind tugging at the massive rigging and involuntarily think of our miserable tent pegs which were all that prevented our tent from blowing away.

But all night long we could hear a mysterious noise as if an anchor were continually being weighed. Were we putting to sea already?

Are we homeward bound? Were we mistaken or dreaming that the ship was not supposed to sail until tomorrow morning? No, it was not the anchor being weighed; it was the noise made by the sucking of a pump. It had a secret, furtive quality, something insidious about it, as if it did not want to be heard. But it originated from a normal operation which goes on throughout the day.

Whale oil was being transferred via long hoses into the ship's large, built-in tanks, as quietly and secretly as if it were gold. And it is indeed a valuable commodity. It is gold, derived from 800 blue and fin whales. 4400 barrels of oil are transferred every 24 hours from the tanks on shore to the ship's tanks.

But when the gurgling of those volumes of oil penetrated to my wide-awake ears, which were attempting to interpret every noise on board again, the mental swerve which my aroused senses made that night was a natural one. I found myself thinking of the natives of colonial powers whose sweat and blood, health and customs, like the blubber and entrails of the whales, are converted by the white man into copra and rubber.

Around noon on 13 May the captain called us to the bridge and reported that we were now abeam of Cape Buller and hence were passing our old campsite in Bay of Isles. But we did not get a final glimpse of it. Shapeless grey veils lay over the island, which was wearing its normal apparel – one which no longer disturbed us.

While the sea was calm on the first day, the next day brought vicious weather. From 5.00 a.m. a storm raged, with northwesterly winds. It was an unpleasant day, which we will never forget. The heavily laden ship had to heave-to; a rudder on the afterdeck was smashed and washed overboard. The seas smashed in the doors on the starboard side and surged into the saloon so that in an instant I found myself in water to above my knees. The experienced bosun came within an ace of being swept overboard by a wave.

But we had often experienced this sort of thing before and endured it as a necessary evil, a tribute to be paid on voyages in southerly latitudes. We were homeward bound!

The sky cleared next day. A starry night over which a

new moon cast its light. Silvery paths and roads ran across the ever-moving waves.

We were homeward bound. It was a magnificent voyage. During the day the sun blazed down, becoming warmer by the day.

Should I say something about the city of Montevideo, which hundreds of travellers have already adequately described? What are its strong points, which are its finest streets and buildings? Whether it has a museum and whether the women are pretty? What is the price of meat? Or how the subtropical zone can intoxicate strangers? No!

I simply prefer to relate how Director Jakobsen of the Compañia Argentina de Pesca welcomed us and made our night in Montevideo pass very cheerfully, and that once again we were back with him on South Georgia. And to say that he loved the island as much as we, having been active there for seventeen years at a stretch.

I have nothing to report about the remainder of the voyage home. It passed like all long ocean voyages and after a further 31 days brought us to Sandefjord in Norway. For many it passed too slowly; many thought it was as if we were steaming through glue, when in fact, without any serious obstacle from winds, we were ploughing through the water as if it was the lightest soil. Everyone patiently counted the rising tally of miles and was delighted to see the remaining fraction growing steadily smaller.

We smoked and chatted all day long; life was easy now. When the waning moon climbed above the horizon like a ripe pear one could not help thinking that the stars were flying and cruising through space and that our own world was just a little human star.

We reached home in Brake, where the ship delivered part of her cargo, on 20 June and on the 21st we were sitting in the Bremen Ratskeller, as if enjoying our first or our last rest. Naturally we bought newspapers, the first ones from home in 11 months. Half a dozen of them of every stripe and of every party. We were so hungry for any kind of news after our period on the island! But we soon realized that no matter how busy everything seemed, in an uproar over things whose significance may have escaped us, the world was still turning on the same axis.

Maps

SKETCH OF THE SURROUNDINGS OF

COAL HARBOUR

Benitz-Geltscher-Benitz Glacier
Coal-Bucht = Coal Harbour
Durchschnitts-Höhe 300–350 m = Average height 300–350 m
Eisspitze = Snow Peak
Else bucht = Elsehul
Frida-hole = Frida Hole
Hessegipfel = Hesse Peak
Johann-Hafen = Johan Harbour
Kap Paryadin = Cape Paryadin
Paryadin-Kamm = Paryadin Ridge
Tal der Hoffnung = Hope Valley
Undin-Bucht = Undine Harbour

E. Pinguinen Kol. = Gentoo penguin rookery
Gestuftes Vorland mit Klein-Seen = Terraced foothills
Lager = Camp
See-Elephant Kol = Elephant seal colony

Note: the other place names in German were given by Kohl-Larsen but have not been accepted as official names

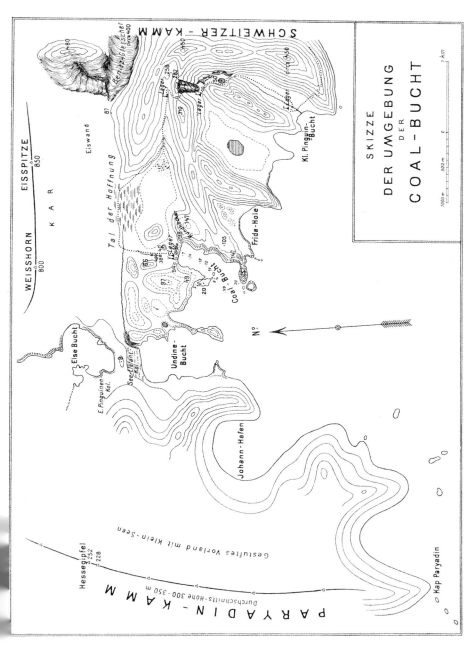

Sketch map of the vicinity of Coal Harbour

SKETCH OF THE SURROUNDINGS OF THE BAY OF ISLES

Albatros Insel = Albatross Island
Allardyce Bucht = Rosita Harbour
Beckmann-Fjord = Beckman Fjord
Brunnonia-Gletscher = Brunnonia Glacier
Grace Gletscher = Grace Glacier
Kap Buller = Cape Buller
Kap Woodrow Wilson = Cape Wilson
Lukas Gletscher = Lucas Glacier
Olav-H = Prince Olav Harbour
Possession Bucht = Possession Bay
Prion Insel = Prion Island
Seeleoparden Fjord = Sea Leopard Fjord
Sunseth-Fjord = Sunset Fjord

Konigsping. Kol. = King penguin rookery
Landungstt. = Landing place

Note: the other place names in German were given by Kohl-Larsen but have not been accepted as official names

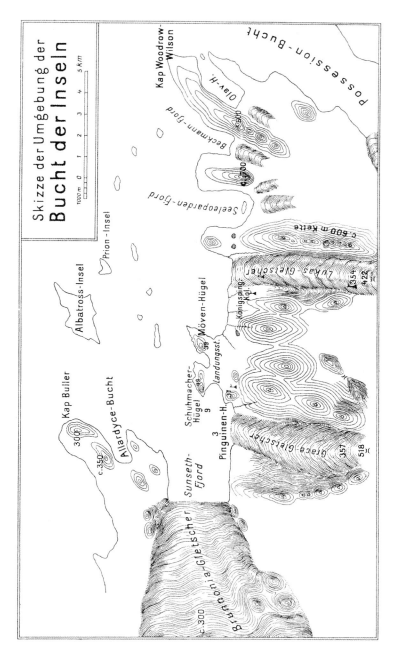

Sketch map of the vicinity of Bay of Isles

MAP OF

SOUTH GEORGIA

*Based on the English maps of 1920 and 1927
with special consideration for the glaciers of the island*

Annenkov I. = Annenkov Island
Antarctic-B = Antarctic Bay
Bjornstadt Bucht = Bjornstadt Bay
Bucht d.Insel = Bay of Isles
Coal B = Coal Harbour
Cook Gletscher = Cook Glacier
Cooper B = Cooper Bay
Cooper I = Cooper Island
Cumberland B. = Cumberland Bay
Discovery Bucht = Adventure Bay
Drei Brüder = Three Brothers
Drygalski Fjord = Drygalski Fjord
Eis-Fjord = Ice Fjord
Elefanten B = Elephant Cove
Else B = Elsehul
Esbensen B = Esbensen Bay
Fortuna Gl. = Fortuna Glacier
Fortuna-B = Fortuna Bay
Georg Bucht (Hunde B) = Hound Bay
Godthul = Godthul
Gold Hafn = Gold Harbour
Grün I = Green Island
Haakon B = King Haakon Bay
Hamburg Gl. = Hamburg Glacier

Herkules B = Hercules Bay
Holmestrand Horten Bucht = Holmstrand and Horten
Husvik H = Husvik Harbour
Johannesson H = Diaz Cove
K.Alexandra = Cape Alexander
K.George = Cape George
K.Paryadin = Cape Paryadin
K.Robertson = Cape Robertson
K.Saunders = Cape Saunders
K.Vahsel = Cape Vahsel
K.Vakop = Cape Vakop
Kap Best = Cape Best
Kap Buller = Cape Buller
Kap Charlotte = Cape Charlotte
Kap Darnley = Cape Darnley
Kap Demidov = Cape Demidov
Kap der Enthäus = Cape Disappointment
Kap Nord = Cape North
Kap Nunes = Cape Nunez
Kap Royal = Cape Harcourt
Kap Woodrow Wilson = Cape Wilson
Kl.Pinguin B = unofficial name
Kochtopf-B = King Edward Cove
König Gl. = König Glacier
La Roche Strasse = Bird Sound
Langestrand = Cheapman Bay
Larsen Bucht = Larsen Harbour
Larsen P = Larsen Point
Leith Hafen = Leith Harbour
Maivik B = Maiviken
Maud B = Maud Bay
Merton Klippen = Right Whale Rocks
Neu Fortuna B = Ocean Harbour
Neumayer Gl. = Neumayer Glacier
Nordenskjöld Gl. = Nordenskjöld Glacier
Novosilski B = Novosilski Bay

Ost-Bucht = East Bay
Pinguin B = Sacramento Bight
Possession Bucht = Possession Bay
Reithwal-B = Right Whale Bay
Rok-Bucht = Rocky Bay
Royal Bucht = Royal Bay
Sandwich B = Iris Bay
Schleiper B = Schleiper Bay
Shackleton Gl. = Shackleton Glacier
Slosarczyk B = Slosarczyk Bay
St Andrews B = St Andrews Bay
Stromness H = Stromness Harbour
Süd-Undine H = South Undine Harbour
Südwest Bucht = South West Bay
Sunseth-F = Sunset Fjord
Undine B = Undine Harbour
Vogel I = Bird Island
West-Bucht = West Bay
Wilkomm-Bucht = unofficial name
Wilkomm-I = Welcome Islands
Willis I = Willis Islands
Wilson-B = Wilson Bay
Wirik B = Wirik Bay
Zuckerspitze = Sugarloaf
Zuckerspitzen Bay = Newark Bay